Oct. 1963

NELSON'S LIBRARY OF THEOLOGY

General Editor
H. H. ROWLEY, M.A., D.D., F.B.A.
with the collaboration of
C. W. DUGMORE, M.A., D.D.
for the Ecclesiastical History Section

REASON IN RELIGION

Reason in Religion

Nels F. S. Ferré

Abbot Professor of Christian Theology
Andover Newton Theological School

NELSON

THOMAS NELSON AND SONS LTD
Parkside Works Edinburgh 9
36 Park Street London W1
117 Latrobe Street Melbourne C1

THOMAS NELSON AND SONS (AFRICA) (Pty) LTD
P.O. Box 9881 Johannesburg

THOMAS NELSON AND SONS (CANADA) LTD
91-93 Wellington Street West   Toronto 1

THOMAS NELSON AND SONS
18 East 41st Street New York 17, N.Y.

SOCIÉTÉ FRANÇAISE D'ÉDITIONS NELSON
97 rue Monge Paris 5

First published 1963

Printed in Great Britain by Thomas Nelson (Printers) Ltd
London and Edinburgh

To
Nathaniel Micklem
who has dared to probe
the meanings and mysteries of reason
both inside and outside faith

Preface

Clarifying the relation between faith and reason seems to be my life assignment. The invitation to write on this subject has given me the opportunity to rethink afresh their relation. I have done so, keeping traditional and contemporary problems as a background, by a direct confrontation of the main four divisions: the relation of reason to the knowledge of God, to man's knowledge, to history and nature, and to the religions of the world. The work will have to speak for itself. Interestingly enough, I have myself been surprised at some of the conclusions to which I have been led!

I am deeply grateful to Dr H. H. Rowley, the religious books editor, for the privilege of this participating in the production of the Library of Theology, and to Thomas Nelson Publishers for their support of the undertaking. My son, Frederick Pond Ferré, who has specialized in linguistic analysis, has acted as a stern but sympathetic critic, and my wife has not only helped with the typing but has suggested numerous stylistic improvements. I am deeply thankful to both. Mrs Robert Suddath, in spite of a heavy work schedule of her own, was kind enough to take on the typing of the final draft. My deepest gratitude is to God, for I have never felt more called into his service than in the writing of this volume.

Nels F. S. Ferré

Newton Centre, Massachusetts
June 10, 1961

Contents

Part I Reason and God

I A Definition of Reason   3
II A Definition of Religion   16
III The Relation between Reason and Religion   28
IV Perspectives, Presuppositions and Postsuppositions   39
V How can we Know that there are Realities beyond
     ordinary Experience?   49
VI How do we Know what is beyond ordinary
     Experience?   61
VII The Moreness and Otherness beyond ordinary
     Experience   74
VIII God's Relation to the World   85
IX Can we 'Know' religious Reality?   96
X Religious Knowledge and Philosophy   106

Part II Reason and Man

XI Relativity and Reliability   121
XII Sin, Sainthood and Sanity   160

Part III Reason in History and Nature

XIII Can Reason Find Meaning in History?   195
XIV Nature and the Problem of Evil   236

Part IV Reason and World Religions

XV Can we Establish rational Relations among
     Religions?   283
XVI The normative Event and concrete Religions   301

PART I

Reason and God

Chapter I

A Definition of Reason

Reason and Religion are coeval with the history of man. Their relation is his permanent problem. To help solve this problem is to allow both to help man more.

By reason I mean the ability to identify, to discriminate, to evaluate, to interpret, to test, to order and to direct experience. By religion I mean the conviction that there are realities and powers beyond ordinary experience that can help and harm man. Our task is to determine what place reason has in religion, how religion can be helped or hurt by reason, and whether religion can assist reason.

Reason is an ability. It is a capacity of the self. A person can identify, evaluate and direct what he experiences. A person, of course, can also will and feel. It is the whole self that reasons, wills and feels. No normal self is bereft of these basic capacities. A self that is aware of itself as in some way a separate being responds to a world which it recognizes as not being itself in that it is unable to feel the feelings of others as its own and to order the world it experiences as it orders its own experience. Reason is man's organ of interpretation. It is the self interpreting both itself and its world. Reason, then, is a function of the self.[1]

One aspect of reason's function of interpretation is its ability to identify. Man is aware of his reasoning as continuous. By reason he can identify persons, things, ideas, functions and forces. For our purposes here it is needless to ask why or how this function is performed. Man knows. He makes mistakes, thinking a straight stick in water is crooked; but mistakes can

[1] Reason as a function of the self depends upon the endowment and the development of the self. The nature of this endowment and development we shall discuss in Part II: 'Reason and Man', Chapter XI. In any case, reason should be understood not abstractly as merely a method, but concretely as an organ of interpretation.

3

be seen for what they are and corrected. Man learns. To doubt primary knowledge, and even more to deny it, is to repudiate reality and to substitute for it some construction of the mind.

Identification depends on man's remembering. Man recalls that this tree is the same one he passed by while he was going in the other direction. He recalls the tree in the context of its environment.[1] The same thing has identity of meaning through man's capacity to remember. He also can classify. Things are alike. All oak trees in some respect are alike. One function of reason is to identify kind. Oak trees are enough alike to be of a kind. Maple trees resemble oak trees closely, yet are of a different kind.

Another function reason performs is to discriminate.[2] A basic aspect of its work is to differentiate. It can not only identify, but also distinguish. Part of primitive reasoning is the recognition that there are many things, ideas, forces or persons of the same kind and of different kinds. As far as either the origin or the status of particulars and universals goes, either as experienced or in the final analysis, both are part of primitive human reasoning. They are given in the experience itself.

Words are basically names we give to general identities in experience. The realities are independent of the words as such. The child who has tasted sugar reaches for it even before he can master the word. Different peoples use different words, but the experience can be identified and the word translated. A Frenchman who knows only *chien* and fails to communicate by means of the word can point to the animal and learn that in English it is called 'dog'. The same procedure cannot be followed in the case of 'gene' or 'God', but unless there is some sense in

[1] The possibility that he shares with animals this capacity to identify is irrelevant to our purposes in this setting, unless, possibly, for the purpose of warding off the interpretation of such recall in terms of some more abstract and advanced kind of judgment.

[2] My use of the word 'reason' as a subject does not involve using it as an independent entity. It is incorrect to make a 'thing' of an organ, an aspect of the self, or the self functioning in a particular way for a particular purpose. But language is for correct communication. No self, either, is a subject as an independent entity! Such use of the self as a subject involves a spurious substance philosophy, disregarding the larger interdependence. Such substance philosophy depends upon a deceptive nominalism, holding that separate objects alone are the nature of reality. I use reason as subject, rather, only in the sense of 'man in reasoning', or 'the reasoning process'.

which such words stand for some actual referents, these referents cannot be included as part of the basic world of reality which reason can recognize,[1] nor can they be discriminated as genuinely different from, and other than, the rest of the actual world.[2]

The capacity to identify includes creative imagination. 'Reason' can identify persons and things; and ideas, functions and forces can be experienced directly. Ideas are produced in experience. In the reasoning process man discovers likeness among things and repetition among occurrences. These are remembered and become independent objects of thought. They can be conceived as well as perceived. Reason gradually gains a degree of autonomy as it builds up a rich world of ideas that are free of the immediate present. The reasoning function becomes a somewhat independent force.

Man can reason concerning any present or any remembered world by comparing and discriminating. He thus partially transcends the world of immediate experience. By creative imagination man can identify similarities and differences, applying his storehouse of free ideas to what he has experienced or is experiencing. By creative imagination man's world has kept growing, but the growth has been authentic only in so far as his imagination has identified something true or desirable, or both. Imagination can open, relate, and creatively rearrange the world, but it cannot create it. Increase in true knowledge is basically discovery.

---

[1] Identity should not stand for 'the same in all respects', but for recognizable and dependable sameness with respect to the natural intention of the word. A poodle and a collie are both dogs and in this respect identifiable while in other respects there can be considerable range of reference for experience!

[2] This analysis allows for the proper use of words with respect to fictitious or imaginary content, like 'unicorn', for connectional words like 'and' and 'but', which relate thoughts or experiences, and for conditional words like 'if' and 'perhaps' which do not involve direct experience. Basic words, however, refer to experience. This analysis, of course, in no way limits or excludes reality beyond man's experience of it! The words 'gene' or 'God' may be useful even if both referents were to be proved fictitious. If nothing else, they are historical words! But they are not basic words unless they refer to some reality that can be experienced or to some reality the knowledge of which results from the correct interpretation of experience. For the time being we leave this question open. Realities implied by experience may be known as more than mere concepts. Experiences of certain kinds may depend partially upon and follow the accumulative interpretation of experience.

Reason reaches the world of the desirable by its power to evaluate. The self experiences persons, things, ideas, functions and forces as wanted or not wanted, and as more or less wanted or not wanted. It calls them 'good' or 'bad'. They appear to help and satisfy or to threaten and harm. Thus arises in experience through evaluation a world which is deemed good and evil, to have values and disvalues, to offer constructive and destructive realities. At the centre of this work of evaluative reasoning concerning experience is human need. Desires become distinguished from needs. What life authentically requires is generally experienced as good even though it may not necessarily be considered most desirable. What threatens life at its central needs is for the most part interpreted to be bad.

There is obviously no legitimate equation in immediate experience of the desirable and the true. Whether in the last analysis the truly desirable and the true go together is perhaps life's profoundest question. The rest of this work will be devoted to answering it in one way or another, but unless all genuine needs can be adequately met in some demonstrable way, this question seems beyond answer in terms of knowledge.

Man needs, in any case, to become fulfilled as man. Without physical sustenance and shelter and without adequate expression of basic human drives, man becomes frustrated. He then interprets such experiences as evil. The fulfilment of these needs is generally a satisfying experience. But since man is a whole, he can be thoroughly miserable even with all his physical needs fulfilled. Some, on the other hand, seem more content without certain physical satisfactions than do others with them. Man needs more than physical satisfaction. Such satisfaction can even be frustrating if it conflicts with the fulfilment of more basic human needs.[1] Reason registers these experiences in memory and adds them to its reservoir of free ideas.

The experience of seemingly the same thing or idea varies from person to person and even from time to time in the same person. The world is difficult to evaluate in terms of either a common or a steady experience. Taste, for instance, seems both

[1] What these deeper needs are we shall examine in Part II.

6

unusually variable and yet related to some common basis in experience. An infant, for instance, experiencing for the first time a passing garbage truck, wrinkled up his nose with dislike, but made no such response when carried through an apple orchard in bloom. Reason's power to evaluate, as well as to identify, relates it directly to life. Reason is in some way life's light informing it what is and what is not truly desirable. Reason is life's counsel. Man can find life good and use reason to enjoy it. Man can find life hard and use reason to escape it, perhaps into a world of ideas. Man can find life challenging and use reason to improve it.

One of man's deepest needs is to know whether or not his experience is genuine. As experience fills ever fuller its reservoir of ideas and of preferences or dislikes by means of which reason works, it becomes an ever more difficult task to know what is actually experienced and what is constructed out of free ideas. In becoming more free from the world man also becomes less sure of it. Therefore he continually needs to check his experience in order to know whether it comes from the world he meets or from the ideas he is continually constructing and putting into the world of his own interpretation.

Each man, besides, becomes basically confronted with a world of already interpreted experience from which he learns. All advanced or developed interpretation of experience is learned mostly from the history of man. Inasmuch as the interpretation, at crucial points, may differ widely and significantly, each person must either choose among ready-made forms of interpretation or try his best to find out for himself what the world he experiences is really like.

To interpret the world is to organize one's images of the experienced world in such a way that they go together as far as possible. The self seeks unity in its view of the world. Such unity is easy to obtain if merely created by the mind. To interpret the world is not to create unity by imaginative construction, but to discover the actual unity outside self. In this sense to interpret is to find coherence of thought inside self by uncovering whatever coherence actually exists in the world, while not hiding, of course, any lack of it, actual or supposed.

To explain is to account for experience. A person stumbles unexpectedly and explains it at least partially by finding a roughness in the road he had not seen. He confronts a hostile neighbour and explains the sudden hostility by his having accidentally destroyed his neighbour's cherished peonies on the border of the plot. Explanation is more than interpretation; it is giving proper reason for a function or an act. Explanation rises to its most complex form when purpose is invoked. No 'why' may be needed to account for countless occurrences once directly referred to human or divine intentions and activity. Real care must be taken at this point. To interpret, then, is to organize one's images in the light of one's totality of meanings. To explain is to account for happenings in terms of causes or purposes. Later we shall discuss ordering one's world as a further step of freedom from the world into creative and responsible selfhood.

The task of selecting and checking experience, especially as it is given to us out of the riches of the past, is mostly an informal and unconsidered part of experience, but it is never totally lacking. In exceptional instances checking can become strongly deliberate; it can become a disciplined co-operative undertaking. Science to a large extent is the discipline of selection by testing. Part of man's task as man, in any case, is continually to check the veracity of his experience. Since we shall devote a whole chapter to this question, it is enough merely to indicate here the proper place of testing in the life of reason. We learn by challenging experience in our evaluation, interpretation, and perhaps explanation of it. Such challenge involves a trial-and-error process of reasoning where checking is of utmost importance, not as a negative attitude, but as a positive venture of discovering what is true and good. Testing is necessary in the life of reason by appropriate means within proper attitudes all the way from scientific experimentation to the 'testing of the spirits'.

The quest for truth and value is native to reason's task in evaluating, testing and checking experience. Evaluation constitutes a primitive part of reason's drive, together with identification and discrimination, but interpretation and checking are

8

indispensable to any advanced and mature reasoning. The only givenness of reason seems to be its inherent drive toward factuality outside and self-consistency inside the self. The basic problem of reason comes from temptations to disregard either or both of these drives under the stresses of the self as it goes beyond mere interpretation of its experience into the higher order of functioning.

Perhaps the fundamental task of reason, furthermore, is to order experience. By ordering I mean the total function of organizing experience. The power of reason presupposes the direct capacity to experience the world in terms of identification, discrimination and evaluation. But these acts by themselves do not constitute reasoning in the full and proper sense of the word. To be sure, delayed response is of the very stuff of reason wherein the immediate world of perception is surveyed in the light of the reservoir of relevant free ideas. Such a survey makes the response more than a perceptional reaction. In any advanced or mature sense of the word, reasoning involves a deliberate, even though not necessarily a self-conscious, ordering of the world of experience. Such reasoning includes interpretation and testing of some kind. The self responding always transcends the world of immediate experience, not only in terms of an accumulative stream of interpretation directly focused on the immediate stimulus, but in terms of a self that has become in some sense a separate free world of its own in terms of its interpretation and organization of the world it is experiencing. This creative freedom of the self in ordering its world becomes increasingly important with every new level of complexity of interpretation.

Every person organizes his own world. He does so from the material he experiences in the context of the interpretations he has been taught. No-one can live on the level of only direct responses to the world itself. To be human means to inherit a world or worlds of interpretation, to confirm or reject such interpretations and to choose among interpretations, including one's own. To reason in the full sense of ordering one's world presupposes the availability of abstract worlds and the necessity for each person to fashion his own world by the history of his own interpretations. Every person keeps shaping a configuration of interpretation, from within which he responds to the world. Every response is pregnant with such previous reading of the world, and the responses, in turn, help to mould the living configuration for interpreting, which is the living self thinking.

Every person, then, orders his own experience. First he interprets his world. He does so by experiencing it, accumulatively building up a world of abstraction retained in memory. The world of ideas, issuing from previous interpretation, becomes focused by man's main purpose (or set of purposes) in his response to the world. This purpose (or these purposes) may be unified and focused, or multi-centred and vague. It may be steady or shifting. The world of ideas, in any case, becomes organized around life itself. The ideas become associated and graded around the meaning of the self. The chain of man's choices is strung along the self's basic evaluation of life. Thus the interpretation of the world is not only of the experienced world directly but even more of the world of the experiencer. Interpretation increasingly becomes fulfilled within one's process of ordering the world. No-one sees the world only as it is. Everyone sees it also through the lenses of his own history of interpretations.

In this sense reason is creative beyond descriptive interpretation. It arranges experience and gives it inner unity and direction. Such creative use of reason comes by the selection from the world of experience of what is most important and most real to the person. Some reality governs life by becoming the centre of life's organization, specific and deliberate or diffused and drifting. For the most part, life is an inseparable mixture of informal and formal reasoning. Man learns by trial and error in relation to some main configuration of interest and interpretation. Most learning, however, is informal and imposed by living. Some small part is planned and controlled.

Reason orders life by organizing experience in line with the main motivation of the self. It lives by making hypotheses concerning what is experienced and putting these hypotheses to the test. Informally this process of reason involves its selection

10

of ideas from its rich storehouse of interpreted experience and its use of them to organize life. Ideas are continually tried and sifted. Life is a stream of such testing of ideas in relation to the experienced world. Some ideas shed more light than others on the meaning and purpose of life in the informal sense of man's continual making of choice by the very act of living. Mature growth in reason means a maximum fitting of ideas to the world and the organizing of the world of interpretation around ideas that both satisfy life and prove true to experience. Man's needs to live and to interpret are wed. They mature only within a marriage relation. When the needs of life and ideas fail to come together, some people open their lives to a reorganization of interpretation and response in the light of experience. Others prefer the inner consistency of ideas, as they have built them, and ignore or distort the world they meet. Man himself is master of the use of reason. He must order as well as interpret his experience.

When reason assumes its formal and 'school' function it deliberately keeps studying how ideas go together (the deductive function) and creates hypotheses, testing them according to prescribed rules and under controlled conditions (the inductive function). Inner consistency and outer factuality still govern reason's quest. By the way in which reason both identifies and orders experience, all discrimination and evaluation presuppose the need for external reality and for inner harmony. The primitive levels of this need call for factual accuracy and logical rigour. Man cannot live well, however, without both standards being met in some genuine way, however far reason may advance beyond these primitive levels. Even though the formal function of reason is proportionately only a minor appendage to the great body of reason's informal ordering, moreover, the appendage can be of an importance that immeasurably outmatches its size. Reason is a strong rudder, but that captain gets farthest and fastest to the goal who best knows the weather!

The main problem of reason is to keep the outer and the inner world together. The outer world of facts, functions, accumulated ideas and persons presents the world to be inter-

11

preted. The inner world is one of personalized ideas, the ideas selected mostly from man's history of experience and made one's own, which the self strives to put together into a meaningful picture. When the outer and the inner world pull apart or when one threatens the other, life itself is damaged in its capacity to respond. Reason is injured and insulted.

Man deems his reasoning real and right, within his total experience, only when he can feel confident that the world his ideas point to is a genuine world; when he is assured that the organization of interpretation within is somehow proportionately and authentically related to the outside world; and perhaps, besides, when he feels that his task of identification, evaluation and ordering leads to fulfilment rather than frustration of life. Reason is part of life and shares its rewards and penalties. Reason produces an inner world of abstractions that is meant not only to portray the outer world, but above all to guide the whole self in its search for fulfilment of life. The ordering of experience is reason's work within the total quest of the self for fulfilment.

Part of such fulfilment involves the satisfying of reason's nature in seeking outer fact and inner consistency. Each of these drives has its own partial but real right. Intellectual curiosity as a minor aspect of reason is that far an end in itself. Such curiosity can be concerned with things as they are and may be symbolized by what is called pure scientific research. Little research is ever 'pure' in this sense, but intellectual curiosity is part of the original drive of reason in seeking fact for its own sake. Science, informally and formally, is always more than merely practical. At its best it is the blossoming of native reason in one of its branches.

The other main branch of the life of reason grows out of a craving for consistency of ideas. This drive is symbolized by the task of philosophy. Like science, philosophy is only the formal discipline of one of reason's main drives. Later we shall consider whether philosophy can also deal properly with the world of fact. It is, in any case, the flowering of primitive reason into a deliberate and controlled act of self-study. The main function of reason, however, is its steering of life. Even informally it is life's rudder, no matter how well or poorly the captain may then use the helm. The climactic task of reason is the directing of experience.

Reason is the rudder! Life is the ship! The self is the captain! The ship does not need constant steering. It has its own momentum. But where we arrive and what we find on the way depend upon the steering. Sometimes the ship seems to stand nearly still or merely to continue its course, but constantly that course must be corrected and often changed. Such actual steering is what we mean by the direction of experience. No directing of life is apart from the identification, discrimination, evaluation, interpretation, testing and ordering of reason. Without the directing function of reason in any and every part of life the captain is adrift in a rudderless ship. Life is not reducible, of course, to choice, nor is choice to reason, but both life and choice involve integrally the reports of reason, especially the drawing from within reason's memory on its stored treasures of experience. To direct experience is to bring to bear reason's total ordering of specific choices which confront the self.

Not all reason is practical in the sense of problem solving, but all reason is in the service of life. Whenever reason becomes an end in itself life is that much parched. Life seeks truth for fulfilment. Truth is rightly a value-laden word. The quest for truth cannot bypass either knowledge or value. The problem is how, if and to what extent they go together. Life is focused at its centre on the quest for truth as knowledge that matters for life. Even if truth should threaten life at its very core, in its most passionate thrust for fulfilment, it matters profoundly to life.

All attempts to separate knowledge from truth are doomed by the nature of the life of reason itself as part of the total self. There can be minor motifs of knowledge as sheer intellectual curiosity, but at its centre the drive of reason is within the needs of life. This fact constitutes both the greatest strength and the most dangerous weakness in the final reaches of the life of reason. The very fear of self-deception gives untold power to man's longing to have truth removed from the drives of self. Such longing is legitimate as a warning sign, but fatal as an accepted goal of reason. There is no life of reason where evaluation and ordering of experience are not intrinsic aspects of the process. Consistency and correspondence, logic and science, matter profoundly to life, but they matter most within the whole context of the life of reason. The life of reason is the whole self examining its whole world within life's actual nature and needs.

Reason exists to interpret the world, to help relate the self to the world, to enable the self to enjoy the world, to warn it of danger and frustration, but most importantly to assist it in the life of choice. The reasoning process eventuates in its directing of experience. Reason provides alternate choices. Response is delayed until man can weigh various choices. 'Reason', to be sure, cannot determine the nature of the choosing. Man does. But the reasoning process by opening up possibilities for choice can help to clarify, classify and compare choices, and provide context for action. Reasoning thus helps to direct experience.

Especially important is man's power to accumulate sets of choices through memory of previous experience, to order them into some total context of life and interpretation, and then to use this context, containing these sets of choices, as a searchlight thrown on the immediate confrontation of the world. Reason has the dual function of going from the particular to the general in experience and from the general to the particular. These opposite processes go on at the same time in the continual use of memory and fresh experience. Reason identifies, discriminates, evaluates, interprets, tests, orders and directs experience ever anew by learning from the past. Most of such learning is from the community of man's experience, but no person can finally escape shaping his own life by choices, in the making of which reason plays an indispensable role.

To say that reason has no relevance for religion is, therefore, to say that religion has no needed place in human life. At no place is life apart from reason, for according to the level of life, reason is its appropriate light. On the human level, at least, there can be no life without a major function of reason. Although to define religion we need not reduce it to the sphere of reason, no religion can be known, distinguished, evaluated, structured, and applied unless reason plays its own intrinsic role.

Reason's role in religion is no isolated, academic function in terms of which religion is judged true and good or false and evil. The test of reason must rather be the lively identification of what religion is, the discrimination of it from all else, the evaluation of it for life, the ordering of it within the context of life, and the use of it in the directing of life. The life of reason and the life of religion must be studied together if both are essential elements of life as a living whole. Reason in religion is the role reason plays within the religious dimension of life. We now turn, therefore, to the definition of religion. After such definition we can begin to try to see how they relate to each other.

Chapter II

A Definition of Religion

Our definition of religion is 'the conviction that there are
realities and powers beyond ordinary experience that can help
and harm man'. We can draw no legitimate definition from the
mere word 'religion'. By derivation it means either to bind or
to rethink. Religion is thus the way man is bound with or into
the world; or what he discovers at the end of his deepest
ponderings; or it can mean the way in which everything is
bound together, or the way man in his profoundest moments
sees how the world itself is bound up with what is important
and real.

Definition comes from description. In studying the nature of
religion through the history of its many forms we can find
something in common that is essential to all of them and call
such a discovery 'religion'. The only adequate definition is one
that fits the facts. No genuine religion can be omitted or unexplained. At the same time, there must be something in religion that distinguishes it from all other forms of experience.
Our definition of religion will have no application and will
consequently be useless unless there is something in experience to which the word corresponds. Every definition of
such a world-wide and age-long experience as religion must,
in any case, be intuitive. The test of the definition will be its
power to account for the experience associated with the name
and to commend itself to other interpreters.

Religion is a conviction. It arises in man's attempt to interpret, to order and to direct his experience. No conviction is
mere description of what is. Religion cannot therefore be
primarily an experience on the level of identification and discrimination. Nor is religion mere evaluation. Nor, again, does
religion stop with being a way in which man interprets and

16

orders his experience. Religion involves all these but includes the direction of experience in the light of the reality interpreted as religion. Religion as conviction involves response in the light of interpretation and evaluation.

Religion is no merely theoretical conviction. It is the organization of experience under the impact of some reality that calls for a basic response. Man relates himself to the outer world as he feels himself bound up with what matters there. His deepest probings into the interpretation of what he is experiencing or can experience make him develop some stance toward the world in terms of which he responds to it. Religion is thus a conviction that organizes the inner world of interpretation in the light of, and under the pressure of, the outer world. Such organization for satisfactory living requires the inner consistency of reason and the experience of authentic outer reality within the wholeness of total experience.

The religious conviction concerns realities and powers beyond ordinary experience. Unless religious convictions correspond to outer reality they contain no authentic interpretation. Religion as an historic manifestation has aimed at and claimed objective reality of some kind. This statement is true at its centre regardless of how varied, partial or mistaken concrete religions may have been. To define the word in terms of mere subjectivity is to betray its own distinctive, historic intention. If religion is man's way of producing an unreal world within his inner manipulation of free ideas in order to escape from the real world, it is a mental malady. If it is man's way of organizing his experience with courage and faith rather than with doubt and despair, religion is doubtless a useful function in life, but it is not what the main stream of religious intention has meant by the word.

Unless the historic religious intention is generally accepted as mistaken, the definition must be true to the main line of man's use of the word. If the historic assumption of religion that there are realities and powers beyond ordinary experience proves false, then religion ought to be redefined in the light of its authentic meaning. For an adequate definition now, religion concerns realities and powers beyond man. It involves psychology, for instance, because it is a matter of experience, but only as all experience is psychological, like botany and medicine, or history and astronomy.

To define religion in line with its main intention, its claimed nature, must not mean, however, any limiting of the definition to the only true religion in the light of what man actually experiences. The religious intention has been too broad to exclude all forms of religion except the one that is considered true. If, on the one hand, then, religion is interpreted as being merely inner experience, the main stream of religious confession is violated. Religion, in such a case, is defined contrary to its own main claim. If, on the other hand, religion is defined in terms of some religion which alone is claimed to be true, like faith in a personal God, or even in a supreme Being, major streams of religious confession are arbitrarily eliminated. To define religion in terms of the conviction that there are realities and powers beyond ordinary experience that can be truly experienced is to follow the main confession of religious experience while leaving as open as the history of religions the kinds of realities or powers beyond ordinary experience that are claimed for the religious experience.

The realities and powers beyond ordinary experience have been variously interpreted. Primitive peoples have believed in the existence of realities and powers behind natural phenomena. Animism is at least a widespread stage in man's spiritual history. There have been—and are—many shades as well as kinds of it, but in all cases the faith and worship have been directed to the reality expressed in and through them. Primitive people worship trees or animals no more than the Catholic worships the saints before whose images he prays. In all cases abuse is likely because of the makeup of human nature, but the main religious intention is clear: to be in touch with the most basic powers of life.

The same is true of totemism. Identification with animals on the part of a person or tribe is not with the particular beast or bird that man can kill but with the power at work in it. The example is more complex in the case of the heavens or the heavenly bodies like the sun, for surely in this instance faith in, and worship of, the literal objects become easier, but the main intention is still directed toward the realities and powers that give light, heat and life.

One main line of interpretation of these realities and powers beyond ordinary experience is that of spirit. The object of worship is now no longer merely felt or informally posited beyond the objects of the natural and animal world. With his capacity to produce free thoughts beyond the world of immediate experience and to manipulate these ideas, man has now interpreted the realities and powers to be some dynamic force, some free power that is more than, and other than, the experienced world. The discovery of the category of spirit is no mere accident from dreams or some conceiving of the gods in the likeness of the wind, but a result of the feeling for the underlying, unifying force of life. It is the work of reason in distinguishing the experience of religion from ordinary experience.

It is hard to know at what point or to what extent men differentiated such realities and powers as separate from, and yet in, the world of experience. American Indians worshipped the Great Spirit. Previous to such an advanced stage of abstraction men generally conceived of the realities and powers more vaguely in terms of the spirits of trees, of brooks, of the dead, or even of vague spirits-in-general. The main line of religious intention in its striving for some life-giving and unifying reality behind and through life had to advance with age-slow steps as man learned in the depths of his experience to order his world. In such a complex world as this, developing man could not easily or quickly put together the drive or inner need and the demand of outer experience.

Some came to interpret the realities and powers beyond ordinary experience as personal in nature. The moving force seemed to them to act not only as some vague spirit but as sustaining a purpose. As the ideas of law and order developed in history, the power behind and through the experienced world also seemed to partake of law and order. There were seasons in nature and dependable ways of behaving toward it. Cause and effect also increasingly coloured the interpretation of religious reality. The force behind and through the objects

19

of nature and animals took on more than the form of spirits. The free, dynamic reality of spirit came to be understood as responsible and even as righteous. The spirit seemed in this sense like a person. The prophet Amos, for example, became so overwhelmed by this aspect of life that for him God became the righteous God of history.

Thus arose faith in the living, personal God of history. Somehow no natural object or animal, no mere force or wind, not even law could adequately describe what man took to be the dynamic reality behind and through all that he experienced. Spirit was living; spirit had purpose; spirit was personal. At least in Palestine and Greece a few men dared to think of the realities and powers behind and through ordinary experience in terms of a human father. As they considered the father to be the strength and wisdom of the family, so they could conceive of the living God as no less the strength and wisdom behind and in the world.

Judaism connected man's relation to God as well as to man in terms of love. Even as high a notion as overflowing goodness was used by Plato in his view of God. Jesus interpreted God centrally as the Father of our spirits who is Love. He lived as well as taught such a life of love that his followers began more and more to interpret the realities and powers behind and in the world through him. His kind of life showed them most truly what God was like. God was not only a righteous Father, merciful to those who loved him or to those with whom he had made a sacred covenant, but the personal Spirit of Love who cared fully for all people. Such a view of God is man's loftiest interpretation of the realities and powers beyond man's ordinary experience.

The more God became interpreted in terms of good, however, the harder it became to explain or to deal with the evil side of experience. Such a view of God seemed good, but too good to be true. Man's fear was also so basic to his experience that he needed some way of dealing effectively with the evil which threatened him. Generally man interpreted God on the level of his need according to his stage of development. The fearfulness of God was therefore usually far more real than his love. Man's solution was often to bring God low enough to deal with evil, in which case God seemed to be both good and evil, or at least not to have full power over evil; or he added to this view of God belief in demons or a personalized devil. Another form of handling the problem of evil was to keep the view of a good God, but to judge man as so utterly depraved that God had to be angry most of the time. In the light of such facts, no interpretation that we now make of the main intention of the religious drive can, in any case, legitimately cut out or minimize the evil realities and powers beyond ordinary experience.

In comparatively recent times, some sophisticated thinkers have conceived of the realities and powers beyond ordinary experience in terms of some aspect of personal experience such as thought. God for them is the original thought behind what is, or God is some inner structure or pattern of the cosmic process. If God is only thinker the problem of evil is not so sharp as if he is a personal Spirit of Love. Man can avoid the problem even better by thinking of God in terms of some inner structure or mere pattern for process. Such sophisticated interpretation helps to hold together man's inner consistency of interpretation with his outer experience of a world like this. But when the understanding of God approximates too closely to the world as it is, the main religious drive is also forfeited. Religion is never mere interpretation. Its whole history shows that it is search for power to overcome the evil side of life even more than it is the gaining of understanding of what life at its centre means.

The extreme step in the process of religious interpretation is in terms of sheer mystery. In this view, inasmuch as God is other than experience, he cannot be known in experience. God is infinite and cannot be understood by the finite or in terms of the finite. God is unconditioned and cannot be contained within words. To define is to limit, and God is the unlimited. God is, therefore, sheer mystery. To speak of God is to speak of the great unknown realities and powers which experience presupposes but which can never become part of such experience. Such an understanding of God logically leads to complete

21

agnosticism. God, if there be one, is then unknowable, and complete mystery has no content of knowledge at all. Even the affirmation that the world of experience is not self-explanatory cannot legitimately lead to any knowledge of there being some other reality behind this one that we cannot grasp. If interpretation means some holding together the inner world of consistency of thought and the outer of the experienced world, the definition of religion as sheer mystery must accordingly be thrown out of court as illegitimate. Since it can never be an interpretation, it can never be discussed. Nor can it ever be genuinely in experience as man quests for the realities and powers beyond ordinary experience that can help and harm.

Some, however, have used this concept of the empty infinite as a logical limit of thought based on experience and have then tried to use the infinite negatively as a principle of interpretation. To call God by any name in experience, in this view, for instance, is to misinterpret him. To worship anything in experience or through anything in experience, in any definitive sense, is to make idols of the finite and to refuse worship to the infinite God. All human loyalties and principles of interpretation are subject to constant criticism since they are finite.

Such interpretation, however, is not only a negative way. It is no way at all. It never leads to any positive religious interpretation. The definition is strictly formal with no possible content. To define God as the unconditional is to destroy religion at its mainspring. Any proximate or secondary interpretation that may be used in connection with the main formal definition is then illegitimate since the infinite can never be known in terms of the finite. Therefore this whole approach is itself definitionally illegitimate and meaningless in the light of the main drive of the religious intention. It is an actual denial of religious interpretation and a direct frustration of its main experience.

The reason, however, that these definitions have been acceptable at all is not only lack of clear thinking and honest facing of man's problem. The very nature of religion harbours the seemingly impossible contradiction that the realities and powers beyond ordinary experience are both more than and

22

other than the experience itself. We turn, then to confront this grave problem within the religious intention, namely that its realities and powers are both beyond and yet in, that they are both other than and more than experience.

Religion is a conviction, so goes our definition, that there are realities and powers that go beyond ordinary experience that can help and harm man. Ordinary experience is of natural objects, animals, the wind, and persons. Religion centres in none of them, nor in their relations, but in something more than what is experienced. Identification of these objects leaves discrimination to affirm its insistent: 'not these'. Yet the religious man uses the same experience of identification and discrimination in trying to get at and to get right with what is more than the ordinary experience. Thus at the same time religious experience affirms enough 'more' of the same kind to be known through, and to work in, these media, and also some 'other' that cannot merely be these media or only more of them. What is thus experienced as religious is somehow both of the same kind as, and of a different kind from, what is ordinarily experienced.

What can be known of such religious experience is, of course, only what is of such nature as to be accessible to experience, some 'more than' which is the extension of what is somehow first previously known in experience. The nature of religion is to find the full reality and meaning of this 'more than'. Although not all experience is consciously aware of some such end-limit or limitlessness as the absolute, the ultimate, the unconditional, or the infinite, the religious experience is always of the more-real-than and tends toward ultimate reality, meaning and power. Such has been the development over the ages of the religious interpretation. The mature and universal religions in their leading interpreters speak of the Spirit, the Person, the Father, the Ultimate. The task of our inquiry is to ascertain whether and how such terms may be used legitimately in the full context of the reasoning process.

The 'more than' can be conceived of spatially. The gods of some African tribes were pictured as dwelling behind a great mountain range which for them was out of bounds. Many peoples envisioned God as in heaven beyond the skies. Or the spatial 'more than' has been extended to mean more than any particular space. God is not limited by space. He is equally everywhere and anywhere. God is omnipresent. Or all space is in God so that no space excludes or exhausts him. Thus the religious experience can think of God as beyond a particular area or as the ultimate container of all there is.

Similarly religious experience can order life as a trial which is in the present but which had a perfect origin and will have a perfect ending. The golden age lies behind and before man. Eternity can lie before and after time in the sense that time comes from it and disappears into it. For the Hebrews eternity was simply a long time. One Greek theory of eternity was in terms of endless cycles. Or eternity may mean all the time there is. It may mean endless time. God's time is, then, more than man's time in the sense of the fullness of it. The more-than of religious intention regarding time may be drawn to its ultimate conclusion as the illimitable extension of duration. God is the container not only of all space but also of all time. These illustrations show some preliminary ways in which the religious 'more-than-ordinary-experience' can be employed.

The spirits likewise are not simply man's spirit but vague, free agents that visit man in dreams or in unusual events. The 'more than' is of the same kind sufficiently to be known by the experiencer and to affect life. The 'more than' can then be raised into the unifying, ultimate Spirit, the unknown Mover, the Sovereign Lord of history. God is not man's spirit, but more than man's spirit. And yet he is, somehow, the same kind of Spirit as man's spirit, as its Source, its Sustainer, its Guide and its Fulfiller.

The experience of the personal realm, moreover, can be extended into belief in demons and angels, or in the ultimate Person, the eternal Self, the Father of all persons. Or again, religious interpretation has constructed faith in creative patterns for the world as well as in one ultimate Creator. Depending upon interpretation there can be ultimate ideas behind all earthly objects or one ultimate Thought beyond all experience. There can be some general power that makes for harmony of experience beyond ordinary experience or there can be God as Love, the Supreme Concern.

On the other hand, the more than ordinary experience seems to require some 'other than'. Perhaps the ultimate may be such a category. On the one hand, man is fallible, God is infallible. Man is mortal, God is eternal. Man is limited by space, God contains all space. But there seems, on the other hand, to be some insistent demand within the religious drive that religious reality be other than in the sense of no mere moreness. Religious experience for vividness, reality and power seems to crave mystery as well as meaning. The 'more than' has to be both indefinitely apprehensible and yet also by nature incomprehensible. If revelation gives new data to reason in terms of which to interpret its experience, what is thus revealed is now known and therefore no longer mystery.

As a consequence, religion seems to require some fenced-off realm where reason cannot enter. Some side to religious reality seems to have to go beyond knowledge. If God is revealed, some precaution seems necessary to keep him yet unrevealed. If God in Christian faith is known through the Son, nevertheless he cannot be known as he eternally is in himself. If Christ is known through the mystery of the redemption in one such view, he must not also be known as the inner nature of Incarnation. If God is known as the forgiver of sins, then he must not constitute the explanation of things. If man can know God's answer to the problem of evil because of God's gracious acts, then he must not dare to know him by thought. If the revelation gives light, then it is still basically man's deepest mystery. The religious drive, regardless of in what form we may later have to account for the fact, has always tried to combine these two sides of God revealed and God hidden, of meaning and mystery, of more-than and other-than.

This double craving for both meaning and mystery is the deepest problem that religious knowledge must face. The realities and powers beyond ordinary experience are claimed both to be known and to be unknown. Religious interpreters have tried all combinations to solve this central problem of religion. They have tried to make the religious reality wholly other, a 'not this, not this'. But in so doing they have failed to point to anything real and relevant to the needs of life, except for the need for the moreness of mystery which seems inherent in religious experience. Others have offered both religious explanation and power for life in terms of the moreness of the best we know, but have been repudiated by the religious world in general because they have failed to convey the sense of the eternally receding horizon of mystery. Others, again, have tried to combine both mystery and meaning within the same interpretation of religious reality and have usually been rejected by advocates of both rival positions. They have also all too often failed to give to their followers the stimulus to full religious zeal that comes from an exclusivist position. For them, too, the nature of mystery that is not meaning has been an unsolvable problem for knowledge.

All that moreness in terms of 'other than' seems to mean for knowledge is negation of finitude. God within this drive for mystery is not limited to space at all, for space belongs to a finite world of relations. Or God is not eternal in the sense of the container of all the time there is, but he is timeless. Time has no place within the infinite. Nor can God in this view be a spirit, nor personal, nor love, nor anything nor any kind at all that thought can handle, for God is entirely other; he is qualitatively beyond ordinary experience.

When we look at this drive for mystery, we can see that mystery, on its knowledge side, amounts to sheer ignorance. The unclaimable is claimed without content, and therefore not legitimately as knowledge. No negation gives genuine moreness. The peculiar fact is that religious experience insists on affirming such otherness. We include it, therefore, in the original definition and shall have to investigate later whether such mystery cannot, even so, have significant meaning provided that it is rightly related to the basic religious claim.

The realities and powers beyond ordinary experience, finally, according to our definition, can help and harm man. Religion is never merely theoretical. It is always related to life. The religious drive springs from man's central desire to protect himself from evil powers, to be on good terms with helpful

realities, and to be rightly related, in the totality of his interpretation, to whatever reality beyond experience is most
responsible for it. Beyond all particulars of ordinary experience
man feels for, and has generally felt that he has found, some
other and greater power to help and to harm. Some force or
forces of good he believes are 'out there' that he can accept;
some evil is also there in some way that he needs to placate;
or some great God is there who deals with him to help and to
harm according to his own behaviour. Religion is thus beyond
man's deepest 're-reading', if this is confined merely to ponder-
ing on ideas, for it is the re-reading of life at its centre, the
inner organization of life with relation to its living dependence
upon and response to what is most important and real. Religion
never merely describes and organizes experience; it never
merely evaluates it; religion is man's wrestling with reality at
the centre of life with regard to life's profoundest meaning, its
severest penalties and its most satisfying rewards.[1]

---

[1] The discussion of this chapter has been a matter of clarifying our main explanatory definition of religion as 'the conviction that there are realities and
powers beyond man that can help and harm'. I append a few supplementary
definitions that can be used to enlarge and illuminate the one already offered.
None of these definitions is adequate in the light of the boundless experience of
religion throughout the world and in all ages, but they all aim at some aspect of
the main definition that tries to include what is central to man's religious experience.
  Religion is man's way of relating himself as a total being to what he values the
most and considers to have final power over him.
  Religion is man's adjustment to the mysterious aspect of life, his wrestling
with it to find meaning and satisfaction.
  Religion is man's attempt to relate himself to the unknown, to wring from it
meaning and fulfilment.
  Religion is the faith that the world of ordinary experience is neither all nor
final, and that there is another reality with power to change it.
  Religion is man's attempt to be at home in a strange world and to discover and
appropriate the true world.
  Religion is man's courtship of life.
  Religion is man's drive to secure and enhance what he treasures most by means
of powers that cannot be conquered.
  Religion is man's attempt to placate the powers that threaten him and to enlist
the help of friendly powers beyond his control.
  Religion is man's reaching out to be right with himself and with his world of
experience in terms of dependable realities and powers.
  Religion is man's struggle to accept or to change his lot in life.
  Religion is man's wrestling with the fact of death in life and at the end of life,
his grasping for true life that death cannot hurt or destroy.
  Religion is man's search for security and permanence.
  Religion is man's quest for freedom from circumstance, his transcendence over
the fickleness and fugitiveness of time.
  Religion is man's pursuit of total and final fulfilment.

Chapter III

The Relation between Reason and Religion

Having provisionally defined reason and religion, we turn to the relation between them in terms of faith and reason, for faith is the distinctive function of religion. Faith is the whole self trusting. Faith as the characteristic expression of religion is the whole self trusting what is beyond ordinary experience. Faith is an attitude and activity of a self and a community. Human faith at its fullest is trust in the highest dimension we know of ordinary life and beyond ordinary life. A leading scientist once upbraided a theologian for not making more use of faith as power for explanation. The whole history of evolution, he said, bears witness to the reality beyond ordinary experience that faith finds. Fish, for example, pressed upward and succeeded in living under conditions impossible for fish. Land animals proved the reality of faith. There would be no drive of faith within unless the reality beyond could satisfy the aspirations it had awakened.

Human faith, in any case, is power for life. It is required for ordinary experience. It underlies the very will to live. The highest reach of such faith is the conviction, be it drive or thought, that ordinary experience is not all there is and can be changed. This conviction is the mainspring of civilization. The outside world can be known, can be used and can be improved. Thus the physical world has been explored, utilized and improved. Earth, sea and sky serve man in ever new ways. Similarly the world of the mind has been ordered and extended. But also man's faith in what is beyond the physical and the intellectual has grown and been refined. In the long run the three dimensions go together and depend upon each other. The need for wholeness within calls for wholeness without. The world that can be found beyond ordinary experience consists

28

not solely of fuller reaches of material and intellectual help but also of realities and powers that can help and harm man where he is most fully human.

Faith as trust has three basic sides: faith as acceptance; faith as commitment; and faith as choice. No part of faith is without reason. Without reason in its identifying and discriminating functions faith is empty. Without reason in its evaluative and ordering powers faith is blind. Every basic separation of faith and reason is a denial of both. Both are indispensable servants of life. A basic help reason gives to faith is to provide information. Such information comes overwhelmingly from the history of faith. Within man's knowledge as an agelong social act there is a heritage of faith. Knowledge preserves for ever-coming generations acquaintance with what, how and why previous generations have trusted what is beyond ordinary experience.

Reason thus preserves in depth memory and in knowledge how people in the past walked in the way of faith and how they fared. It transmits the story of men of faith as well as the history of faith itself. Through its power to describe and recall, reason offers faith as embodied in personalities and developed in positions. The present context is not the place to distinguish between faith as believing certain propositions and faith taken as trust. Naturally, faith 'as embodied in personalities' and as 'developed in positions' should not be assumed as being of the same order.

Faith from history can become faith in life. Faith is an attitude that takes on structure through continued interpretation. All life is a struggle between faith and fear, between trust and dread. The child learns the history of the race not only by learning speech but by incorporating the emotional tones which accompany the life of man. Especially important are the psychological sets of the members of the child's family. Within all these there develops slowly the way in which the child characteristically responds to the outside world. Part of these emotional and behavioural patterns the child accepts from its social heritage; part of them the child acquires from its own experience. Taught faith is never real until it becomes lived faith.

A primitive child who has been taught faith in witch doctors and fear of medical men has had to reconstruct its whole inner response when the former failed to heal the hurt and the latter succeeded. Another child who had been brought up in the complete confidence of God's protective care and who, watching her own father, as a member of a snake-handling cult, permitting himself to be bitten by a rattlesnake to the glory of God, saw him swell up and die, lost her socially acquired primitive faith, and clamoured for a source of trust that would stand the test of her own experience.

But the personal testing of faith is seldom as dramatic and as clean cut as these incidents. It crawls forward in the inner depths, usually below conscious recognition and choice. All through life faith is tried and found true or wanting. Even inner experimentation within ordinary experience, especially at its more general levels, is complex and difficult and seldom arrives at a settled result. Faith in the realities and powers beyond ordinary experience is all the more hard to assess.

One primary function of reason in the realm of faith, then, is the preservation and recall, through record and memory, of past faith. Reason in this respect is mainly a social function. For the most part transmission is 'from faith to faith' within communities of faith. Religion works mainly through institutions. Exceptional personalities first experience the faith, especially in its highest reaches, and then groups of worshippers receive, elaborate and perpetuate the faith. Oral tradition and written doctrine perform their vital functions within the passing on of faith, but the basic organ of continuity is a special community within which the faith lives. Faith originates on its human side in seers and prophets, but is continued within the cult.

Faith provides reason with new material for creativity and criticism. Experience, not reason, is the fountainhead of faith. This new material always comes within the total involvements of experience. Such experience, in turn, presupposes both the general and the special histories of the faith in question. Of peculiar significance are the integrity, competence and balance of the man who originally had the new dimension of religious experience and insight. To judge among faiths, on any developed level, is well-nigh impossible except for men of such stature in the realm of faith and in the capacities and training of reason that they can enter into significant sharing of the human sources of faiths. Very likely such personalities will have some experiences and interpretations of their own of the mysterious depths of what lies beyond ordinary experience, further to confuse people in general! Such is the case of a creative genius in any field, and all the more on the subject of the final realities and powers that underlie and govern our total experience and knowledge. For this reason community life and the cultic expression of religion must ever dominate its continuation.

The further fact also becomes understandable that some people know and confess that they have had experience of what lies beyond ordinary life; others are not sure how much experience, if any, they have had nor how true is their informal testing of faith; they therefore put their trust in those who, they believe, have been in position to have religious experience and knowledge. Still others fail to find anything in their lives that they would consider to be distinctly religious and testify to this lack in their lives, some with bitter disappointment, some with seeming indifference, others with hostility toward those who seem to them either deceived or dishonest. We therefore shall have no easy task when we come to weigh, as best we can, the claim of religion to truth!

Before so doing, we must go beyond the discussion of the preliminary function of reason in describing and transmitting faith, socially and in persons, and try to set forth the three distinctive functions of faith itself. The primary nature of faith is trust as acceptance. The outside world comes to man either to be trusted or to be feared. Every person, deep down, wants to be accepted, to belong, to trust. The world of experience for a large part fulfils this drive. Another part frustrates it. What happens to man both helps and harms. Religion at its deepest dimension is a reaching out to make contact with realities and powers beyond ordinary experience that can be trusted.

Such trust as acceptance may take the form of complete

acquiescence. Man may 'surrender' to whatever he worships. He may receive as having nothing of his own. He may let himself be acted through as though he were nothing on his own. His main stress may be on complete obedience, the giving up entirely of one's own wish and will. He may feel absolute dependence on the reality that gave him life and sustains him. The main direction of his religious action and understanding may be a matter of 'let go and let God'. People have aimed in their religious experience at selflessness, at the destruction of the ego itself, at finding God where man is not.

Or trust as acceptance may take the form of participation. Man may identify his will with what is real and right. He may want to co-operate as well as acquiesce in a way of living that is consistent with his understanding of the realities and powers beyond ordinary experience that help and harm. Man, then, directs his religious drive not to any destruction of the ego, but to its transformation and fulfilment within religious reality. In either case trust as acceptance is central. No religion is without such trust. Religious experience centres not in man's striving, but in his finding and receiving the realities that reach beyond his own willing and control.

The second function of faith is commitment. Even in giving itself away the self acts. Even in the acceptance of a primary reality for co-operation and creative self-fulfilment there is a secondary movement of the self toward the source of trust. No self can be merely passive in the religious experience. Passivity itself is acceptance by the self. Thus trust, on the one hand, is a matter of receiving; on the other, of letting oneself receive.

There is also a more active element in many instances of faith. There is a thrusting as well as a trusting faith. Faith can be a matter of courage to be and to do. Religious faith is man's resolve regarding what he finds most important and most real in and beyond ordinary experience. Faith is perhaps basically a state of serenity engendered by authentic trust, but faith can also be a fight. Faith can be the inner struggle to accept what it needs rather than wants, what is real rather than rationalized. Faith usually contains both these elements: rest in reality, and conflict in the finding of and in the remaining with that reality.

An intermediary function of faith is choice. The past parades its many objects of faith before each person. Man confronts a long history of faith, a widespread spectrum of differing faiths in the present, and his own history of faith as well, with its crowding of persons and positions to be trusted or feared, to be accepted or rejected. Life with no trust is impossible. To live is to believe something concerning the world, and to go on living is to relate oneself positively in some way and in some measure to what is given in experience. Life is a continuous stream of experience calling for choice as to its reality and meaning. To choose one person's faith is to reject the interpretation of others. To trust according to the directions of one position is in effect to declare other sources of trust or ways of accepting false. Man lives in some measure and manner between trusting and thrusting faith. The life between is the life of faith as choice.

The claim is sometimes made: all live by faith, therefore all are religious. It is true that all, to some extent, do live by some faith, but not that all are therefore religious in the sense of believing in realities and powers beyond ordinary experience that can help and harm man. The fact that all peoples in all ages have had religions does not require the further fact that all people have shared and lived by the faith of these religions. Religion is more than a quality of life; it is an affirmation concerning the nature of life, namely that the realities and powers that govern life are both more than and other than ordinary experience. Not all people have confessed such convictions and many have claimed not to have them. Their testimony, too, must be respected.

Obviously religious reality, if it is to be experienced, must be subject to the general conditions of experience; therefore, being also beyond experience, it can never be the direct report of experience apart from the history of its interpretation and ordering. If religious realities and powers, that is, are not a matter of ordinary experience they can be known only through the ordering of experience. They must be needed in order adequately to account for ordinary experience. Once they are thus understood, man can direct his attention to them and experience them through the wholeness of experience while at the same time understanding them as having a dimension and reality of their own. Religious reality is known both as mediate and immediate inference from the wholeness of experience and as a separate reality that can grasp, confront and affect the worshipper. All complex experience, depending upon a history of experience, is, of course, thus known. It may be surprising to observe how much of experience, in fact, depends upon the very concepts of interpretation and communication which are brought to it in the act of knowing.

If my analysis of religion later proves suggestive, and, as I hope, convincing, the knowledge of there being both more-than and other-than dimensions to religious knowledge will have to depend on the demand of what is experienced in religion that there be more of it and that it have an other-than-what-is-experienced side to it. If this more-than-experience which is found in experience shall be given any right to being ultimate or fundamental to ordinary experience, it must not only be real and relevant to experience but also in some way have basic meaning to explain it and basic power to correct and fulfil it. To make such propositions acceptable our task will be to show that such claims are suggested and satisfied by the nature of the wholeness of ordinary experience.

There can be no denying the fact that countless people fail to affirm their ordering of experience in such a way that the religious interpretation becomes a necessary part of it. Countless others believe that they experience such reality mostly because they have taken over by faith the report of others, whether of exceptional religious personalities or of the community to which they belong. If the religious claim to reality is authentic, this lack of religious experience and interpretation can, of course, be attributable either to failure to avail oneself of the faith offered or to the freedom to make a negative response to it.

None of the three functions of faith can by itself, nor can all three together, rule on the reality of the religious claim. Nor can faith, as faith, make anything but an arbitrary choice for trust and commitment. The light of faith, however, is reason.

Although reason has no material at all in the realm of religion except within faith, neither has faith any way of knowing and choosing apart from reason. In the realm of religion faith and reason are inseparable. Faith relates itself to the religious reality; it reaches up and out beyond ordinary experience for that which can help man and, if abused, harm him as well. Reason identifies what is there and distinguishes this from the rest, but only within the full process of evaluation and the ordering of experience as a whole. Similarly to faith, reason, as reason, has three distinctive functions within the workings of faith. They are appropriately related to the life of faith. Faith as trust in its distinctive nature as acceptance engenders the creative use of reason, whereas faith as choice and commitment calls forth the descriptive and the critical powers of reason.

When man's main attitude toward the outside world is trust, he directs his reason to find whatever can help him. Trust and creative reasoning go together in all areas of life and knowledge. The primitive man who first bent nature to his purposes acted positively by both faith and reason, even as does the highly trained scientist who asks the most sophisticated questions of nature in his quest for its aid. The philosopher who believes in the value of the clarification of the processes of reasoning or in the discovery of general truths for life and knowledge employs the creative reason within the attitude and activity of expectant faith. Man's continual knocking at the doors of outside experience to find and to accept more truth and help from it illustrates the organic working together of faith and reason. Obviously, such outreach uses description and involves man's commitment, but the fullest drive and direction of reason is led by faith.

The highest and most daring use of the creative reason is in the outreach of faith to find whatever is most truly real, important and right. Convinced by its long history of discovery in every realm of knowledge that what is now known is not all there is nor all that can help, man keeps reaching out by faith, directing the enterprise by reason. Religious faith is man's deepest trusting—aided by a history of description of previous findings of faith and man's courageous commitment to go on finding—that the nature of the more-and-other-than ordinary experience is good for man to know and well for him to accept. The nature of religious experience is such that the way to find the religious dimension has been a matter of living oneself into the reality or into the condition of being reached by the reality. Thus the religious experience of a devoted life of worship and prayer, of concern and rectitude have yielded the fullest finding for the religious claim. In such lives reason has become creative and has accompanied faith into its highest flight of discovery.

We have already discussed the descriptive function of reason as it provides the material for faith from the heritage of faith and from the past appropriation of personal faith. Especially strong, as we saw, is the function of the descriptive reason within religious communities and institutions where faith is formulated into doctrine. Faith in such a setting displays steadiness and balance. In just such a setting, however, the creative and the critical reason have the least chance to do their proper work. They are all the more needed because they are the less wanted!

The critical reason labours to keep the self unified within and in right relation to the outside world. Without the proper work of the critical reason, faith in the long run becomes unbalanced and unrelated. It neither satisfies the self nor works, even though one who shuns the truth may want to make himself believe that faith satisfies and works effectively apart from the critical reason. The drive of the critical reason is to find self-consistency of interpretation and correct relation of such ordering of thought to what is outside self.

One aspect of the task of critical reason is, then, to find consistency of thought. By far the largest part of this work is the silent, continual work of reason below the deliberate decisions of the self. Most of life is lived and most knowledge learned without explicit intent and without focused intellectual activity. Formally, this function of reason in finding the rules and processes of consistency is called logic. Logic can provide the rules for finding the game, but can never supply the game. The rules of logic, too, must analyse the processes of intellectual consistency in such a way as not to substitute these rules for what is genuinely outside the self. Such self-restraint belongs to the proper function of logic.

As to the second aspect of the function of the critical reason, namely to find consistency in the empirical world, it may be that the world outside is not consistent in itself. Then reason should not find it so. It may be that the world outside does not correspond to the kind of consistency reason expects from within but has some other form of cohesion. Then reason should not falsely impose its own unity upon the outside material. It may also be that the primary experience of a group or a person refuses to be welded into some smooth unity. Some experience may seem true to identification and yet not go together in thought. In such a case, reason must recognize that it has worked at identification and discrimination, that it has also worked at evaluation, interpretation and testing, but that it cannot order its knowledge so as to find the same consistency outside that it can construct within its own world of free ideas. The two deep drives of reason are for correct interpretation of information and for inner consistency. The critical reason can be developed into a sharp tool of analysis to guard self and society against false faiths. However complex and far-reaching faith becomes and however important it is to keep open and courageous the creative reason, no faith will be strong and real that has not passed through the hottest fires of the critical reason.

We shall shortly develop and discuss what the powers and the problems of the critical reason are, as we come to weigh the claim of religion to knowledge beyond ordinary experience that is yet related to it. Even in this general analysis of the relation of faith and reason, however, it is obvious that the three great temptations of religious knowledge are (1) to develop faith solely within the drive of creative reason and not to subject it to the tests of the critical reason; (2) to live by a descriptive faith, centring in the past, especially of a concrete community of faith which provides a faith that is kept immune from both the creative and the critical reason; and (3) to be so centred in mood and method in the critical reason that the life of faith itself is undermined. Neither life on any plane nor the life of religion can be strong and real except as both faith and reason work together livingly in the creative, descriptive and critical realms. With respect to method these three realms remain, but the greatest of these is the creative. In the creative realm, as we shall see, both faith and reason find their fullest effectiveness and fulfilment of nature.

Chapter IV

Perspectives, Presuppositions and Postsuppositions

Before we discuss the nature of what is beyond ordinary experience and how it can be ascertained, we need to raise the question in another form as to the relation between the inner and outer aspects of knowledge. The problem is how presuppositions are related to postsuppositions.

There is no such thing as totally presuppositionless thinking. All new experience becomes known in relation to previous experience. Past experience is ordered experience. Every self shapes its own world of interpretation by selection and arrangement of material. It both chooses and creates a context. The self is the constant context for all personal knowledge. This context is an accumulated result that cannot be reduced to or tested by any one set of immediate experience and no number of experiences can add up to its total sum. But it is far more than a stream of choices that can never be reproduced. It is a creation by the self from among its reservoir of free ideas. It is indeed the synthesis of faith and reason as we have just described their respective functions. A presupposition as the choice and creation of the self can therefore never be proved. The processes of both creative and critical thinking unavoidably involve presuppositions.

If a presupposition could be proved it would no longer be a presupposition of knowledge. It could be proved only in terms of some other presupposition, in which case the former presupposition would no longer be a presupposition, for it would have been in fact originally a false presupposition. Logically a presupposition of experience can never be proved. Lives have presuppositions as well as thoughts; the presuppositions of a religious life are especially beyond proof. The realities and powers of such a life are whatever are beyond ordinary experience in such a way that they can never be proved by it. They could not be 'more real than' and certainly not ultimate unless this fact were true. All live by faith in terms of the analysis of experience. All live by presuppositional contexts that in their wholeness cannot be reduced to proof.

Although not all men are religious in the sense that they confess the experience of what is beyond the ordinary content of life, all are religious in the sense that they live by a faith, a context of life, a presupposition that cannot be proved. We seem now to have mixed two kinds of definition of religion: one claims content beyond ordinary experience; the other claims only inescapable involvement in a presupposition for life, an unprovable faith by which all live.

This apparent mixture, of course, is the central problem of religious knowledge: how religious reality can be both beyond and yet related to experience. Every person takes a stance toward the world he meets. Every person develops a posture of living. The way life is both lived and interpreted depends upon the self's shaping of life. Neither the self nor anyone else can prove the final correctness of such shaping so as to rob any person of the freedom to choose and to create context.

The question concerning such stance-presupposition is whether it is only choice and creation, or whether in fact, deepest down, it is not also discovery of what is more than experience. What is more than experience may be the presupposition that overarches both the self and its world. In *Faith and Reason* I began with the definition that religion is 'whole-response to whatever is considered most important and most real'. Since presuppositions are inescapable in actual life, all (by this definition) are religious. The only question under such a definition concerns what constitutes a true faith. According to the definition of the present volume, however, people are not necessarily religious in their choice of context. Irreligion is a genuine choice. Man is free not to respond to God in the creation of his context of life. But such freedom does not imply that all may not in fact be related to God and choose concerning him. It means only that man is free to have an ignorant or a rebellious faith, that man is free to rationalize as well as to reason. The true circle of reality may still compass those who deny it, and our investigation aims to establish that the weight of the evidence tends to such a conclusion.

Religious reality claims to be the presupposition for life, the 'more than experience' that has power over it. Our problem is exactly, therefore, to investigate the nature of this presupposition. Is there a true context for interpreting the world? If this context reaches beyond the individual experience and is indeed true for all interpreters, is there some common element in man that testifies to this fact; and does this common context, if discovered and correctly employed, most genuinely and helpfully order the world of experience to what is beyond it?

Certainly such presupposition of life is for all of life. Therefore it cannot be merely theoretical. Any analysis of knowledge that cuts the lifeline between reason and life is analytically inadmissible at the start. There must also be the same or some similar presupposition for conduct. Specific actions come from some working wholeness of self. Unless there is some presupposition for conduct, some character of life, there is no responsible self. There will be changes and lapses in character and activity, but always some unity can be presupposed in the case of every normal self. To be sure, thought and action are not identical. The ordering and directing of experience are by the same person but are distinct functions. Therefore faith and life can diverge as belief and action. Interpretation and application can conflict. For this reason the presupposition of life is more than either theoretical or practical. The level of motivation where the self chooses and creates context and determines its line of conduct lies deeper than either context or conduct. All these matters we shall have to investigate in our section on man and reason, but for our present purposes it is necessary to keep in mind that the religious presupposition is for all of life.

This governing presupposition is the meeting-place for all perspectives on the outside world. The self looks at what it finds from within the major unity of its own chosen and created centre of interpretation. Each person sees everything from a total stance that breaks up into various perspectives in relation to differing subjects. Each perspective, in turn, helps to give

41

meaning to what is seen. It provides a context for interpretation. The facts become related within a given discourse of meaning. The world is seen from a concrete angle of vision. Each person views his experience within the pattern of his own vision. All knowledge depends upon the presupposition of the self and upon the perspectives stemming from this presupposition. These perspectives are not mechanical, equal in intensity, or entirely at once. The self who is the living knower shapes in some sense his own presupposition by his own choosing and creating of context; he also fashions the perspectives livingly from within his own activity. This is the reason that thought and conduct can go apart even while they are both basically interdependent upon the creative activity of the self from within his own dynamic presupposition of life.

One part of knowledge, in any case, is the experience of the objective world. The outer world is not created; it is found. It resists man's attempt to make it conform to his own interpretation. In a dream a man can walk through a lake without getting wet or fly through the air without falling. In real life he gets wet and falls. In general, man's sense of reality corresponds to the maximum correlation of tested experiences, personally and socially. The outside world is stubborn and penalizes whoever disregards its actuality.

Three aspects, therefore, enter into all legitimate knowledge: the presupposition, the perspective and the outer world. The presupposition and the outer world are the two given elements of interpretation. The perspective is the mediating instrument which is often torn between the two actualities. The main problem posed for religious knowledge is to what extent the perspectives help to shape the presupposition as well as the presupposition the perspectives; and to what extent the perspectives shape experience from outside so as to make it conform to the interpreter's own inner demand for self-consistency, or are themselves given by what the self genuinely experiences as outside.

This question naturally brings up the main problem of to what extent the presuppositions are themselves postsuppositions. To what extent is the presupposition that is shaped by the self given from within experience, as part of the person; to what extent is it created by the person out of his own free ideas flexibly received from experience; and to what extent is the presupposition the result of accumulated experience of the outside world historically and personally? A presupposition for living and interpreting that is mainly derived from the accumulatively descriptive experience of the outside world is a postsupposition. Something is presupposed because of the knowledge transmitted by the history of the race and the particular group to which the interpreter belongs. The same thing is equally true of the history of the individual person in so far as his presupposition is mainly the stored result of what he has previously experienced of the outside world.

Language itself is a presupposition for knowledge, and language is the long product of the patient ages. All concepts distilled into language, apart from which creative knowledge would be impossible, are postsuppositions. All methods of dealing with knowledge that are used in further interpretation are largely postsuppositional. So are the moods of any age that direct attention to certain aspects of its problems and not to others. To what extent, then, is the presupposition of any life, or the presuppositions of schools of interpretation in effect postsuppositional? In what way and how much have the perspectives that are the joint products of the self and the actuality of the world entered into the make-up of the presuppositions that in turn keep shaping knowledge?

The more knowledge reaches advanced levels the more serious this question becomes. Schools of thought keep building interpretations from within their own presuppositions, looking at all new facts along their own predetermined perspectives. Communities have prescribed sets of conduct that become standard for all personal action. Religions become defensive and conservative. The interpreters of each religion are strongly predisposed to look at life and knowledge from within its own given context. Thus the self is itself shaped more than it is shaping. Given patterns for right living, for instance, almost force themselves, informally if not formally, on the interpreters of ethics. Although doctrines and codes vary widely and religions differ scandalously, the question is to what extent such divergence results from differing circumstances in objective experience. To what extent is such knowledge in fact post-suppositional? Or to what extent is it created as well as chosen by the self, thus bearing little relation to the real world of experience? I shall treat this fundamental question later with relation to man, history, nature and other religions, but it is especially of decisive importance here in our discussion of reason and God.

The theme of this book is that, if we are to find truth, no initial and no final separation between the inner and the outer aspect of experience is legitimate. We know no inner experience apart from the experience of the world, either in the history of the race or of a person. To begin by isolating the person from the world is to court the disaster of artificiality. No subsequent analysis can be adequate because instead of the given, living relation the analysis will deal partly not only with a corpse but with an imaginary and unreal individual. Nor can the outer world be isolated as though it could ever be discussed apart from the knower. We know no such world. It is created by imagination, not given. Analysis is correct only when it first turns its attention to selected elements for the sake of closer scrutiny, and then further examines each part both in its living function and in its interrelation with the whole.

It is impossible ever to say what is given in the self apart from the world or what is given in the world apart from our living knowledge of it. It is equally impossible to determine what comes merely from discovery apart from creation, and what comes from creation apart from discovery. There is only one world of interpretation resulting from both foundational contributions to knowledge. The most we can expect is to see whether some common interpretation is possible that can do justice both to what the self is and to what the self finds, personally and communally. In so doing we may come to see that there are not only self and the world of ordinary experience, but also a reality with the right to be presupposed in the ordering and directing of experience—a reality both more-than and other-than ordinary experience that can help and harm man.

If this result be sound, the relation of presupposition to post-supposition will become clear as they in turn relate to the perspectives for seeing the world and to the world that is seen.

Parables are always dangerous and often misleading. If they are used at all they must be taken for the main point which they are trying to make more vivid. No doubt the details will usually lead far astray! Nevertheless I am going to introduce an illustrative parable for the sake of hammering home the main line of my exposition.

Once upon a time there were people who lived in what seemed to them an endless forest. They had not always lived there. In the long, long ago countless generations had made their way into the woods by diligent and ever accumulative levelling of trees before them. They had thus made a wide road along which to work as they made their way ever more deeply into unknown territory. They had gone so far that now no-one could ever retreat far enough to live in the land outside the forest, but they had to live and interpret their living from within the depths of the forest itself.

(The interpretation of the story thus far is that man has made his way into the civilized state of speech over an incredibly long time. He is now in the land of speech and propositional communication and he can no longer return to whatever land was once his origin. Man's main vantage point for interpretation, that of a species of being that can think and communicate, he now simply assumes. This fact is a main presupposition that is in actuality a postsupposition.)

The forest is full of new things to discover. Some people have branched out in one direction while others have chosen their own paths to clear. As they have moved into different regions they have come upon differing kinds of territory. In many inviting regions they have cleared vast fields for settlement and have stayed there for generations, except for minor pioneering around the edges of their habitations. They have even set some of their number to tell them what it means to live in the forest and what can be done to improve their living conditions. These have described the life in the forest, gone back as far as they can into the broad highway from which they came to see if this could tell them more about where they now are, and tried to venture a distance ahead in the woods to see what more could be expected for the people if they continued their journey.

(This is to say that after man once became man with speech and learning, differing civilizations arose. The peoples within these civilizations developed fixed ways of living, settling down in them. They also set out to describe the meaning of life from within their own experience. Religions arose, too, in man's attempt to know how life could be bettered. Some went back to history the more fully to understand the present; others faced the future rather than the past. The main attitude, however, centred in living where they were and there improving their condition rather than going beyond the boundaries of ordinary experience.)

As this search for meaning and improvement grew more intense and exciting, some of their number set out in search of the peoples who had gone in different directions. They found much to their astonishment that the territories which they had reached were different, but the interpretations that these other peoples have made of the meaning of the woods were more different still. They compared notes, trying to come to some general meaning of the forest which would be more true and helpful than any separate description and explanation of its meaning. Occasionally there was some real coming together in understanding, but usually the interpreters found that the other interpreters could not describe their place aright because of the meaning that they had given to living in the forest in their own place. Sometimes they could agree on facts and sometimes on interpretation but usually they were far apart in both, although the woods, with beech here and chestnut there, were still the same forest.

(To interpret: history has produced differing civilizations, and widely different religions. As peoples come closer together in the modern world they try to understand each other's view of life. Sheer description of fact or analysis of meaning are easier subjects for agreement than the meaning of life, especially in the depth dimension of religion. When even facts are compared in the light of religious presuppositions they begin to take on differing colour tones! Thus presuppositions affect perspectives which in turn affect the interpretation of what is actually experienced. The problem is how to arrive at some unity of perspective that will allow some coincidence of perspectives that will in turn make possible a significant measure of community interpretation of the world we inhabit.)

Finally great spirits arose who craved fuller meaning for themselves and more common meaning for the separated peoples. At great cost to themselves and by unbelievable effort they made their way up a high mountain from which they had a unique view of the whole surrounding forest. From this view they could chart the lie of the whole inhabited land and see how the different areas were related. This over-all view helped the various interpreters to understand their own situation, to correct their interpretation and come to closer agreement with the interpreters of other peoples. But best of all, in the far, far distance they saw the end of the woods.

(This part of the story seems to propose direct religious experience, or at least vision, whereas our previous analysis has been basically in terms of the implications for ordering experience. But even here we suggest that the seers depend upon the work of previous generations even for being in the woods at all! Is not all immediate confrontation mediated by previous knowledge? I mean to suggest only one point, the relation between presuppositions and postsuppositions. In any case, the ordering nature of knowledge does not by itself reduce experience to that of concepts rather than to concrete content.)

Seeing much clear land, mingled with woods and lakes and bordering on an ocean, these intrepid souls encouraged the people not only to live the better where they were, but also to prepare to continue travelling at great cost of work and sacrifice until they should reach the better land that awaited them. But most of the people, dreading the hardships of further pioneering and content to enjoy life where they were, and indeed observing that many others doubted the reliability of their great seers, refused both to believe the report and to make preparation for moving.

(Prophets and seers, saints and saviours, have claimed an

47

experience that goes beyond ordinary experience. They have confessed to being in contact with realities and powers that can most deeply help and harm man. The religious dimension for them has been the way to understand the meaning of life. That vision has given context to all their further knowing of this world. And it has let them know in various ways that this life is not all there is to reality. Better lands await man if he will but find them. Many people have found help from these men of faith even in the interpretation of this life. They have discovered new ways of relating thought and conduct. But innumerable people desire neither knowledge to unsettle them about this life nor fanciful promises about any life beyond this. They have therefore refused the vision offered them and rejected the challenge. But a few have trusted the seers and have started out on the further journey toward the promised land. A very few have even climbed the mountain and have seen for themselves the good land in the distance and the bordering ocean!)

Chapter V

How can we Know that there are Realities beyond ordinary Experience?

Now we turn to the most bothersome question: how can we know what is beyond ordinary experience? The question splits into four main aspects: how do we know that there is anything beyond ordinary experience; how do we know what is there; how can what is there be related to ordinary experience; how far can we know what is there?

Faith is one thing; knowledge, another. They should go together, but they often go apart. Faith can create an imaginary world. It can create an antidote to fear's imaginary threat. Many remember how as children they frightened themselves into seeing animals behind the distant bushes in the dim light of an autumn evening and how they then began to hear help coming along the lonely path in the isolated woods. Or if they were less given to make dream worlds, they may at least have found a protective story when they broke the china heirloom! After a while the story seemed almost more real than the truth. Faith found a world to protect the threatened self from its crushing fear. But faith did not produce facts. No help came walking down the path; and the fancied world collapsed before the parental tribunal. No mere wish, or hope, or faith can produce solid knowledge of a world created by the imagination. Cosmically speaking, men are frightened children. If religious faith, therefore, is to be credible to mature thinking, it cannot avoid finding a satisfactory answer to the problem of knowledge.

How, then, can we know that there are realities and powers beyond ordinary experience? The world that we know is a process that has grown over the vast ages. It has not been made in the sense of having been manufactured. No external accretions, previously unrelated, have been pushed into process

49

New levels or dimensions for knowledge have continually been added, but not in the fashion of a house to which additions are made for further use. Even if the skeleton of this universe, so to speak, came suddenly into being all at once billions of years ago, as some scientists think, the manner of its coming to be is not settled. Such intensified or concentrated creation, then, constituted the continuum within which new creations would appear. Even if the original universe may have come from elsewhere, the history of this universe since then has been a process of development.

Wherever the new came from and of whatever it consists, was not there as such before it entered the process. At least it was not visibly present. Life was not always on the earth and man came here much later. No amount of examination of what was there before can explain why and how the newness itself came to be. If chemists will soon produce life in the laboratory, for instance, the chemical elements will not account for life. Prediction of an event based on previous observation is not explanation of the event. *Post hoc* is not *propter hoc*. Neither does biological generation explain life. Life simply is more than, and other than, what was there before. Yet every new becoming has proved not only to belong to what was there before but even to help fulfil it. With each arrival of a fulfilling novelty the process as a whole reached a new high. Such fulfilment can be seen, of course, only from the point of view of the new which both made use of what was there before and added a new dimension to the process.

If usefulness is one criterion of meaning, the process itself thus took on meaning increasingly. What was previously in process was presupposed and used by the new. Somehow the process consists of parts that are interdependent and mutually helpful at least in reaching and maintaining the kind and degree of unity which the universe now exhibits. The process as a whole has been thus far orderly and has added new, fulfilling dimensions which were not there before. Each new appearance not only added a new dimension for knowledge beyond the previous, ordinary world, but it also showed new capacities on the part of the former order that could accept and facilitate the new as actually belonging to the previous process even while going beyond it.

The highest level of becoming is human life. It presupposes and depends upon the previous process as a whole. Discontinuity is never apart from a solid base of continuity. Physics, chemistry and biology have their several rightful claims in the interpretation of what human life is. But they do not exhaust it. Man experiences understanding. He makes symbols for communication and uses tokens for future rewards. But no creative power to produce speech built on the capacity for abstract meaning and for using complicated symbols for communication concerning worlds which are not present to sense, can equal man's ability to order his world in such a way as to understand to some real extent what experience itself means. The dimension of meaning in the sense of explanation, of seeing the inner relation of experienced realities, is unique to human beings among all the created life we know.

To discuss the meaningfulness of the process is, therefore, first of all to discuss man's meaning. Such meaning is no mere feeling concerning the world, but is a way of describing the inner way in which the process hangs together in itself, as a history of man's development, as a supporting continuum of man's life, as a world to give content and challenge to man's present experience, and a world for ordering and directing future experience. Man's life is inclusively related to the process as well as being its highest point of arrival. If the process has general meaning it must be in terms of man's life and for man's interpretation of it.

Does this fact, however, help us to know that there are realities and powers beyond man's ordinary experience that can help and harm him? Such is in fact the case. If reasonable interpretation is to have solid meaning, the new cannot come from nothing and from nowhere. To believe so is to forfeit faith in reason where it counts heavily in its need to understand and to be at home in the world. The new must have some ground, some secret power for coming to be. It must come from some place or from some reality with power to produce the new.

We are not proposing some simple solution of cause and

51

spatial location. At this point we must exercise great critical care. These categories may be far more difficult to fathom than we can imagine. In ordinary experience there is continual newness. The springtime and the baby keep coming with fresh growth. Nothing stays quite the same with the lapse of time. The hidden possibilities for growth and change in what we know are pregnant with newness. Why, then, should not cosmic newness be merely one more manifestation of the bubbling reservoir for novelty that seems to characterize process? Cannot the process that generates newness within itself generate newness of itself? How do we ordinarily relate possibility for newness within the process to the added dimensions of novelty which the cosmic process as a whole illustrates? Is not creativity a general power of the world we know?

All ordinary newness occurs within observable laws of growth and change. If all that we knew merely came and went, grew and decayed, then a reasonable interpretation would be that this is a world where potentiality continually eventuates in actuality. The newness of growth, in such a case, could be one aspect of ordinary experience. Persons, too, could be included as the highest example of complex growth and decay. They could be classified as the flowering of cosmic growth. The incoming or outcropping of new levels, however, witnesses to the fact that the process is no mere container of events, some of which grow. Rather, the very process grows beyond itself.

Something new beyond previous growth within process happens to process itself. New levels occur, however gradual may be the process of their appearance, which previous process cannot explain. The newness as such, which, as we shall see, is no mere matter of the reorganization of elements originally apparent in the universe, witnesses to the fact that even as what is within process must have some environment and means of growth outside itself, so process itself must have some 'environment' and means of growth outside itself. Otherwise reason is severely truncated by some far less adequate faith which in the last analysis involves that new things come from nothing and from nowhere. The cosmic process itself involves every kind of reality we know, some of which were not originally visibly present; unless we accept this basic fact we discount the use of reason.

The appearance of newness is, of course, not a matter of spatial incoming in some external sense. For this reason we can say 'incoming' or 'outcropping' equally well. What matters is the irreducibility of the new as such. The problem is not where life starts in the process, whether a virus, for example, is 'alive' or not. The question is not whether some animals have 'minds' or not, but whether mind as such is a quality irreducible to matter. Water is something as such, more and other than hydrogen and oxygen. When water appeared, the history of evolution revealed the fuller dimensions of nature. We know no consciousness apart from bodies, but consciousness is a quality of experience revealing a further dimension of the nature of process.

Whether we call the point of origin 'outside' or 'inside' is unimportant provided we do not treat the new as some un-related external from 'the outside' and reduce it to some verbal 'possibility' or potentiality 'inside' nature. All aspects of process have to be treated seriously. The only question is how they can best be understood in their togetherness: as a process of becoming, as working together, and, possibly, as expectant of further disclosures and developments. No matter how the analysis turns, the upshot must be that the history of evolution is the history of the disclosure of the fuller and richer reaches of reality, especially from the point of view of meaning. To be sure, the problem of evil, since such is the case, becomes intense; but there is no problem of evil until meaning is born and life becomes significant. Reason is honoured when it is trusted with all the available facts and meanings.

It does us no good at all, however, to say that whatever we know within process we know by comparing one thing with another, but that in the case of the total process we have nothing with which to compare it. Knowledge, to be sure, has grown out of a history of comparison. Apart from such a history there would be no knowledge in any developed sense. Knowledge is the product of the history of the race in its total interpretation of differing aspects of experience. But if there are processes of growth inside experience as well as organic interdependence and mutual helpfulness, and if the world in which we live exhibits the characteristics of such growth, reason can do no other than think in the terms of its most reliable kind of interpretation. Such metaphoric and analogous thinking is legitimately at the call of reason.

If it is to order its total interpretation and if it is to face seriously the religious question, reason cannot ignore its most fruitful and solid suggestion concerning the nature of the process as a whole. Obviously such suggestion is neither proof in terms of direct logical consistency, necessarily involved in its own integrity of entailment, nor proof in terms of direct identification of an outer world. The suggestion is, rather, reason's most creative and reliable work within the need for an ordering of experience in line with the fullest and truest faith. Such a conclusion from the total ordering of experience is therefore neither logically compelling nor factually necessary. It is, rather, the knowledge of faith's choice at reason's behest where any other ordering of experience or failure to order experience would be a less full faith. Obviously there are various kinds and uses of knowledge, but as far as man can, he must live by whatever kind and measure of knowledge serves to interpret his total world of experience.

The claim to religious knowledge, namely that there is a dimension of reality and power beyond ordinary experience that can help and harm man, is strengthened by the fact that the incoming or outcropping into process of the new constitutes a series. If into a settled process there came something new that was of such a nature that it already both fitted into it and enlarged its meaning, we should indeed marvel and wonder at such an incredible happening. If such incoming happened repeatedly, moreover, until it became evident that this was the nature of the process itself, we should be well advised to look for a purpose as well as a ground for becoming. The series of becomings into the cosmic process works according to some principle, the facts suggest, and in line with some goal.

Not only are there organic events within the process; the process itself appears to be such an event, growing not only in

54

an environment and by means of resources beyond itself but also according to some inner or outer goal-seeking. The inner direction and the ingression from beyond itself indeed point in the same general direction by their belonging to each other or being made for each other, so to speak. There are both increase and enlargement of meaning in terms of organic togetherness of increasing complexity, and finally of interpretative meaning. The co-working of the inner development and the series of novelties adding to process bespeak some common reality and power which are increasingly disclosed by the history of the process itself.

We may call such conspiracy of events a working according to some plan. No machine by itself originates planning. A plan is purposed. Within the cosmic order of coming to be and development there is, therefore, what we ordinarily call purpose. The process exhibits no mere chance increase but development according to some principle. A principle is itself descriptive, not explanatory. The history of the fulfilling new dimensions of process that have made it what it is, suggests strongly, therefore—according to the most creative and critical use of reason within faith's endeavour constructively to interpret and order life—that there are realities and powers beyond ordinary process that are responsible for the nature and the direction of the process. The world of ordinary experience in this way points to the world beyond ordinary experience. The history of creation is in fact a history of the revelation of its fuller dimension of reality. The history of process reveals what is potential to process and yet not within the resources and powers of the process as such.

It is possible, of course, but not legitimate, to account for all potentiality in terms of process; this is like accounting for the sun in terms of the potentialities in the growth of a leaf! The sun is hardly reducible to an aspect of the life of the leaf. Similarly, if our analysis is right, the final frame of reference will not be the process itself.

An amazing fact, furthermore, is the incredible spurt of comparatively recent process. From the point of view of the kind of meaningfulness that man can find in the development of the process, the order of things was fairly constant over the vast ages, and all changes were preparatory and incredibly slow. Billions of years made ready for the birth and development of life. Life itself crawled over the immense stretches of cosmic time. Even primitive man took his patient time to develop into historic man. Then, with a comparative speed that would make the fastest interstellar rocket seem practically to stand still, historic man zooms into advanced civilization. The pencil line of a few thousand years has been the measure of man's historic life in terms of self-conscious, advanced meaning.

The age of the great religions is slighter still. The last five hundred years have revolutionized man's living and thinking. And now he stands in less than a hair's breadth of time at the verge of revolutions in inner and outer reaches that baffle the wisest of our age by their startling suddenness. If time has any meaning in the ordering of life, the perplexing power for changes within process suggest its relation to realities and powers that differ from ordinary experience. The answer to the power and pace of process does not lie within process itself but in its environment, however conceived, out of which and by means of which it received its power and direction for change.

But how do we know whether what came into process came from outside or inside? No-one ever saw it come! In one way, these terms therefore have no meaning. We know only the fact of demonstrable newness. Even these facts are retroactive conclusions through analysis. The history of science itself is a huge venture of inference. In another way, directional thinking is spatial thinking and spatial relations represent the plurality, but not the inner unity of things. Even the term 'within' is spatial, involving extensive togetherness. As a matter of fact, our final choice of frame of reference for reality will be from 'within'.

We are going to consider things as containing a hidden possibility, a secret power, an undisclosed aspect. Even to discuss whether the new came from 'inside' or 'outside' is to pose the basic problem spatially. To substitute dimension for direction is no solution. Direction may seem to require thinking on levels whereas dimensions go through the same point. But a dimension involves points of reference both for being and for seeing. A dimension both is and can be observed as adding a new aspect to something. Dimensional as well as directional configurations involve extensive thinking.

Nor is appeal to possibility a solution of the problem of the becoming of what is new. Without substance, 'possibility' is a mere verbalism. Either the new was present in process all the time, in some manner consistent with the power and the purpose of its coming to be, but could not be observed, or it was not there.

If it was always fully present inherently, but not visibly, there is never anything new. The history of becoming is then the history of the disclosure of what always is. The new, in such a case, is only a matter of discovery. The history of creation, at bottom, can then be nothing but the history of the revelation of static sameness. Becoming, in such analysis, is unreal. Even if reality is conceived of in terms of a dynamic flow of events, this flow is always the same; it comes from nowhere, it goes nowhere. If the new from beyond or within process is denied as new in order thereby to deny miracle and mystery, becoming is denied in principle, creativity is refused a hearing, and we are left with some underlying permanent order beyond change that is disclosed by the history of creation.

Or even this knowledge can be denied—for the history of creation involves change—and with it the history of development as pictured by science. Such a conclusion leaves us with experience as an illusion in its capacity of ordering its world. Reason can, therefore, never approve of a conclusion that goes thus contrary to the main facts of organized ordinary experience. To deny the new altogether in view of the facts we have is not only to undermine experience but to do violence to reason in its native capacity to interpret and to order its experience.[1]

There is, to be sure, a rebellion of the mind at the coming to be of something that we cannot understand. Such revelation robs us of our final control of knowledge as well as of reality.

---

[1] With regard to this question, the *ontological* problem, all statistics, as for instance population statistics, are irrelevant. No number of chances for creative combinations can produce the primitive power for becoming.

A depth dimension of miracle and mystery is added to meaning. Time in such a case tells of what is more than our time. Therefore the natural temptation both of orderly knowledge and of security in knowing is to ignore or to deny the reality of anything new. But such procedure lands us, as we have just seen, in the eternity of all things, where all coming and going, all birth and death, all growth and decay are illusory. There is no creation; there is no history; there is only eternal reality, self-same and unchanging. In such a case the religious problem becomes how to find what must be the unchanging reality beyond the falsity of experience, whether or not there be such reality, and whether one should identify oneself with it beyond the illusions of experience or get lost in the eternal void which itself is more real than the illusions and sufferings of life. Some religions have taken these choices.

If we are to interpret possibility as neither a mere verbalism nor a pre-existing world merely disclosed by process, the possible may refer to an order of creative reality where the new has a genuine aspect of newness while still not lacking causal relation to previous reality. In such a case we have to accept as the most orderly and adequate account of evolution, the fact that the history of creation is the history of revelation. What is revealed, however, is not a self-same eternal reservoir which discloses to us in nature and history only an infinitesimal bit of its depth, but an ultimate creative reality with power and purpose to create and to direct creation to a goal. We may no more than glimpse this goal, if we see it at all, but it is the only perspective that can give meaning to the whole process of creation.

The problem is, therefore, not whether what is new comes from outside or inside the previous process, but, rather, whether it is real or not. If we accept the new that has come in a creative, accumulative series in some real sense, and in some aspect of its reality as not previously existing, as not having been 'there' before it became, the natural implication is that it comes from a creative reality with power and purpose to let it become or to make it be. To say that it comes 'from' this creative reality is, of course, to spatialize our thinking. In one sense such a statement is legitimate as well as humanly necessary since we know only within a diversified order characterized by simultaneous otherness as well as genetic otherness.

But there is also some inner unity and togetherness which underlies all this diversity in space and time. If this creative ground which accords most naturally and most adequately with the facts we know, is rightly called 'God', it is arbitrary and weakening of thought to connect him only with unity and not with diversity. We know no unity apart from all diversity. We arrive at the concept of unity from within and through our own unity of experience and the unity of the universe, such as they both are. It is one thing to say that God cannot, of course, be merely one item along with other items in time and space. It is quite another to say that God is merely some aspect of power and unity who is totally incomprehensible within or even to space and time categories.

Since we know no undifferentiated unity as such but only the power for being and for togetherness which not only underlies but characterizes all things, we must somehow know God in some reliable manner through the ordering of these things in our experience. Mystery is not thought. It can preclude a premature meaning in terms of thought, but it cannot take the place of thought. The statement that God is not finite is no explanation, and is significant only as a guard against the confusing of categories.

If 'to exist' is confined to mean 'to stand out' from other things in space and time in the sense of merely being among other things and being one of them, then obviously God does not exist. He is not a finite being alongside other finite beings. Such a God is an idol. But 'to exist' in God's case means not to stand out among other finite things, but to stand out from all finite things as their creative ground, power and purpose. Existence in finite terms must basically be defined as 'standing out from' God, as being diversified into separate beings with no capacity for total unity. The power for total unity, in terms of which all finite realities exist, is God. In this sense he is separate. He is not their power to be but the power for them to be. He *is*, in the only full sense of the term; and he is not any of the finite objects, events, or persons. He is the invisible reality and power beyond ordinary experience that can most basically help and harm man.

'Beyond' in this sense is spatial in that God is not one item in creation. He is beyond them all. He is eternal and never created. He is the constant source of newness without himself ever coming to be. God is not spatial in the sense that he occupies any space among other spaces or alongside all other spaces. He is the creator of all space and time, and also is with, in and alongside all space-times. He is the power for unity and the power for diversity that is more real than any object and all objects, events and persons in their totality, and he is best seen in terms of the purpose exhibited in our most adequate ordering of experience in line with the goal observable in process.

'Ultimate' reality is to be seen not as space-time existence but as its ground and continuing power and purpose, and, therefore, through space-time existence. Space-time can be a means whereby we indicate identity and difference in God's relation to the world. In a real sense, God is always both present and absent, for he is the power to be and the power to change in all things without ever being any or all things. He is both in and separate from all things. How such a double relation can obtain we shall discuss under the subject of God's relation to the world, but even here it is well to be aware of how much is involved in such terms as 'within' and 'without', 'possibility' and 'existence'.

Three main questions remain on this subject: how do we know what this reality is; how can it be related to the world we know; and how can we test by our critical reason such a proposed ordering and directing of experience by our creative reason within our chosen stance of faith?

Chapter VI

How do we Know what is beyond
ordinary Experience?

How do we know the nature of what is beyond ordinary experience? A series of novelties severally and accumulatively
fulfilled by each other in such a way as to constitute an evolving
universe bespeaks a prior ground and purpose, whose nature
we are now charged to depict.[1]

The only way that we know what is beyond is by means of
what is within. What is more-than and other-than ordinary
experience we can know only from what is already available to
knowledge. If such were not the case, we could not know what
is beyond either as more than ordinary experience or as relevant
to it. Knowledge is a matter of experience, at least in so far as
all knowledge is in experience. What is entirely beyond experience is also entirely beyond knowledge. Whatever this
unknown could be, for us it would be equivalent to total irrelevance and non-existence.

The case for the knowledge of religious realities and powers
beyond ordinary experience that can help and harm man should
never be put as a matter of these realities and powers being
either outside or inside the ordinary world. Since they are
religious, they must in a decisive manner be beyond experience,
but in order to be known they must be inside experience as
well. Thus in some sense religious knowledge must refer to
both what is within and what is beyond experience. Such
knowledge should, therefore, be put as a question concerning
what aspect of this evolving process can best illuminate its
total nature. Such an aspect could also be basic to and in this
sense beyond the rest of the process.

[1] The survival of the new as well as the arrival of the new indicates an order
of being as well as power for becoming. Unless reason is to be discounted, the
history of creation is the history of revelation of reality.

61

Why can we not claim, however, that what first appeared in process, namely the inorganic realm, most adequately explains the rest? Any attempt at such explanation lands us in an unfactual reductionism that amounts to the most incredible as well as the least usable faith. As a matter of fact, the interpreter explains himself away. If thought is serious, thought itself must have cosmic status. It can be neither accident nor illusion. It must be the evolvement of something real. The only way in which this procedure of appealing to the inorganic realm as a basis for explanation can be carried out with any seriousness is to claim that, to begin with, there was much more to what came than what first appeared. Such a claim implies an unknown realm in, with, or under the known that affirms subsequent cosmic history to be the history of revelation of the fuller and more important nature of the realities and powers that were always there. Thus we must reject the inorganic realm as a basis for explanation.

But can we, instead, select the present stage of the process as the best indicator of the true nature of the total process? Following such a line of reasoning, we have to face immediately the question why, if we can accept the present stage, the process should now have come to a stop. Such an ending to the process of revelation of reality becomes factually preposterous in view of the fact that the latest infinitesimal segment of cosmic process has revealed immeasurably and incomparably more meaning than the rest of the whole cosmic process put together. If we take this fact seriously, we arrive, on the contrary, at the conclusion that cosmic process is about to burst into sudden bloom after the long growth underground, the slow development of stem and leaves, and the protracted budding. The real problem is perhaps, conversely, how a kind of environment that can labour long to produce a gorgeous flower for a day can then have its bloom almost immediately shredded by insects. Nature, indeed, must surely yield to history as the main basis of explanation. The main evidence of process, in any case, points to a surge ahead, to the disclosure of fuller realities and powers somehow already present but not yet fully disclosed. Therefore neither the beginnings of process nor the present stage of process seems best to indicate the ground and purpose of process.

What is beyond ordinary experience can best be seen, rather, in terms of the highest arrival in process of meaningful life. This is our thesis. The main thrust of process, now suddenly erupting beyond all comparison with previous millennia or billennia, is the creative realization of human life and history. The minor counter-argument concerns the nature of the destruction which threatens the creations of this thrust. There must, of course, be no winking at either evil in life or evil in death. But our task now is to discuss the nature of the highest arrival in cosmic process in contradistinction from the slow beginnings of the creation of the conditions for meaningfulness and the present stage of incredibly swift moving process.

The highest arrival in process we know best by the fact that while it is meaningfully related to the process as a whole it can be explained by nothing else. The pinnacle of the mountain relates to its far larger base but is not the base. Nevertheless it is of the same kind of material as the rest of the mountain. The pinnacle of human history, on the other hand, also relates to the rest of human history which is its base, as well as to the flat country of nature, comparatively speaking, on which the mountain itself rests; but what makes the pinnacle of human history, besides its general continuity with all else, is the radical difference between its nature and the rest. As far as the aspect of its novelty goes, the highest new is irreducible to previous process. Life and love are simply not merely more matter.

Such newness in itself, however, would be a matter of indifference unless it mattered organically and profoundly to previous process. The new must relate to the total process, giving it its most inclusive and highest meaning. Even the dark shadows must somehow themselves be due to the nature of the total process in the light of its highest meaning. The highest new must meet the test, as far as the nature of the test —and what is to be tested—will allow, of inclusive relevance in terms of explanatory power. If we refer to our illustration in discussing presuppositions and postsuppositions, the highest must be the peak from which the whole woods can be most reliably surveyed, but must offer, besides, the view of what lies beyond the forest.

The facts of highest discontinuity and most extensive relevance are not enough, however, to establish the highest arrival in process. Life needs more prescription than description. We need to find out not only what is, but what is wrong and what to do about the wrong. The highest arrival must by its own nature intrinsically be the standard in terms of which what is evil can be discerned and what is good can be prescribed. It must, in short, provide a standard for the transformation and the fulfilment of life. The highest must cut the most deeply into human evil, both to throw light on its nature and reveal the remedy for it. If the highest arrival within cosmic process, and more particularly within human history, is to represent the realities and powers beyond ordinary experience that can help and harm man, it must, however, be more than even the fullest explanatory power and the truest standard for human good. It must also possess the power of human transformation and fulfilment. If we understand, accept and apply this power aright, it must somehow constitute the most effective remedy for human ills and the most beneficial reality for human improvement.

Requiring such conditions of history's highest in no way makes man central to religious reality. Man is the one to be explained, not the explanation; man is the one to be cured, not the remedy; man is the created actuality standing in constant and immeasurable need, not the creative reality and power that can finish and fulfil the process. Therefore it cannot be said that the explanation is man-centred. Such conditions, nevertheless, do demand that the religious realities and powers be not the imaginary idols that are unknown or impotent in the face of man's actual problems and needs, but the true God who alone can explain, judge and save. No mere model will do for religious explanation, only a model so rightfully selected from experience itself that it most fully represents both its actuality and its potentiality. Religion is at its best the more it thinks and lives in the light of reality.

We conclude these suggestions, therefore, by the assertion that we know that process most strongly suggests realities and powers beyond itself, not yet seen and accepted in their plenary presence; that what is beyond must be seen from within human experience; that the highest arrival fulfils the demands that these religious realities and powers cannot be explained from what came before in process, can most inclusively and relevantly give meaning to the rest of the process, including its evils, and can best illuminate what is wrong, prescribe for its cure and provide the power for both its cure and fulfilment.

We have now come to the point where we must discuss how the highest arrival can be found in concrete history. When we have performed this task we must go on to discuss how the highest arrival can then be known in its relations to the total process, and finally in what way and to what extent we can support our claims.

If what is beyond is to be seen from within cosmic process, more particularly from within human history, and most especially as the highest arrival in terms of total meaningfulness and power for fulfilment, we must choose this arrival from among personal events. We cannot choose from events lower than life, which are blind to interpretation; and among lives, we must choose the most fulfilled life that can be set up as standard for other lives, making available for faith the fulfilment of life. Whoever lived the most meaningful life, or at least whoever saw and accepted as a conclusively fulfilled ideal the reality and power that can most fully meet human need to such a degree that his life became an effective illustration of it, can alone provide the kind of life that is the most adequate standard and power for all the rest of human life.

In the next section we shall make a further study of human need as indicative of the nature of the environment that elicited and elicits it, and also consider the fact that there is a common human nature; for both these implied affirmations are presuppositional for the present analysis. Without cosmic process meaning is a prerogative of human life. The most meaningful life is the one that can provide the answer to what human nature is and what it is all about, what it needs and how this need can

65

be met. The highest novel emergence in such a case, although unique on its arrival, must at the same time most fully indicate the deepest potential of human nature as such. The most fulfilled life indicates the kind of life that is the meaning of life.

If such a life came in the past, unless it was at the time too far ahead of life-in-general to be relevant, it must have impressed other lives with its relevance and power. It would thus in all likelihood have become the centre of religious interpretation. Such a life could be lived, in the first place, only because in its depth experience it had seen a new reality and related itself to it. It had come in contact with, or had been invaded by, what is beyond ordinary experience up to this point, and had thus made what is beyond a matter of being also partially within ordinary experience. In so far as this religious reality is also relevant for people inclusively and fulfillingly, in so far as it came within human history in this pioneering person of faith, it also became available for people in general.

The likelihood is, therefore, that if such a life has been lived it has become the centre of a historic religion. Every centre of a universal religion should consequently be studied as a candidate for the true universal. The last section of this book will be devoted to such a study. To be sure, if no historic religion offers an adequate candidate, living personalities should be studied for their understanding of the meaning of existence and the way in which this understanding is not only a matter of theoretical construction but should also have the full relevance and power of an embodied life. If neither the past nor the present offers such a living meaningfulness in terms of a personal event, we must, of course, live by the best we know and keep trying to understand and to accept the realities and powers beyond ordinary experience that can help and harm man.

Even if such a meaningful life can be found, moreover, it cannot prove what is beyond. From within process there can be no proof. Only at the end of process, or for one who can know the end of the process, can there be knowledge of the nature of the fulfilment of process. At such a time or for such a being, however, confirmation is unnecessary and irrelevant.

We are not now discussing the nature of proof or the measure of possible confirmation of religious truth. All we are doing in this context is pointing out the fact that the choice of the highest arrival in history constitutes a faith judgment suggested by some solid knowledge as to the nature of ultimates. The choice, in any case, is among the faith judgments of actual religions, or possibly of leading religious personalities, past and present. What we seek is the kind of life that can most effectively make clear its meaning for the rest of us and can point us to the way in which such meaning can be obtained.

The highest arrival of meaningfulness in human history, I suggest, is the life, teaching, death and resurrection of Jesus, called the Christ. The highest I have found is the love of God as lived and taught by Jesus. I cannot see how anything can be higher than the all-inclusive, unconditional and eternal love that was at least conclusively suggested by Jesus' life and instructions. If anything can be higher than that, I am of course open to its revelation and ready thankfully to accept it.

That Jesus lived and taught such love there can be little doubt. The two great interpreters of his life, the author of the Johannine writings and Paul, make love central. Such love came from God. God so loved that he sent his Son. Whoever remains in love remains in God and God in him. God's eternal purpose in Jesus Christ is to reconcile the world to himself. Nothing shall ever be able to separate us from the love of God which is in Jesus Christ. Jesus' death on the Cross and his return from death were the workings of God's love for man's salvation.

The parables and teachings of Jesus in the Gospels are understandable only in the light of the central love of God and man. God in his perfection sends his rain on all regardless of their desert; and just so should his children act to become mature. God is like the father of the Prodigal Son, ready to forgive and restore. God's final judgment is always according to the standard of the spontaneous love that gives and helps without being aware of gift and action as meriting any reward in the sight of God. The labourers in the vineyard find that God, in paying for the day's work, is concerned with their needs, and that he pays according to this standard and not merely according to justice.

In man's relation to man, love to neighbour is also defined in terms of the neighbour's need, and crosses all barriers of religion and nationality. Within the community founded around this personal event of Jesus, called the Christ, the members should have the same care for one another. They should weep with those who weep and rejoice with those who rejoice. From God's love, seeking the least and the last as the good shepherd seeks the hundredth sheep even when ninety-nine are safe, all the way to man's forgiving his fellowman his small debts as God has already forgiven him his unpayable large debt, the theme of love shines forth out of the New Testament in concentrated focus beyond all specific words and sayings.

This kind of love is centred not in human effort, but in faith. Jesus prayed to the eternal Spirit whom he called Father. The three main characterizations of God, according to Jesus and his interpreters, are Spirit, Father, and Love. Day and night Jesus was in contact with this Spirit of Love whom he named Father after the best human name he knew. He came to know and to accept the nature of God through his commitment in faith from his earliest life onward, through frequent and long praying and through living out the concern he found in God. Trusting faith and responsible commitment provided for him the content for his creative reason to interpret God as universal love.

Surely Jesus' evaluative response and his ordering and directing of experience were not entirely new. He made use of the best in the Old Testament, the religious history of his people, where there were close approximations to God as universal concern; he also very likely made use of an environing Greek atmosphere of universalism, and in all probability he received some influence from the Essenes, and possibly through them or in other ways, from Oriental winds that seem to have refused to die down before they touched on Mediterranean shores; he may even have had some Egyptian heritage from the sun-worshipping Pharaoh who defied the narrower religion of his people. Creative thought is never brand new. It only adds

68

something new of content or dimension, of context or organization, some new way of evaluating the old experience and of ordering and directing it accordingly.

But this new dimension of universal, unconditional and eternal love, which became at least suggestively dominant in the life of Jesus, became decisive for the understanding of God by human reason. It revolutionized the understanding of the nature of ultimate reality. The living, personal God of the Old Testament was still the same and yet also radically new. He was still understood as judge, but judgment now was not for the sake of vindication or even for justice. God's love came not to condemn but to save the world. Righteousness was not done away but lifted into a matter of love's right relation with God and among men. Wisdom remained respected; not the wisdom according to the old world which was passing away, but according to the meaning of Christ, a foolishness and stumbling-block to the old standards.

This new understanding and acceptance of God presented man, too, in a new light. The new universal and unconditional standard made man hopeless in terms of his self-sufficient attainment of religious reality and rightness. Man instead was shown up as a sinner beyond self help. Equally impotent seemed the old kinds of community to rescue man from his wrongness and get him right with God and man. But to man in such a predicament God offers instead the good news of willing acceptance, forgiveness and power to become right. Even the burden of religion itself is off man's back. The law as the threat of an impossible attainment is done to death.

To be sure, Jesus himself came to know God through his response to God in prayer, life and thought. How well he knew God we cannot know. The specific details of Jesus' life and teachings are beyond reconstruction. We know only the general outline of his life and teachings. But these by their unity and power witness to a concrete historical figure who shook not only his own world but world history. That he knew the nature of God to be love is clear. He would not have lived and taught accordingly otherwise.

To what extent this driving, evaluative judgment had permeated explicitly the whole ordering and directing of his life and thought we cannot know. Human beings seldom become a consistent system in respect to both life and thought. Inherited remnants of inconsistent teachings may have remained in Jesus' life to crop out in less elevated moods, for discouragement engenders its own dragons of cross-purposes. But these he shared in common with the whole previous process. The radical and redeeming new is what mattered in its creating a truer picture of what is beyond man's ordinary experience with power to help and harm.

Jesus was a man of primary religious experience. His creation of thought was, we shall see, discovery of reality. His thought was close to life. Those he taught were not trained formally. Besides, the main stress of Jewish religion was historic and concrete. It was mostly a matter of people and persons, of the living God and of ways of living before him. Therefore Jesus never used his insight as a theologian and philosopher would have done. He never applied his central theme to man's general problems in any systematic fashion. Even though his thinking sprang from the creative centre of God as love, he lived and applied this thinking mostly in terms of concrete instances, whether of action or of creative artistry.

At a time when faith in the living God was taken for granted within a devout community, and before man's general questions had been raised insistently and comprehensively by seekers from within and attackers from without, such a personal and practical approach was enough. Today, when many centuries have been used to bring to the bar of man's judgment the adequacy of the faith, especially now in the light of man's burning general questions as to the meaningfulness of life as well as in relation to other living religions, it is necessary to reassess this faith judgment that Jesus' life and teachings, death and resurrection—indicating God to be universal, unconditional and eternal love—actually do provide the answers of creative reason to man's problems of suffering, of sin, of incompleteness, of history, of nature and of the relation of one faith to other religions. Only after these questions have been discussed can we entertain the probings of the critical reason. But first let us conclude our suggested content for history's highest arrival of meaningfulness by pointing out the bearing on this suggestion of Jesus' death and resurrection.

Jesus went to death because in the experience of his very being he knew that God was love. God was Father and he knew himself as son. To claim such a relationship with God was to upset the existing religious order and indeed to blaspheme against God. Therefore Jesus was doomed to death. According to our best information, Jesus could have refused to go all the way to death with his testimony. Like Socrates, who chose death to honour the law rather than escape, Jesus chose death to honour God. Deep down he could not refuse his Father's will, recant or escape. Countless people, of course, have gone to death for what they believed; many have refused escape even out of sheer stubbornness. It was not Jesus' going to death that matters most to our theme, but his faithfulness unto death within the outgoing love of God which had become his own.

If God in fact is love and if God had become the centre of Jesus' life and thought, the main originator and continuer of Jesus' ordering and directing of his experience was God. Jesus was in line with the will of God. He lived the will of God and died within the will of God. The authentically human by such living expressed the genuinely divine. The life, teaching and death of Jesus thereby became one whole testimony to the nature and the way of God.

As such, this personal event, Jesus called the Christ, could become for his followers the context of insistent, embracing love by which to evaluate, order and direct their own experience. The struggle to do so, in persons and in the new community, is portrayed in the New Testament, parts of which reach both lofty heights and practical concreteness. Thus the story of the life of Jesus lends itself to a pattern for interpreting the meaningfulness of life. I believe and shall later undertake to indicate that it shows most fully what life is about, where it has gone wrong, and how it can be helped.

If death had ended that life, however, it would be an example of human nobility, to be sure, but equally one of ultimate

F   71

futility. It might then have aroused admiration as to the nature of man, but would have told us at the same time of the impotence or unconcern of the realities and powers beyond ordinary experience that can help and harm man. It could even suggest the inimical, invidious character of what is beyond. If such a life could have been held by death, death and evil, and not life and good, have the final say. The ultimate meaning of life then is tragedy.

But then also we should have to push aside the main direction of process, its highest product, and declare the accumulative unity at the centre of the stream of cosmic history to be meaningless. In view of all other evils in nature and history, we can with some real right come to such a conclusion. The natural and preferable ground for ordering and directing experience, however, is the main line. In the light of the total direction and sudden spurt of process, it is more reasonable to come to grips with the contrary facts than to make the contrary facts deny the main evidence.

As it happened, the God whom Jesus trusted brought him back to life to assure his followers that they were not mistaken in their basic faith. Discouraged, persecuted, hiding men turned bold to witness to their experience with and of Jesus in his life, death and return to life. What actually happened we cannot know. The historic details are, as we should expect, confused and tangled. From the beginning of the spread of the movement, however, men risked their lives for the fact of the resurrection. These men had seen the healing and helping power of Jesus. They had been astonished by the reality of his teaching and living. They were taken aback by his kind of death and worldly defeat. But when the drama of Jesus' life finished in the kind of victory that was consistent with all that he lived and taught, and consistent indeed with the heart of his own faith, the followers and friends of Jesus found the faith natural that led them to their death in the same cause of the love of God.

For those who have evaluated, ordered and directed their experience consistently along the lines of Jesus' life and teachings, the resurrection is not the problem it must be to those

72

who have centred their interpretation of life within earthly experience rather than what is beyond. Without a trusting faith in the Creator in the first place, the new creation in this life and beyond is unreal. With such faith, however, the ultimacy of this world seems contrary to all demands of both the creative and the critical reason.

Such claims, of course, must be scrutinized in their proper place, but in this context, it is needful to stress that the personal event of the life and teachings of Jesus, called the Christ, is not fully understood, even potentially, as the centrality of God as love, apart from both the death and the resurrection of Jesus. If we choose as the faith judgment most indicative of the meaning of life and of all existence the personal event of Jesus, called the Christ, because through him God came to be understood as unconditional, universal and eternal love, the choice must be not only as some ideal suggested by him but as the actual demonstration in human history of the power of the kind of life that constitutes the most adequate context for the interpretation of experience, revelation of wrong, and standard for right relations with God and among men.

Chapter VII

The Moreness and Otherness beyond ordinary Experience

The highest arrival of meaningfulness, we have seen, best indicates the nature of cosmic process precisely by its being more and other than the process as a whole. Now we must deal more extensively with this moreness and this otherness. The final frame of reference for the Christ-event is not human history. The reality of universal love roots in eternity, not in earthly time; and yet that love judges us all and promises us fulfilment.

Before Jesus lived and taught, God had never been understood and accepted as unconditional, all-inclusive and ever faithful love. In Jesus' life and teachings, as portrayed and suggested by the New Testament, such a grasp of the nature of God was at least dominantly lived and conclusively suggested. To be sure, there had been approximations to it, especially in the Old Testament. Even allegiance to law and going beyond the measure of the law lead toward God and away from self-centred living and thinking, whether of persons, groups or nations. Surely long before Jesus lived, there had been definite expansions in the interpretation of God's goodness and inclusive reign. God was already known to act redemptively beyond covenant, law, and particular peoples. Yet no-one had dared to know God as sovereign and eternal love whose outgoing concern is as constant as his very being. Nor had anyone dared to suggest that man's maturity consisted in such Godlike conduct of total and unconditional love.

Such newness was qualitatively revolutionary, demanding an all-or-none response. All religions, all laws, all attitudes, all conduct and all customs: in short, all life, had now to come under this unconditional scrutiny and become radically re-

constituted. All securities and satisfactions now became subject
to drastic re-examination and revolution. A few daring spirits
since then have dared to draw near the centre of this fire, which
threatens to consume the main heritage of the past in every
present, but none has stood at its centre to find there, instead
of the terror and pain of destruction, the saving light on man's
problems, the power to destroy the evils that infest him and
the fulfilment of meaning both for life and for the cosmic
process as a whole.

This new is thus more than ordinary experience in the sense
of both going beyond and fulfilling the past, thus witnessing to
its source beyond previous process; it is also more by being the
fullest potential for man. It was not only new when it came. It
is always new to human experience which must stand under its
judgment and share its fulfilment. As far as human thought can
reach, we can never go beyond the eternal, sovereign faithfulness of God. We can become fulfilled within it but can never
come up to it, let alone go beyond it.

In the second section of this book we shall discuss the way
in which man is fulfilled within the eternal love of God. The
point now is that the moreness which came in Jesus is not only
an historic but an eternal moreness. If God is this moreness—
and we cannot see how he can be either 'less' or 'more'—not
only are the purpose of process and the nature of man disclosed
in the kind of life lived and taught by Jesus, but even more, in
this personal event we see the Ground and Goal of all ultimate
meaningfulness.

If the religious reality which goes beyond ordinary experience
is the God of unconditional concern in whom are the fountains
of creation, the moreness we are discussing with regard to
cosmic process and human life lies obviously mostly in the
future. The sudden spurt of human history, quite incommensurate with the rest of the process, indicates the further and
fuller revealing of what is beyond ordinary experience. Why
the cosmic beginnings should be so low and so slow, as they
seem to us, is beyond our comprehension. God's eternity is a
strange framework for human conceiving. The present attainment in human history even at its best, and accompanied, at

that, by untold suffering and sorrow as well as frustration and failure, can in no way qualify as God's final work with process and history. We cannot know how lost species in evolution fit into any final meaningfulness nor account with any certainty for the fulfilment of subhuman life. If God is the one Jesus saw him to be, however, all pasts become fulfilled in God's final present.

Perhaps all life lives through innumerable existences preparatory to self-consciousness and moral choice. All life can be continually latent in God who works on every level of creation. Our own personalities come out of the depths of natural as well as human history. Perhaps we, too, keep living innumerable lives in this world or in the wide-flung sidereal spaces, until our spirits become free and mature within the immeasurable riches of God's eternal realities. We may, of course, even now be ready to retain such selfhood and memories as are consistent with God's unimaginable purpose for us. In such case, God's future for us would be growth in new lives and in living conditions for our personalities and for our communities of intimate affection.

One thing is certain in the light of the kind of meaningfulness Jesus saw at the horizon of his life: the moreness of religious reality for creation has only begun to be glimpsed even within our best earthly attainment. What can and will happen in human history and beyond earthly existence is beyond knowledge; the time of its happening depends partly upon our freedom of choice; the nature and certainty of God's eventual fulfilment of life, however, are inevitable involvements of the central Christian faith judgment. The truth of the Christian faith is only suggested by the past; it is evidenced more if it proves to be man's most effective way of ordering and directing his life for maximum fulfilment; but since the whole thrust of the central Christian faith judgment, that God is sovereign love, points toward the illimitable future, Christian faith cannot be mostly a matter of knowledge. The main line of meaningfulness focuses on the future, as man becomes fulfilled within the boundless love of God.

Is not our assumption that human beings will eventually be

76

fulfilled a matter of an unjustified making present process central rather than God? May not human beings be fulfilled by being surpassed, as is the rest of creation? Such surpassal, I have suggested elsewhere, may be fulfilment within the subhuman creation. Why may not man be similarly fulfilled in history or beyond our particular environment? Such a thought, indeed, I had in mind in proposing the possibility of 'innumerable lives' either in this world or in world beyond. As human beings we may now be only candidates for preliminary fulfilment, not for final graduation. Or, as a matter of fact, lives may never reach finality of form, but be subject to the endless enrichment of God's creative resources as he co-operates ever more intimately in the adventures of our freedom.

If, however, God is the personal Spirit who is Love, 'the Father of our Lord Jesus Christ', and if we are and know ourselves to be personal spirits within the companionship of God, we seem already to have arrived at that degree of individuation where the moreness of God's creative fulfilment becomes related to a permanent selfhood. Jesus, beyond the grave, seems to have been both identifiably the same and yet also unrecognizably different. What this experience was we cannot know, nor can we know the far future of process or human history. Within the experience of our faith judgment, however, we can know him who is the ground and goal of the illimitable newness of the endless future. What is more than ordinary experience, in any case, as seen in the personal event of Jesus' life, teaching, death and resurrection, is known mostly as a potential fulfilment in the future that cannot be foreseen in its details.

Our discussion of the content of future moreness may be no more right than the feelings of a unicellular life for some future belonging to a complex organism; but if we human beings can know and experience meaningfulness, and if we have seen its Ground through the kind of love Jesus lived, we can predict with some degree of assurance the general nature of the Goal, the context of fulfilment. But how can we know, furthermore, that religious reality is not only more than but also other than ordinary experience?

We can know, in the first place, the aspect of otherness by considering our own limitations. Our knowledge is severely circumscribed even in the case of ordinary experience. How much less can we claim to know the ultimate reaches of religious reality beyond our experience! Religious moreness by its very nature has this dimension. Nor can we know ourselves except as candidates for fulfilment. How we shall know when we become fulfilled we cannot know now. There certainly will be an otherness in our own knowledge which will surpass all mere present moreness. Our knowledge will at last become not only increased but transformed.

Even the moreness of the God disclosed in the Christ event will be no mere moreness, no mere knowledge of the same kind we have now, even at its best, when we ourselves are transformed into the likeness and power of the eternal Love in such a way that we then will know effectively, from within this reality, which is now mostly a matter of otherness. Whatever knowledge we now have, even in the Spirit, is still so obscured and diffused, and very likely severely distorted by our present human nature, that when it is delivered from its incompleteness and falsity the same knowledge will become other.

Then also if God is unconditional, all-inclusive, eternal Love, how can we possibly know as he knows? Such otherness is qualitatively debarred from our knowledge forever. Thus we cannot know either in the full perspective of the togetherness of all things, or, especially, as God knows. In these respects there is an unimaginable otherness to religious reality that man's knowledge can never encompass. There is, therefore, a real point in discussing the otherness as well as the moreness of religious knowledge. We can know, in so far as the Christian faith contains knowledge within its ultimate faith judgment, that there is such otherness, some of which is attainable in future experience while some of it is forever beyond our ken.

Are there ways, however, for religion to affirm through understandable communication both the moreness and the otherness of religious reality? I suggest the following approach:

We must start with knowledge, not ignorance; with meaning, not mystery. Therefore we should start with what Christian

78

theology has.called the Incarnation. We start with the way in which we see God in the kind of life Jesus lived and taught. But if God is not only quantitatively but also qualitatively different from ordinary experience, the event of Jesus' life itself has to be taken in two positive senses. In one way it must be used directly. God is this kind of life. God is this kind of love. God is completely faithful as Jesus was faithful all the way to death. Thus we use a concrete event with definable content to evaluate, order and direct the rest of our experience. In this sense our faith judgment provides a meaningful criterion both for interpreting and for living our experience.

But this direct or 'literal' use of language is obviously not enough by itself. Religious language, to be sure, is basically from within experience and in this sense it must have a primary value of sign language. Without signs there can be no symbols. A sign says; a symbol suggests. A sign denotes; a symbol connotes. A sign points; a symbol means. A sign generally is a matter of sense experience, or at least concrete, directly communicable experience; a symbol is a matter of meaning, only suggestively communicable. A flag is a symbol that can be experienced as a sign (a coloured piece of cloth) signifying a country as a total entity that cannot be directly experienced as a whole, but only as that piece of land or as those people.

Symbols somehow suggest through signs realities beyond concrete experience. Through the Cross as a sign the forgiving quality of God may be suggestively or symbolically experienced. Even if God as symbolized by the Christ-event should be directly experienced, the knowledge in that experience would still be as indicated by the sign-event of Jesus' life and teaching of love. But the symbolic experience, if authentic, can never be reduced to the sign. If Jesus' life is used as a theological sign for God it suggests generally a kind of love which in God is immeasurably richer and deeper than any human event. Therefore direct use of the 'revelatory' event is not enough by itself. Besides, the human event as sign includes all the conditions of finitude which are inapplicable to God. Therefore we say not only that God is the kind of life we have found in Jesus but also that he is like this kind of life, but, of course, on the level of his own being. When we use language in this symbolic way to refer to God we are using analogy.

Both the use of language directly (as sign) and the use of language analogously (as symbol), however, have to be general and supple. Directness becomes a matter of use. It is a way in which we can evaluate, organize and order our own experience and help to do the same for the religious community to which we belong. Every sign is in some respect relative to the knower. When a life is used as a sign, the more flexible and complex nature of such a sign multiplies the problem of relativity. What one person assumes to be direct presentation of objective truth may not seem so to another individual. When this life, furthermore, has been interpreted through a long history, both of original reporters and subsequent interpreters, it becomes even more difficult to arrive at a stable sign as the base for religious knowledge even as a minimum definite meaning. There is, nevertheless, a kind of love central to Jesus' life and teaching which is generally but authentically recognizable.

In the case of analogy, moreover, the problem is enlarged and intensified. There can be no equations or proportions that can be attributed with necessity to such a projected likeness. Analogy is only a means by which we can avoid reducing language about God to the experience of this world. It merely suggests the moreness which is involved in religious reality. Thus direct language is presuppositional for religious knowledge while analogical language delivers this language from its boundedness to ordinary experience.

To direct and analogous use of language we add the paradoxical. A paradox is the assertion of seemingly contradictory propositions. We need such use of language to indicate the limits of knowledge not only of finitude but also of categorical limits. A paradox can be used to indicate our recognition that we are not in position to know God in any sense of fulness, nor as God knows himself, nor in any other categories than those of human beings in time and space. Eternity, for instance, is more than human time prolonged infinitely toward the past and toward the future. Eternity can be considered God's time as earthly time is ours; in such a case, however, eternity must be experienced differently by an eternal being, for we cannot even conceive of its nature as from within God's experience.

If time is real, our creation is new in eternity. If it is God's only creation, God's creating is a quite arbitrary act. Why in endless time, should God at any point choose to cause the finite to appear? Such an assertion of arbitrary creation casts the gravest suspicion on our ultimate. If time is real, however, and this universe is not God's first creation, we must face the problem of a mathematical series of creations. Numerically this should bring us back, however long the chain, to some first instant. But then we are also back again to our original problem! We can, of course, conceive of an endless chain of creations. In such a case our creation is only the recurrence of a link that always is, but is not always here. Or we can think of time as God's continual stirring the same dough, with nothing new except the shape that is new to us, who also are made and remade without end.

If, however, the disclosure of God as love best answers our evaluation, ordering and directing of experience, within our compass and competence, none of these suggestions makes sense. In such a case we simply cannot know eternity. The problems of time may perhaps have begun with time and concern those in time. Time may be real for us and serious for life and destiny without being real in the same sense for God. God may then enter time and work in time without being limited to time. In other words, we cannot now see even what our basic problem is concerning God's relation to time, because we cannot get beyond the presuppositions and perspectives of temporal existence. To admit such a fact is not to appeal to ignorance nor is it to sell reason short. We may use reason to the fullest and by so doing find that there are realities and realms that we can affirm as existing and even as being the Ground and Goal of process and of human history which are still in basic respects beyond the comprehension of human thought.

In other words, where human experience is available, human reason can function. In so far as religious reality has entered human history, reason can deal with it. That same reality, however, is not on our own level of existence, a fact which makes it impossible for our reason to follow it into its own proper sphere. To indicate this fact, particularly for worship and life, paradox seems to have practical importance. Thus the idea that God is both beyond and in time is a paradoxical assertion containing more truth than the bare assertion that eternity includes time, and yet a truth which is beyond us in so far as it modifies God's existence and not ours.

Or, to take one more example, if God is the 'fount of eternal Joy' who shares of his felicity in creation in order to achieve eventually our sharing of his joy in grateful and understanding freedom, then to say that God actually suffers in history seems to spoil or offset the joy in eternity. Perfect joy in eternity and real sorrow in history on the part of a personal Spirit do not go together. We can, of course, refuse to consider knowledge beyond the limits of experience or else try to indicate in direct language that there are unsolved problems; but, practically, what happens is that man's experience then tends almost overbearingly to crowd to the centre of attention and paralyse even the central religious assertions. Therefore, to take our two examples, it may be better to assert paradoxically that God is both timeless and in time and that God the eternal Father does not suffer while the incarnate Son does, although Father and Son are not divided in reality.

The danger of paradox, of course, is obscurantism. Believers with fear-filled and submoral religion or with irrational faith dread to face serious intellectual analysis. The safest hiding-place is paradox. Paradox can therefore be theology's main road block to truth. The religious interpreter must always be aware of this danger and be willing to show the need for using paradox. Nevertheless some of us who for many years have withstood all recourse to paradox can now see the place for its proper use. The right use of paradox is never to indicate knowledge nor to cover up the problem of critical reason in the attempt to help a credulous faith, but, rather, to place the ultimate problems within their proper perspective. A paradox must never be used to fence off any legitimate human inquiry. It can be used only to indicate the fact that if our most careful use of reason within our necessary choice of faith judgments as to the total meaning of experience has found God to be the Ground and Goal of the meaning of existence, some problems arise in relation to him which reason cannot reduce to the level of human problems.

The moreness and otherness of God in relation to knowledge can also be understood in terms of human experience. Those committed to walk in the ways of God can have a pattern for their lives in the life of Jesus and in the love of the universal community. Love effects freedom and faithfulness in fellowship. Love is concern for all and each. With such a context in mind the members of the community can plan their lives. They have a standard of reference for each decision and all decisions. In prayer thay can have the experience of God according to the reality of his nature, or indirectly they can adopt the context of the concerned and creative community. As they thus live, they can come to know more and more of the pattern of meaningful existence and receive more wisdom, maturity and steadiness in their ordinary living and thinking. They are not without a guide into the moreness of religious experience and religious reality.

No such planning, however, can include predictable action indefinitely. No pattern we make, with whatever devotion and care, will fit all new and unexpected situations. Often those who are the most dedicated to the straight course of obedience and who have most diligently fashioned rules and regulations relevant to their lives which express their ultimate allegiance will be up against the otherness of God in terms of the failure of all human planning. Human control of situations in terms of the moreness of our understanding of religious reality may have to give way before the awful reality of the biblical wisdom that God's ways are not man's ways. We may be forced to make decisions that go contrary to our own predictable behaviour, and yet come to know that obedience to the unexpected demand in an unexpected situation was more helpful and effective than anything we could have foreseen.

The prophets and saints of old, in any case, affirm with one voice that God does not act in history according to our expectation, and that his commands in the hearts of those who know and heed his voice may often come with strange biddings. The danger for the religious life is always either that we deny direct knowledge of God and therefore deny all light on our decisions, or else that we claim to have the answers in terms of mere moreness of our present gift of light. When we accept the fact that religious knowledge includes both reliable moreness and also unpredictable otherness, we can plan with confidence without lack of flexibility, leaving the final result of life within a pattern of history far beyond our finite and sinful grasp.

We have now discussed in what sense religion is the conviction that there are realities and powers beyond ordinary experience in terms of both moreness and otherness. Our next task will be to picture how such moreness can be understood with relation to the ordinary world. Can such a relation be conceived at all in terms of reason or must it go beyond it? If our previous analysis is correct, there will be knowledge with respect to and within the relation but not beyond the relation. When this analysis has been carried through we shall turn to the final and critical question of this section: to what extent can such knowledge be verified or open to public inspection?

Chapter VIII

God's Relation to the World

How can we frail human beings possibly conceive of God and his relation to the created order? If meaning on our level of existence is reliable and if God has cared to disclose his nature, we can 'picture' at least reliable indications that can be filled out and corrected by growth in understanding. A kindergartener might not draw a recognizable picture of her father, the birch tree in the garden, or Mount Everest, but we can see that she has tried to draw a man, a tree, and a mountain. Similarly if we know God at all as the faithful love we have found in Jesus, or even as outgoing and creative concern in general, our attempt to describe who he is and how he is related to the world might be on a level far more primitive and crude than the kindergartener's pencil scratches, and yet they must point in the direction of that reality toward which we can keep growing in life and understanding.

If we take the evidence of the order of process and conceive of this order in the context of the highest arrival, we can make the following suggestions, first as to the nature of God and then as to his relation to the world. Creative faith using reason can thus grasp after an understanding of God.

God is the causal ground of existence, the fountain, even perhaps the generator of existence. Energy seems to be the most common all-penetrating universal we can grasp. Such energy may have erupted out of the creative nature of God to form suddenly the creation we know. Or this creation may have come from other creations far beyond our ways of knowing. The universe may be expanding from some reservoir of being. Whether God be fountain, generator or reservoir of energy, he is the causal ground of existence. Such an ultimate is a legitimate abstraction from what we know only as it may help us to

85

order and direct our experience, whether in the science of astronomy, for instance, or in our theological quest for unity and understanding. Thus God can, for our purposes, be thought of as an inexhaustible abyss of energy that contains all the energy there is or is needed, or, to use language more closely in line with the surge of process, as the creative being who generates the new power for any further existence as well as continually generating the power needed for sustaining and motivating what already is. In any case, a capital mistake in thinking of God is to remove him from the causal order, and 'cause' is here used to include material and efficient cause in their ultimate reference and power to work.

God is also the source and standard of structure. He is the power for order, or the ordering power in creation. In the ultimate frame of reference God is also both formal and final cause. The unity of order, that is to say, is very likely due to no eternally existing realm of forms or essences. Order is the outworking of purpose and becomes in a real measure created along with the process to fit its needs. Both energy and structure can, of course, be eternally given, and God may only use them creatively in fashioning the process, but it is simpler to think of a unified dynamic source of both than to conceive of three separate realities that have somehow to work together.

Possibly we could deal with the problem of evil more easily if we posited no ultimate unity of energy, form and agent. In this case evil would be due to inherent defects in the ultimate nature of reality. The same conclusion would follow if there was no full internal harmony in the one creative being; but, as a whole, to conceive of evil as incidental to God's work in time is more in line with the fullest ultimate unity than it is to picture it as having ground in the eternal nature of things. Neither a finally finite God nor a personal devil really helps to solve problems in the last analysis. To court an easy solution of the problem of evil by positing a defect in the ground of being is in effect to preclude the fuller, harder answer which only the larger, more creative faith can give.

The reason for portraying God as creative being rather than as the static point of reference beyond the changes of process,

86

and the reason for preferring a unified ground for our ultimate, is emphatically that static views of God beyond process so shrink him into a mere reference and lure of order as effectively to remove him from the process as the dynamic orderer of it; while all lesser or lower pictures of God than the creative ground of being come too close to the process as it is. They do not provide sufficient room for the pedagogical nature of process and thus leave us no adequate view of God as the reality beyond ordinary experience.

To remove God too far from process is to forfeit the power to explain his relation to and working in the process; to stay too close to process is to forfeit the power for its explanation, especially of its sudden shift into its otherwise unaccountable spurt of meaningfulness. Therefore, considering the evidence we have and the best way to interpret our total experience, especially the development of process, we suggest that God be conceived of as creative being, the fount and generator of energy and the source and standard of structure, who is also the ordering power in creation.

God is also the womb of life and the fosterer of thought and love. Whatever the chemical continuity between organic and inorganic life and whatever the biological links between the two, life is a new level of being with a kind of 'irritability' not found elsewhere. Life simply is no mere matter of chemicals. There is newness in life not accounted for by events below it. God is the source of this newness. It is new in itself either without being unrelated to the ground of being or without being unrelated to the combination of chemicals which release it. Causally and in terms of order it partakes both of the givenness of the universe and of the ground of creation. Thus we keep both the proper continuity to previous creation and the actual newness in relation to its ultimate ground while also allowing for the manifestations in time of genuinely creative being. The temptation is either to reduce life to the activity of chemicals or to rob it of its authentic measure of self-being by attributing it solely to the action of God. While having a true dimension of newness, life is not from nothing and totally unrelated to its material source, nor is it self-caused, but declares the nature of

God. Life comes from life. All life comes from God and is related to God. Thus all dimensions in nature are both real and related.

But particularly God is the fosterer of life and love. He furthers life as a good gardener aids the growth of his flowers. Flowers come to their fruition in beauty and seed. Life on the higher level reaches its maturity in thought and love. Meaning is no mere accidental convention, no chance discovery of a phantom. Meaning springs from an order of being and relations. Meaning depends on existence, ripe for meaningfulness. Meaning, on man's level, is man's sharing the ordering power in creation with the capacity to evaluate and to direct it toward personal and social fulfilment. The ability to think is a gift with great potential for high-grade experience.

God's reality as the prime thinker and his embodiment of thought in creation and for creation give man the precondition for man's use of reason within his own measure of experience. God is the lure and the challenger, the frustrator and the fulfiller, the problem and the solution, for he is ground not only of energy and order, but even and especially of the realm of thinking. God is always beyond and therefore higher than any created being, but he is also the creator and fosterer of good on every level of creation, with thought as one of the highest.

But thought is a servant of life, not life itself. The heart of life is love. Love is fulfilment by wholeness of relations to self, others and to God. This wholeness God offers. God works both by lack and presence, both by search and finding, both by conflict and community. The whole question of the place of love in religion, and of reason's function in the life of love, we shall consider in the next main section: Reason and Man. In our attempt now to indicate the nature of God, however, it is obviously the central concern of the religion based on the highest arrival—the kind of life of love that Jesus lived and taught—to stress that God is love and the fosterer of love. God is the drive behind individuals and groups that makes them become themselves, by their fearing and fleeing the love that fulfils, but God is even more the invitation and the attracting power of the kind of love by which people can become genuine persons and communities.

Do these definitions of God imply that he is not necessarily personal? If the invisible reality out of which the process and the development of process comes is called spirit because of its all-penetrating reality plus its unitive power, and if the nature of this spirit is love, do we need the personal concept in our definition of God? Is not spirit energy directed by purpose? If spirit is the final unity and universality of energy, is it not energy motivated by love? Can we not know that this spirit is love by its highest working in history, and therefore know God enough without attributing to him the limitations of the human form of created spirit?

If the personal category suggests the limitations of created beings, to be sure, this category should not be applied to God. The human form is not final, even for our own future, and how much less so for the nature of God! At the same time the human spirit is the highest form of love we know; we know no love higher than the kind of love indicated by Christ; therefore we call God the highest kind of life and the highest kind of love we know. The ultimate energy is not formless, nor without purpose, nor without concern, and therefore we picture God best by the use of the highest life we know.

At the same time God is the creator of all life below and related to it, as well as to all possible existences beyond our present human form. Therefore God in his nature and relations must be understood in wider categories than the personal without in any way minimizing the ultimacy of his eternally faithful concern. God is fully personal but not only personal. He is personal spirit but not spiritual personality. I have purposefully defined God, therefore, in this instance, as the womb of life and the fosterer of thought and love, not as life, thought and love. I believe that we see God reliably through and in his highest manifestation and that therefore he is in some direct sense such life, thought and love.

And yet we know God, we must remember, through his presence and work in the created world, and for this reason I have preferred not to try to suggest final understanding but authentic indications as to the nature of God. In other words, I have tried to include our reliance on analogy and paradox along with the direct basis for definition. 'Mother' is defined in terms of the child, but hardly is put on the level of child on that account! She is more than this relation. In the case of God, we can conceive of him only through his relations to the world, but our imagination can attribute to his being in himself independent and, to us, unknown powers and realities that are in no way exhausted by his relation to nature, history, or even incarnation.

The more our understanding of cosmic process and life expands, the more necessary it becomes both to take seriously and to live by whatever faith-stance gives us the most reliable knowledge for ordering life, and also to avoid limiting God to our frame of reference. Perhaps the truest sign of maturity is the kind of confidence in the truth we have which makes us increasingly humble before the gaping depths of the truth yet to be had.

God should also be understood as the goal of process and life. God is nature's and man's destiny. In their proper places these questions will be treated at some length. All that needs to be suggested here is that if any process were eternal, process would be ultimate. But our evidence is for a developing process, a finite process. If it has a beginning in time the conclusion is probable that it will end in time. Then, too, if process were ultimate, there would be no power beyond it to fulfil it. The main thrust of process, however, is toward a goal. The thrust indicates power beyond the process. The goal is God as the fulfiller of life. Since he eternally is, and is beyond every process and every point in process, he is the resting point for man at any time.

Life is not all movement. It has a fixed focus not only toward the future but also beyond itself in the present. God is thus the eternal reality and Father of man's spirit in and with whom man can transcend the flux of process at any point. God is who he is, as well as the One who becomes as he shall become. He is both beyond and with process, and therefore he is the possible point for rest beyond process as well as the power for work within process. God is thus both the goal of process and of life, which gives meaning and zest to the living in it and to the fruition of it, and also the One who eternally transcends process not only to give it direction but also to afford man rest in every present.

If God is the ground of being, the ordering power in creation, the womb of life, the fosterer of thought and life, and the goal of life, God is, so to speak, the sharer of his own being. Perfect love must be beyond singularity and plurality; it must be unity in diversity; it must be beyond subject-object relation in external terms and beyond subject-subject relation in internal terms; it must be unity as community where oneness flows out into manyness and where manyness is known in oneness. Such life of love we attribute to God who cannot be described in terms of our oneness or manyness, but only as their source and goal.

Such perfect life of love must be pure joy. It is this joy that is God's reason for creating. His joy at times spills over into finitude to be shared in love within the fostering of the community, which through freedom and conflict and through suffering and satisfaction eventuates in the understanding acceptance and incorporation into the life of God. God then must be the ground of being, the thought and love of being, and the full joy which is life's ultimate meaning both as source and goal—How, however, can we ever relate such a view of God to a process and life like ours?

God is related to all things by all things being in him. Existence 'stands out' from God, the invisible source and standard of all things. To 'stand out' is the etymological meaning of existence. The word 'existence' is, of course, confusing. If existence is taken in the sense of derived being, 'standing out from', only finite things exist. In this use of the word the ground of existence, God, does not exist. But existence, on the other hand, is often taken to mean simply 'to be'. Perhaps it might be well, therefore, to make sure of our meaning by rephrasing the thought in the following manner: created existence is maintained in some real sense distinct from God's creative existence.

But such standing out or distinctness from God in separate existence is, therefore, only partial. Although man in a dependent sense is creative too, eternal Being, creative and dynamic, is still the ground and goal upon which all else depends and by whose power it operates. God is definitely God, and not man. There can be no question, in this view of God, however, of the absolute's not being able to become related to, or to be within creation, since then it would no longer be absolute but would become relative. There is no ultimate, closed, unconditioned reality, for God is ultimate reality who is the creator, sustainer and director of all. The infinite Love by his very nature produces the finite and perfects it as well, not by its becoming infinite but by God's own pedagogical accommodation in love to the finite and by his final achieving for and in the finite its perfect relationship to him, and within its own nature.

God may be thought of as the total field of all actual and possible relationships. Within the totality of this field there are dimensions of being, not spatially separated, but qualitatively distinct. If 'innermost' is considered in terms of fullest self-being rather than spatially, shall we say that God is innermost himself as the power to remain selfsame and to control the other aspects of being? God, then, at his innermost centre is the burning joy of perfect love. In this joy of love God shares his being in creation, not by emanation or by bestowing the eternally self-existent on the created realm, but by producing the conditions in nature and man for the understanding and acceptance of the meaning and power of the divine community. Creation is still in God but as an objectified realm which is qualitatively external to God.

The, invisible non-spatial reality of Spirit transforms or creates energy into a visible, spatial order. This order is qualitatively incapable of self-sufficient, self-same existence, or of by itself knowing and entering into relations with such existence. God in himself, so to speak, is the eternal centre of everywhere. His presence as he is in himself is a qualitative matter. There is no time nor place where God cannot equally well disclose his real presence. Such disclosure depends on the nature of the qualitative capacity and response of created beings. Since created beings can never become God, what determines the relationship is God's wisdom as to its appropriateness and man's requisite preparation according to God's requirement.

We can think of creation, then, as objectified existence, standing out from God in partial self-being. God may be considered as related to this realm according to three qualitatively different functions. Inanimate and subpurposive nature is related to God mostly by his sustaining and directing activity, which for the overwhelming part is merely letting nature function. We shall devote a main section of this book to a closer study of God's presence in nature. God operates on the level of purposive creation, moreover, wherever this line be drawn, mostly through a purposed passivity. When God has once created purposive creatures, he lets them learn mostly for themselves through the complexities of their experience. At the innermost reach of this second 'level' or dimension of creation, God becomes present as personal and public conscience, urging the right and warning against the wrong. In neither of these realms, however, is he present in his unconditional and all-inclusive love. The very innermost layer of creation, if such spatial terms must be used pictorially even in the qualitative realm, consists of those who have come to know who God is and to accept for their lives his very being.

Perhaps we can think of God's relation to the created world first in terms of a mostly sustaining and directing activity; then by a mostly purposed passivity which is an appropriate partial presence; and finally by his becoming the Companion of persons and community. The third stage in essence is the beginning of the fulfilment of man. Man is fulfilled by his presence in God and God's presence in him. This mutual immanence is more than God's being everywhere present in some sense. It is a qualitative mutuality in the Spirit in which the Infinite Spirit finds the satisfaction of goal-reaching and love-sharing, and the finite spirit finds its fulfilment by entrance into its eternal destiny. To whatever extent there is a real beginning of such relationship, the qualitative barrier between God's innermost being in love's joy is done away and, qualitatively speaking, God becomes all in all. Such fulfilment involves no losing of

93

created reality, genuine selfhood or community, but only their being perfected within their right destined relation to God.

We have been troubled by terminology. Clearly God is eternal being, and as the ground and goal of all being is not reducible to a part of nature nor to any aspect or dimension of it. He simply is not merely some dimension of depth or the authentic being of all existing lives. He is no merely logical prerequisite for the unity of creation and no mere given power for unity within existence. For this reason classical thought has made use of the word 'supernatural'. This term suffers from the fact that it defines God in relation to the natural, as though the natural were more certain, or at least of primary reference. It also suffers from being a spatial term. But there seem to be no expressions that do not conform to our thinking in time and space.

Directional or level thinking may give way to 'dimension' as more adequate, but even 'dimension' has spatial reference. This term can equally well be used to reduce God to an aspect of existence. Perhaps the biblical affirmation that God alone has immortality might serve to call attention to the incommensurable primacy of his being. Perhaps we can also make use of the scientific concept of unity and universality where oneness and diversity in singularity and extension are not separate layers or external events, but characteristic of everything. In our own case, however, the primordial and foundational unity and universality would root in God and only be reflected secondarily in creation. Otherwise created being becomes the main reference for the eternal ground and goal of all things!

If such is the nature of reality, God can be eternally self-same in his innermost being. His joy in love is never marred by its overflowing. God goes out in creation and to creation. On all preparatory levels he works toward the level of love without violating the proper level of freedom on the part of the creatures. Such suffering as there may be in creation is accepted by God as appropriate, and experienced with the strength and joy of anticipation. Suffering on the inner levels of creation is joy's redemptive identification.

God cannot know suffering in his innermost being, however,

for joy moves out sovereignly to effect its goal. The more the creatures come to know and accept God's love, the more they may suffer in a new way. But human anxiety and finite pain are not part of God's experience. They can be means to the finding of faith's assurance of love's final joy. God's love in history when facing suffering is always 'the joy set before' the Cross. The more God is in man, the more joy for creative and redemptive living is present. Such men 'rejoice' with Saint Paul 'in all their afflictions'. For God and for those who understand the eventual goal of all creation, love counts life all joy whatever happens on the way to the eternal destiny. The ecstasy of life's premature transfiguration is the only participation man can have in anticipation of the innermost life of God.

Chapter IX

Can we 'Know' religious Reality?

The thorniest problem for reason in religion is the question whether or not we can know the powers and realities beyond ordinary experience that help and harm man. Can there be religious knowledge? Is not the basic nature of religion so much a matter of faith that the term 'knowledge', if not totally inapplicable, is at least grossly inept? Is not knowledge something that can be confirmed, 'verified', and in denial proved untrue, or 'falsified'? If faith by nature is creative, whether in terms of trusting or thrusting, can it allow more than its own use of reason, or in principle submit to the demands of the critical reason; and, on the other hand, if knowledge is conceived of in terms of public verifiability, can knowledge ever admit the reports of faith as genuine parts of its own domain?

If we are to respect human experience and the use of reason within it, both faith and knowledge, however, must be elastic terms. Faith without reason is irrelevant and unreal. It becomes an empty attitude and a phantom creation. Faith exists as genuine human experience only in dynamic, controlled relation to the totality of experience by means of the identifying, evaluative and ordering power of reason. Unless faith is a requirement of reason itself, indeed reason's highest reaches for ordering experience creatively, it has no authentic part of life. Such ordering is in the last analysis dependent upon the ordinary experience, not in the sense of receiving its reality or its authority from this experience, but in the order of knowledge, since we come to know even the religious realm only through our experience and its need for being interpreted and directed. Thus faith, if legitimate, cannot be divorced from knowledge, reason's interpretation of experience. Not all may have such faith as has been related legitimately by means of

96

reason to the totality of knowledge, through which process it was also derived in the first place; but neither do most people have any other form of knowledge except derivatively and through trust in those who know. Faith's knowledge is by inner necessity loosely elastic.

But knowledge, too, is by nature elastic. Knowledge itself is based on faith in man's rational capacities and on the dependable nature of the world to a measure so remarkable that we take both of them mostly for granted. No-one can prove these things; yet when such faith in reason is gone or when the worthwhileness of intellectual activity is undermined, the pursuit of knowledge suffers. No developed knowledge can be proved in any final sense and certainly not by consensus. Nor can the point where knowledge begins or stops be drawn with definiteness and satisfaction. Logic will not do without the logician. Science cannot prove itself, but depends upon the scientist. The psychologist will feel that there is some knowledge resulting from his investigations, even though persons cannot be reduced to pigeons, nor pigeons to physics. Indeed, the history of knowledge testifies that individuals have seen a knowledge that was at first seen by exceedingly few and opposed by consensus. Yet they saw and knew, and made what they saw and knew a matter of accredited knowledge.

The historian, the statesman and the religious seer, at their most creative and in their most important efforts, deal with intangibles that are ever harder to verify, yet they could not render their service unless they dealt in some sense with knowledge as the veridical interpretation of experience. The mathematician may have an all-or-none set of mind and refuse to admit that a physician has any knowledge; yet in calling him in for treatment the mathematician admits by implication that that physician has more than an unfounded faith or merely speculative fancies. As a matter of fact, the medical man may feel that the edge of knowledge in the field ends with his profession, only to find ever-new cures by the study of folk medicines in different parts of the world that have been based, however inadequately, on the long experience of the race.

Unless knowledge is to be used arbitrarily and as a profes-

97

sional weapon of self-glorification or attack on other fields, knowledge must be used to mean correct identification and interpretation of experience, including its evaluation and directing. Knowledge is, then, and must remain, an open term. Knowledge, like faith, is elastic. Its opposite is unexamined or incorrectly examined experience.

Proper use of the terms faith and knowledge should mean more than clear communication. It should involve proper relation to experience as well. If any group merely defines its terms with care and then allows other groups to define their terms and use them accordingly, there may be gain in tolerance and constructive co-operation but at the expense of truth, for they have then all forfeited their common allegiance to the givenness of experience as the final legitimate reference for language. To treat language as merely conventional is to undermine the ground of community in truth. Truth should be a sacred term presupposing for its finding integrity of investigation and communication based upon competent interpretation of experience. Truth is a value-laden, ideal term which correctly should stand for what authentically is, integrity and competence of search for it, and clarity and fullness in the communication of it. Faith and knowledge should both aim at truth.

To put the matter in different terms, faith and reason should both be grounded in knowledge, but elastically, according to their different functions in experience. The surest way to undermine both language and knowledge, and, indeed, the whole creative interpretation of experience, is to fence off usage into segments of experience without a common base. If usage, besides, is made a matter of convention and correct usage accordingly, the nerve of responsible interpretation of experience is cut.

Practically it is far better to suffer war over interpretation than to relegate the interpretation of experience to meaninglessness. Practically it is better to keep sorting our false or partial conclusions, even within an elastic and confused situation concerning both faith and reason in relation to knowledge, than to shut out the possibility of knowledge in man's most vital

areas of decision by some arbitrary and, in the end, both un-
livable and unreal definitions of knowledge in terms of verifica-
tion or usage. The real test for knowledge is always with
reference to experience and its proper organization. Tests are
secondary and exist for the sake of eliminating false and partial
interpretations, and to make room for truer ones.

Religious knowledge is vision. It is insight into the meaning
of the wholeness of experience. Each person and group with
religious ends in view must interpret experience for the sake
of making response; and all experience is involved in any interpretation of life's total meaning. The fact that there are
inadequate religious responses does not do away with the fact
that religious responses are constantly made. The more adequate the interpretation according to our analysis, moreover,
the less it can be subject to tests by reason in its critical capacity.
Synoptic vision cannot be proved by partial perspectives, much
less by isolated facts. The whole, in its meaningfulness, is
unique in the kind of totality that can imply what is beyond but
cannot be proved by what is below. Veridical insight cannot be
assumed by anything outside itself and does not need to be.
For genuine vision of meaningfulness the critical reason is
irrelevant and even gets in its way. That ultimate meaningfulness cannot be proved by anything less than itself is a fact both
logically and psychologically sound. We are more grasped by,
than we grasp, true faith.

Precisely on account of its ultimate nature, however, creative
faith needs the critical reason. It feels no need of it, but there
are too many candidates for ultimate faith, all claiming the
proper use of the creative reason, not to demand that the true
faith meet the test of sound criticism. These candidates make
too divergent claims for them all to be true. Faith is not only
a matter of trusting and thrusting, but of responsible choice.
There should be some grounds for choice, however little the
choice can then be brought back to its ground. Man's mind, by
its nature, is made for the testing of all interpretation of experience on the level of the ordering and directing capacity of
reason. A fundamental drive of reason, we have seen, is to
discriminate. It examines the correspondence of its ideas to

the world outside, and it scrutinizes the self-consistency of the organization of these ideas.

Unless we use our reason with the fullest freedom and competence to perform this critical work, we become frustrated in part of our being. When the full use of reason is suppressed, and, even more, repressed into the subconscious, we experience guilt and a sense of insecurity about our faith. Within such guilt and insecurity we become both falsely defensive and aggressive. Fear produces destructive zeal, often behind a constructive mask. No faith is ever sound and satisfying that has not used the full range of reason both creatively and critically.

But not only is harm done to faith within. Faith is also made less effective in the facing of the real problems without. Every attempt to interpret experience is going to meet profound and unavoidable problems. A pre-critical faith may be naïvely strong, but not mature in the facing of the actual world. Only a critical use of reason can offer the counterarguments to creative faith that can force it to go more deeply into its own inadequate interpretation. Only a critical use of reason can unearth for faith the problems which those have who do not share the faith. Faith, therefore, is not strong in itself, or for others, unless it has passed through its pre-critical, second-hand stage. It may seem strong and secure, but offers no relevance for those whose eyes have been opened to the evils of the world. Its joy is the innocence of ignorance, not the chastity that has passed through temptation.

As these problems press in on the believer and he retreats into faith rather than opens up to the urgings of reason, he loses the sense of reality and power for living. He suffers dissociation from life. Therefore in some appropriate way the critical reason must have its day and way within the creative life of faith, which, of course, basically employs the creative reason. This, then, is our main thesis: creative faith can never be proved by critical reason; such proof is both logically and psychologically false; and yet neither can faith live healthily within, nor effectively toward, the outer world without some honest and competent employment of the critical reason.

Apart from the general and informal use of the critical reason

within experience as a whole and apart from the specifically
critical use of reason within the religious reasoning proper,
there are two disciplines of knowledge that have to be considered in their bearing on the critical examination of religion:
science and philosophy. Can science constitute a critical test of
reason to confirm, to reject or to select religious content?

Science cannot as science perform this function. Science is
either a particular act of description of things or forces, and
how they work, or a general human attitude and enterprise.
In its dealing with particular fields, science uses specialized
methods and cannot generalize. The approach to correct
description or function is determined by the nature of whatever
is to be described. Physics, chemistry and biology use different
tools and different basic concepts. Neither material nor method
is simply interchangeable. Geology and anthropology are
different areas of investigation with different approaches. The
only general method of science is the determined intention and
practice of describing events and functions for what they are,
by whatever separate methods can best make use of objective
tests. There is thus no limit to science as attitude and approach.
The word can even be enlarged to include a critical, objective
approach to the field of religion. Such a use, however, can
apply only to those events in religion that can properly be
described, like the facts of history, of nature, of psychology and
of sociology.

No facts of description, however, can explain or confirm
critically the total thrust of process. Science can furnish facts,
and these may have vital bearing on religious interpretation.
They may modify theologies open to further truth. Astronomy
may help to change our views of the method of creation, geology
may help us to change our understanding of the preparations for
life, anthropology may serve to alter our interpretation of
man's prehistory and the shaping of history, psychology may
function as an aid in understanding the nature of man's spirit.

The main description by science of the process of evolution
in place of the full-fledged special creation of an older theology
has already altered man's scope of understanding and given
firmer basis for an already existing view which saw man's

101

history as a development up to Christ, fulfilment in him, and the spreading of his truth afterwards. Religions which have been based on the idea that this world has always been the same or on its revolving in cycles can similarly be corrected in their understanding of what is beyond ordinary experience. Theologies with springboards in meaningful history felt, and partially saw, something beyond ordinary experience, but had no genuine basis as yet for their interpretation or for the secondary confirmation of it. These theologies have been immensely helped by the results of scientific creativity.

Science produces facts, not interpretations, of the meaning of experience. These facts are important and must be treated with high respect and never violated within distorting theories of religious interpretation. Proof, in the fullest sense, is not possible within science, but only prediction with more or less high expectation of accuracy. Scientific results, both conclusions and methods, change with astonishing rapidity, a sign of openness of method. The idea that scientific laws have zero probability in terms of the probability calculus, however, reveals the impracticability of abstract thinking uncontrolled by its base in experience.

But if science as such is only probable in the sense of its description and prediction, how much less can sundry facts prove any ultimate meaningfulness that is derived from the interpretation of the wholeness of human experience. No amount of discovery as to the factors which come together in the production of newness, nor any amount of control of such factors, can in any way deny the newness of the new or the general pointing of progress. As far as we can see, these facts are reliable standards at the base of investigation. If man should discover how to create and to control life, for example, he would only be using the materials out of a process which has produced him and furnishes him with both the capacity and the material for such creation and control. In man's scientific investigation in its particular sense, man describes and predicts events and forces, but he neither explains nor prescribes in terms of meaningfulness for life, with regard to what is most important and most real.

But science is not only a way of discovering and describing events and forces in their natures and workings; as scientism it also has become an all-pervasive way of looking at both life and knowledge. As such it is a religion, proffering a total meaningfulness and a central approach to what can help and harm man. It is an implied claim to be the only, or at least the best, way to truth. In such a case, it is no longer science in the strict sense of the discovery and description of particular phenomena, according to their limitations, but a total attitude to life and knowledge. It is a religion.

It is a false religion, however, for it is methodologically illegitimate. Science describes facts and never becomes a meta-physics as such. Facts are needed and should be heeded. But facts must be ordered self-consistently and with reference to the totality of experience. To do so is not the proper function of science. To make a religion of science is to forfeit the creative function of faith in dealing with the forces and meanings not amenable to direct description, yet objectively available and helpful to life.

True religion reaches out for creative interpretation and response by creative faith and reason. Science as a religion centres in the critical reason, in the minor rather than in the major aspect of knowledge, in the attitude of doubt and in-decision. As an attitude and method, science majors in the minimum hypothesis rather than in the maximum true and helpful faith. As a method dealing with sense content to be described and utilized, and not with living meaningfulness up for decision, science can and ought to serve its own proper function, and has, indeed, proved its worth within its own field. Science can be and has been immensely creative within its own method and should not be prostituted as a faith. We must be thankful for its critical care, even in its creative dealing with the field of description. As a method and attitude of total meaningfulness, however, that is, as a religion, science under-mines the edifices of faith, the spirit of adventure that builds it, and the readiness for decision concerning life's meaning which now especially confronts man with deadly seriousness.

If science and the quest for total truth were equatable,

H   103

obviously religion would have to become scientific in method and attitude, but as it is, the legitimate function of science is to interpret the created world and to supply the facts that critical reason can use with religious interpretations. Both religion and science have their proper attitudes and uses. The way of religion is basically the way of faith; the way of science is basically the way of doubt. In religion, the accused prisoner is innocent until proved guilty. In science, the prisoner is guilty until proved innocent. In religion, the young wife is assumed faithful unless proved faithless; in science, she is considered faithless unless proved faithful. Vital life operates primarily on the basis of a trust that cannot be proved, or rationally justified in any sense of conclusive and constant proof. Life is justified in the living; faith in the believing. But there are faithlessness and guilt in life, and therefore as a secondary necessary mood man must be open to critical thinking. Otherwise he becomes a dupe of his own uncritical believing.

Within the mood and method of science, all meaningfulness in life as a whole is absurd. No faith can be proved in all-or-none terms. But life as a whole confronts us inescapable with some choice of meaningfulness. Only a vital and true faith, real and relevant with reference to experience and its total ordering, therefore, can give a basic and satisfying importance to knowledge. Where, then, are we?

Science cannot prove or disprove any faith. It can only produce facts to challenge or to confirm religious interpretation. As separate sciences with distinctive approaches and tools, science can produce discoveries and descriptions that can alter theological content; but science is never a method that can deal with the total ordering of human experience in its decision concerning meaningfulness, nor can it ever deal with what is beyond ordinary experience. When science is used as a substitute religion it is always pseudo-religion. It is used beyond its proper method and nature.

Perhaps religion originally produced the preconditions of science by its sense of the totality of experience and the dependability of the universe. The presupposition of one universe of operation and discourse, where conclusions must be arrived at through a controlled method, is needed to clear the deck of all false, magical, superstitious religions which are grounded in arbitrary revelations and in irrational faiths. Even science as such a total enterprise can be used by genuine religion to prepare for a world-wide climate of expectation of a religion that will respect integrity of investigation and competence of interpretation with a view to common knowledge and the common good. Perhaps science in this popular way has been the greatest force for the demoralization of unworthy religions and the preparing for a universal religion that can answer the deepest need of man for full faith and full reason.

As a formal discipline, science does not deal with the questions distinctive of religion, but can supply, if it is rightly used, ever-new facts, ever-new content, to be interpreted within the context of religion. As an informal attitude and world view it can lend us its openness, its universality of outlook, and its demand for a public investigation of all facts for the purpose of establishing only true facts. Science can be delivered from its pseudo-religious nature and contribute instead to true religion the wider and fuller reaches for its faith. Science should not be used as a religion, in which case it operates with a discipline alien in mood and method, but it should furnish the critical reason with material for its proper use within religion as a living enterprise. Science can also help by providing religion positively with universal attitudes and methods, and with properly established facts, for the controlled use of the creative reason.

Chapter X

Religious Knowledge and Philosophy

If science, as science, cannot constitute for religion its critical reason, either in its limited technical task of description of fact and function or as a general human enterprise, can religion use philosophy to this end? No, philosophy cannot, as philosophy, be the critical reason of religion. Why not?

Philosophy as a formal discipline deals primarily with meaning. The primary field of science is fact and function; the primary field of philosophy is meaning; the primary field of religion is salvation. The realm of science operates in the material world; the realm of philosophy operates in the mental world; the realm of religion operates in the spiritual world. The three disciplines thus deal with the whole man in the whole world of body, mind and spirit. If this is so, however, why does not philosophy fit exactly the function of the critical use of reason in religion? Philosophy has its own field and function and cannot be used wholesale within any other discipline, although philosophy can and should come to the help of both science and religion in its constructive criticism of both.

Philosophy deals with meaning both as the inner consistency of thought and as the consistency of thought to the world of fact and to the world of the spirit. It treats knowledge not as the description of fact and function nor as the delivery of faith, but as a realm presupposed by, and involved in, both fact and faith. Philosophy explores the realm of the mind. In this capacity it can treat mental consistencies in legitimate abstraction from the concreteness of experience. This function of philosophy is distinctive of its concern and responsibility. It is philosophy par excellence. There is thus by nature a peculiar intimacy between philosophy and logic. Philosophy claims logic as its special domain. There have, of course, been many kinds of logic in the history of man's thought, but the abiding heart of logic is the analytical. Logic is the study of proper entailment of ideas, regardless of any application to actuality. Such study aims at exactness and inevitability. There is an inherent certainty in logical analysis that can be found nowhere else, with the possible exception of pure mathematics. This independence of logic as a function puts in question any revision of formal logic, even of the excluded middle, to fit facts of Quantum Mechanics.

This fact of exactness and certainty in analytical logic provides both its power and its weakness for philosophers. The power of philosophy as logical analysis is that it provides objectively a dependable standard and model for clarity and certainty for all other disciplines. We human beings are always looking for clarity and certainty beyond confusion and insecurity. The handling of this field gives the philosopher a sense of knowing what he is doing that cannot be had elsewhere. Consequently he feels inwardly secure. He also feels above the fumblings and gropings of both the kind of philosophy that tries to deal with actual knowledge in experience and above those who in other fields necessarily lack his kind of precision and inevitability. Especially in a world where mathematics and exact science have been both admired ideals and strong producers of progress in knowledge, the philosopher is tempted to go both of these one better by offering analytical philosophy as the model for all knowledge. He has even tried to make language conform to the analytical ideal; language should be as clear and as exact as mathematics. There has been an ardent attempt to produce a symbolic, exact language as the model for all communication.

In this spirit the analytical philosopher has reached out to try to redo even knowledge outside logic and language. His ideal of the knowledge of the external world has been exact science. Such science has been pictured mostly as inventory. The world has been portrayed in the ideals of such philosophers as a world of discrete entities that could be described with exactness in nature and function, and statistically tabulated. Indeed, under the sway of this ideal and motivated by its drive both to clarity and to certainty, some philosophers have actually drawn the line of knowledge at the point of controlled science. Grudgingly they have had to admit, of course, that the actual world, even of sense, can never be made to conform to the ideal clarity and certainty of analytical logic, but that it can at best obtain the approximations of high probability through the most rigorous methods of science. As a matter of fact, however, some did even go to the incredible extreme of limiting the definition of man's meaningfulness to analytical philosophy and strict science.

Thus the very power of the method became the occasion for its greatest weakness. The fact is, of course, that there is a kind of objective, demonstrable certainty, humanly speaking, in analytical logic that cannot be found elsewhere. This truth ought to be obvious and freely acknowledged. There is similarly a demonstrability available to exact science, dealing quantitatively with sense data, that has no objective equal in any other realm of man's experience. If knowledge and meaning are defined solely in terms of maximum public verifiability, knowledge has a right in these two realms that it has in no other areas. The tragedy is, of course, that a heady drive for clarity and security obscured, for such seekers of exactness, the wholeness of the basis of knowledge and the total scope of man's meaningfulness. Method turned metaphysics implicitly. Mood turned religion covertly. There were both intellectual conviction and missionary zeal in the gospel of the narrow certainty, or in the worship of such certainty as the ideal of knowledge.

Much of this conviction, too, was justified by man's need to clarify his terms of communication, examine his flabby arguments, and probe again into his hidden rationalizations of both faith and reason. Analytical logic came with cleansing power at what seems to be a critical point in man's history both intellectually and spiritually. Analytical philosophy brought to bear on religion the accumulative insights of both the scientific attitude and of philosophy proper. But these philosophers in their heady hour lost the sense of proportion. The partial and needed truth became for them a whole gospel. The corrective was mistakenly taken for construction.

Most of these philosophers have now seen the onesidedness of their stress, and are finding their way back from their fancied heaven of fenced-off knowledge to the real world of full, serious responsibility. The fact is, of course, that philosophy does not deal with self-consistency alone, nor is its only concern clarity and complete certainty. The self-examination of the mental realm is for the sake of better understanding its function in the total enterprise of human knowledge. The distinctive task of philosophy is analytical logic; the central task of philosophy is the use of logic within the totality of experience.

Philosophy must therefore keep asking itself the fundamental question of its field: how can philosophy be of use in all the fields of human knowing? How is self-consistency of form related to whatever consistencies can be known, chosen and used within man's total experience? Philosophy must deal with such consistencies not as fact or as faith, but as the presuppositions of method, the perspectives of inquiry and the power for application. It cannot deal with knowledge as a whole in the sense that it masters all knowledge in its several specialties nor as a total world view, but in the sense that it examines the proper use of reason in dealing with these specialties and with any world view offered by faith. Such is the native right and natural responsibility of philosophy.

Philosophy cannot, as philosophy, deal with the specific questions of fact presented by a scientific discipline; but it does have both the right and the responsibility to scrutinize the methodological presuppositions of science, the perspectives accepted by any science, and the way in which reason is used in the applications of scientific data. There is, accordingly, a legitimate philosophy of science. As a matter of fact, there have been great historians and philosophers of science who have been helpful to the scientists themselves in their work on scientific method, for in the sphere of method scientists necessarily turn pseudo-philosophers.

Methodological investigation should be the joint enterprise of philosophy and science. The bearing of the whole field of science on the approach to any particular science is of utmost importance even to the special sciences, and often scientists work with philosophical presuppositions of which they may not even be aware. A great philosopher, by his probing into the deeper relations and reaches of reason, usually causes an earthquake of thinking that disturbs every field of thought. For philosophy to abandon this task is to surrender its own usefulness as a discipline and a responsibility, which must then be assumed by others less fitted by training and attitude for the task.

Similarly philosophy, as philosophy, cannot deal with the reports of faith. The experience and vision of faith is the result of religious commitment and choice. A philosopher has as his task the inspection of the processes of thought in all areas of inquiry. He cannot limit fact or faith to the distinctive field of philosophical analysis, nor can he substitute analysis for fact or faith, but he can investigate the proper use of reason with regard to both fact and faith. We have already dealt with science. In the case of religion, philosophy can likewise criticize the use of reason by the religious interpreter, whether he be the informal believer or the professional scholar. The religious presuppositions should be examined for their inner consistency and for their right use within proper perspectives in the realm of fact. The applications of religious truth to human conduct should also come under the survey of philosophy as to the proper use of reason informally in conduct and formally in ethics. The philosopher, as philosopher, is not a social prophet, but the prophecy of the prophet cannot be exempt from rational examination by the philosopher.

Philosophy cannot deal with experience as a whole but only with the use of reason in experience as a whole. Every interpretation of experience as a whole is up against the fact that as a candidate for ultimate meaningfulness it is by nature within the field of religion. If a philosopher, for instance, chooses to interpret present process as systematically as possible, without hiding the inconsistencies, in so far as such interpretation is possible he has only produced some coherence of the world as it is; but to offer such a view as synoptic 'knowledge' for the ordering of experience is to choose as a faith-judgment a fugitive present without adequate power for self-explanation in the past and without sufficient power for self-realization in the future. Such a procedure is to label as knowledge what is in fact a faith-judgment, and a poor one at that. Such 'knowledge' is no summit view but a glimpse of present process from within its own movement.

If philosophy chooses, instead, the past as the ground and centre of knowledge, it becomes guilty of a reductionistic naturalism which is a stance of faith and not an adequate knowledge of the ultimate nature of things. If, on the other hand, it chooses to call the high report from future fulfilment—as indicated by the highest arrival in process, and the organization of experience around its centre—a 'knowledge' of ultimate things, philosophy confounds faith with fact. Only when the result of process is obtained can it constitute knowledge. Thus philosophy cannot deal with the whole of experience as knowledge of reality, for such knowledge is impossible from within the process.

Philosophy has long been obsessed with metaphysics as its chief discipline. All too long it has failed to see that metaphysics as rational knowledge of the ultimate is impossible. From within the movement of unfulfilled process there can be no mere rational description of the nature of ultimate things. Every choice available to man is a choice of faith with something to be said in its favour and something against it as well. Apart from faith in the meaningfulness of life and of reason it can seem quite natural to assume that since nothing comes from nothing only the original basis of process is permanently real. From this point of view and in this spirit, reason can rule that all later creations are the temporary manifestation of the inner womb of process which alone remains real in terms of self-being. The hidden faith-judgments in this world-view— namely, that all that has come of life and meaning, not to mention the accumulative way in which it has come, and especially the incredible spurt of recent process, have come about without sufficient cause and purpose adequately to account for them— are lost from view in method, and from mind in mood.

Similarly, the choice of the present process as the basis for knowledge of the nature of reality is understandable, since we can see from no other point of view than where we now are. Why not, then, accept ourselves and what we see has happened? Why reduce the meaningful new to a limited past, and why speculate on results in the far future which we cannot live to observe? Thus there is also reason for this stance making it easier to suppress or repress the astonishing faith-judgment that man can freeze the fleeting present into the nature of reality, which, however, up to now has shown such change. Thus a philosopher can think that he is really giving us rational knowledge in terms of coherence.

Likewise the use of reason in line with the main development of process as indicated by its highest arrival and main line of development, can seem to be knowledge to some who call such a view philosophy; but actually the view of the far future is preposterous except as the choice of faith. We cannot 'know' that the process will be fulfilled by God. Philosophy, as philosophy, therefore, cannot deal with the ultimate nature of reality as reported by the total organization of experience and its implications. For this reason philosophy cannot be a world view or a metaphysics. Every judgment concerning the nature of the whole, and the choice which such judgment necessarily involves on the part of anyone correctly and competently informed, is a faith-judgment, and in this sense belongs to the field of religion.

But philosophy, as philosophy, can objectively appraise the reasoning involved in such an interpretation of religion. It can scrutinize the presuppositions of the whole approach. It can weigh religion's use of reason to determine whether or not it is consistent with the facts offered by science, and whether these facts are used within a context of open reasoning or of closed rationalization. If religion and science make different use of the same facts, it can call this to their attention and try to adjudicate any dispute as far as the use of reason is involved. The methodological assumptions of science may be wrong, as may be those of religion. Or the religious interpreter may distort the straight report of certain facts in order to use them as a false support for his religious claims. Thus philosophy deals with the whole of experience not in terms of the construction of a metaphysics, which is always a pseudo-religion and methodologically spurious, but in terms of the proper or improper use of reason, wherever reason is found, with relation to itself or to the interpretation of human experience.

But cannot philosophy, as philosophy, observe objectively the various faith-systems and weigh them in the light of their respective adequacy in the use of faith and meaning? Of course, such methodological objectivity is possible. If it were not, all objective, synoptic knowledge would be impossible. In such a case, philosophy could not help religion with its own critical work. The philosopher in such a task stands apart, viewing and comparing various orderings of experience as a whole. To deny him such responsibility is to imply, if not explicitly to charge, that he is either less competent or more sinful than the theologian. The temptation to self-justification and self-security is involved in all stances of faith. We should not want to deny to philosophy any creative ordering of experience in part or as a whole. The philosopher, after all, is in pursuit of meaning.

But when choice and commitment are made, then religion takes charge. Faith is in the saddle beyond knowledge, even though with the use of it. Within cosmic process knowledge cannot settle the question of the nature of the whole. Thus situationally even within knowledge, philosophy cannot become metaphysics as the overall knowledge of reality. Furthermore, the philosopher is a man, who simply by living keeps making actual choices, whether or not he wants to do so or recognizes the fact. His choice does not in itself close his mind, or else all objective knowledge would be destroyed, but it acts as a powerful personal influence in his interpretative task. Therefore the work of philosophy in the realm of ultimate choices for ordering experience should be recognized as conjunct to religion. Its field and function are the philosophy of religion or philosophy in religion. It is always best to keep lines of approach clear.

Philosophy is not science and does not perform as a science with regard to fact or function, but it must deal with the use of reason by science. Philosophy is not religion and should never perform the function of religion, but it is under the obligation

113

of its own nature and function to watch over the use religion makes of reason. In our next main section we shall study to what extent all human beings are too limited in capacity or too driven by sin to carry out the functions assigned to them by the nature of the field, but for our purposes now our thesis is that just as science deals with fact and not with faith, and therefore cannot function as the critical reason within religion, even so philosophy, as philosophy, deals with meaning as reasoning within itself and with relation to experience, and therefore cannot function inside religion as its critical reason. The philosophy of religion is an important discipline, studying religion's use of reason with regard to both meaning and fact, but it is a branch of philosophy. The full critical use of reason in religion, however, can be carried on properly only as religion's self-criticism within its own stance of faith. No objective, outside knowledge can ever take the place of the living insights of the creative ordering of experience within the necessity of choice and commitment.

Religion, to be real, must be capable of honest and competent self-criticism. Science can provide facts and the suggestions of an open and critical mood and method. Philosophy can supply rules of the game for the use of reason and help to assess the use of it in religion. But to be effective inside the religious stance, reason must be used within the experience, commitment and vision of faith. Such use must be creatively to express the deliverance of faith, and critically to check and challenge faith's right to its claim. The demand on religion is clear. It cannot prove faith from beyond itself. If religion, as our content definition claims, is man's ultimate presupposition for life and thought, there can be no higher court to which to appeal. The god who can be proved by anything else is not God!

At the same time, if the ordering of experience calls for the recognition and acceptance of God's reality, right and reign as the ultimate perspective and power on life's meaning, its deliverance from evil, and its transformation and fulfilment, then, once this supreme miracle has been accepted by faith, there should result from the central presupposition of true religion perspectives on the nature of man, on the course of history, on the working of nature, and on the many kinds of religion that will bestow on these the fullest available meaningfulness, the best prescription for man's ills, and the fullest possible power for salvation. Religion is by nature a matter of faith. The truest faith can be tested only by its maximum relevance and organic fulfilment of the totality of experience. Such meeting the test of critical reason will be no proof of either science or philosophy. Such proof would deny the nature of religion and declare its fraudulence. But such self-authentication based on honest and competent self-criticism demonstrates the integrity and legitimacy of religion as a sober and responsible human organ for interpreting experience.

Where, then, have we come in this first main section: Reason and God? We have said that reason is an intrinsic part of religion. In itself it is the ability to identify, to discriminate, to evaluate, to interpret, to order, to test and to direct experience. Religion, moreover, is the conviction that there are realities and powers beyond ordinary experience that can help and harm man. Faith is the whole self trusting, accepting reality, choosing among candidates for the ultimate meaning of experience, and committing oneself to one's choice. Faith's choice, however, needs to be based not only on the creative use of reason, working out its implications, but also on the critical use of man's mind in testing religious judgments for inner consistency, and for relevance and authentic relations to experience as a whole.

We then saw how presuppositions for thought provide perspectives for interpreting different aspects of experience. Such presuppositions, while they cannot be proved, nevertheless can be partially explained as postsuppositions and tested for their capacity to account for experience and to give it needful direction. Thereupon we showed that the adequate ordering of the full human experience demands its interpretation in terms of what is beyond process, as this is viewed in the light of its highest arrival, which cannot in its newness be accounted for by anything in process and yet is most inclusively and meaningfully related to the process as a whole.

This highest arrival we found to be the life, teachings, death

115

and resurrection of Jesus as the Christ, the exhibition in and through one life of the universal, unconditional, ever-faithful love of God. The nature of the moreness and otherness of religious knowledge was then discussed as knowable and communicable, basically through the direct use of the primary religious event, but also secondarily through the use of analogy to deliver the moreness from crude literalism, and through paradox to preserve the suggestion, particularly for worship, of the otherness of God. We then tried to picture God in his relation to the world as the Spirit of Love, in some real sense personal without the limitations of human personality, and as the Ground and Goal of existence.

Creation, we suggested, is within God, in one sense, and stands out from him, in another, so that he is both the Spirit in himself, and the One within whose presence and power, in some sense, all creation moves, in some measure free and in some measure completely dependent upon its Source and Sustainer. Finally we have discussed to what extent religion can be a matter of knowledge. Our conclusion was that its knowledge is never a matter of science or of philosophy, although science and philosophy can both contribute to religious knowledge and criticize its findings. Religious knowledge must rather be a matter of faith's vision, choice of ultimates, and commitment. Such knowledge can be tested basically only by its creative power to order and to direct experience and by its critical self-examination as to its meaningfulness, relevance and power for salvation.

Before leaving this section we want to stress again and emphatically that religion is not science or philosophy. It is not primarily a matter of fact or of reason. It is a total way of life with main concern for salvation from evil and attainment of good. The philosophy of religion can be of value if it keeps this fundamental fact at the centre of its attention. Otherwise it tries, however subtly, to make a philosophy out of religion and to have it conform to its demands. To meet such requirements would be to declare religion fraudulent at its heart.

Reason is an indispensable part in the religious life and thinking, but reason in every part of life, and especially in religion, is not master and judge, but servant and judged. The function of reason is to provide clarity and consistency within man's totality of experience in relation to reality. If our religious claim is right, such service is more goal than attainment. The truest knowledge of religion is only a signpost to help.

PART II

Reason and Man

Chapter XI

Relativity and Reliability

We have now examined the use of reason in man's search for God. In so doing we investigated the function and powers of reason in general. But reasoning is part of man's total behaviour. Therefore the nature of man affects the working of reason. Two aspects of human life are especially pertinent to the processes of reason. Man being finite, his reason is necessarily relative. Can a relative reason, then, be adequate in the field of ultimates? Can a relative reason deal reliably with religious knowledge? Our first question, accordingly, is the relation between relativity and reliability.

A second and even more serious question as regards the bearing of human nature on reason is the problem of man's sinfulness. If all men are not only finite but also sinful, can reason be reliable in matters of religion inasmuch as reason is not only relative but also distorted? Is it not true that sinful man either accuses himself or excuses himself? In either case he fails to be objective. His thinking becomes either defensive or aggressive. He does not really reason about these things which concern his own security and desire, but rather he rationalizes. Can sinful man, then, ever attain to authentic knowledge in the field of religion? Religion speaks of realities and powers beyond ordinary experience that can help and harm man. Can man's reason deal with, and be helped by, these realities and powers? If it is ill, can it be healed? Can it become reconstructed; and can it perhaps even keep being changed in terms of creative and critical capacity for more genuine knowledge?

If sanity depends upon right adjustment of self to the world it meets within and without, does the peculiar power of religion —faith—contribute significantly to sanity? Does sanity depend upon a certain kind of faith within which reason works? Are not some faiths actual invitations to insanity? Do they not invite a fleeing from or a distorting of the world we meet? May it not be that the fight for sanity is at bottom a fight for a kind of faith? If our findings in the discussion of the previous section were true, wrong faiths should split the self within itself and falsify the interpretation of the world. Sanity, as right adjustment to the real world inside and outside self, would then be hindered by the acceptance of wrong faith, whereas right faith would unify the self and relate it realistically and constructively to the actual world of experience.

The two main subjects for investigation under the topic of reason and man are, consequently, relativity and reliability; and sin, sainthood and sanity. Discussion of these two topics should help both to consolidate our findings and to further our argument.

Granted that man is finite and that, therefore, his reason is relative, how can we assess its reliability? Obviously we cannot do so in any final sense without begging the whole question. The reliability of the reports of reason cannot be absolutely guaranteed, but only accepted from within man's situation and examined from within the compass of his competence. Since man himself is finite, no aspect of his thinking can apodictically be declared certain. It is finite man, for example, who proposes the validity of analytical thinking; even such thinking, therefore, which cannot be isolated from the thinker, is touched by relativity.

Indeed, even the claim that man is finite can be no more than an intuitive, primitive assertion, reducing the very claim that man's thinking is relative to relative status. In truth, man can be partly finite and partly open to the infinite in him in such a way that his thinking can be touched with both certainty and probability, or with both necessity and unrelatedness. There is no final proving the relative by the finite, and therefore no absolute assessing of reliability of knowledge. Apart from claims to inerrant revelation and avowals of complete scepticism, neither of which can be proved by virtue of their own claims, we are left with the more sobering task of trying to ascertain in what measure finite man's relative reason is reliable for the purposes of religious knowledge.

122

The two main choices for pursuing the examination are the way of faith and the way of doubt. The successive stages in the pursuit are surely those of total doubt or total faith in immediate experience; doubt or faith in all but self; doubt or faith in the interpretation of our ordinary experience within our time and space order; and finally, doubt or faith in the realm of religious affirmation in the terms of our definition as going beyond ordinary experience. Doubt and faith within our present context of discussion refer, of course, to the reliability of reason in its task of interpreting, ordering and directing experience.

Before beginning our examination it is well to affirm again that total faith-in-general and total doubt-in-general have no relevance for discussion. To trust the human mind for full and invariable truth is so basically to deny the fallibility present in experience that such groundless faith seems nothing but psychotic. In effect it amounts to an uncritical solipsism. It is equally out of the question to accept some total revelation which constantly informs reason infallibly. To do so seems a direct denial of our humanity, an attempt at escape from our actual finitude. After all, the recipient of the revelation is finite!

Similarly complete doubt makes any and every affirmation of no truth or value, precluding serious intellectual discussion. Perhaps a man of letters has the right to accept as his confessed faith that all is absurd and then proceed to play with ideas to the effect that since if all is absurd it is logical to die, the devotee of the absurd will go on living because such action is more in line with the absurd. But our best intention, at least, is to carry on a serious investigation into the limits of relativity and reliability, and therefore we have to rule out as relevant for our discussion the two contradictory, absolute claims to total doubt and to total faith.

There can, however, be a rationally acceptable doubt of immediate experience as giving us any reliable knowledge. 'And behold he awoke and it was a dream.' In the moment of experience the world pictured in a dream can appear more real than any waking experience, and yet the awakened person can doubt that the dream contained any reliable experience. It may have done so, of course. Dreams may tell us of our unconscious depths. But if so, what actually was experienced at the moment was not, as such, reliable truth. We may be totally convinced in a dream that we can walk over telephone posts in mid-air, only to find our waking attempt to do so disappointing. But unless we invoke the rule of total scepticism, we must grant that at least some knowledge comes through immediate experience in one form or another. To be totally sceptical about all immediate experience amounts, therefore, to total scepticism. The continuing basis of, and contact with, experience is the person himself, who lives centrally in the present, so that the total man, even sleeping, 'has' a dream.

The man with an illusion in one moment comes to the more continuing kind of present experience which is real or sane. The man knocked unconscious has no known present consciousness, but a continuing presence of experience which sustains him even apart from consciousness. Thus there can be legitimate doubt as to the reliability of any particular present experience, but none as to the reliability of immediate experience in general.

Completely opposed to scepticism is an alternative point of view regarding the reliability of reason in immediate experience: complete faith in its reports. What is experienced directly is true. There may later be wrong interpretation of what was experienced, but the experience as such was entirely reliable. Therefore error is ruled to be the result not of reason's direct awareness in experience, but of its judgment in experience. The examination of evidence at this point is both difficult and of critical importance. Unfortunately for this view, however, the fact seems to be that separation of reason's awareness and reason's judgment cannot be based even analytically on the evidence of immediate experience. Sometimes awareness and judgment acquiesce and sometimes they diverge.

One may actually experience and judge one's train to be pulling out of a railroad station when suddenly the last car of another train which had been actually in motion comes into view and almost immediately one finds oneself still sitting in the station. In such a case immediate awareness and judgment agreed. Or from previous experience one may be aware of the danger of such a mistake which necessitates suspension of judg-ment as the immediate response, until one can ascertain which train is actually moving. On the other hand, if, while attending a motion picture, one is suddenly confronted by a man walking upside down on the ceiling of the screen, the experience and the judgment may diverge. The immediate judgment in such a situation may be that the picture is turned upside down.

Every immediate experience comes coloured with previous interpretations which bear on the nature of the judgment. A child who does not know that a stick under water looks crooked may judge that he broke the stick upon hitting the bottom; at the same time there was an absence of noise and of the ac-customed jar of breaking in the hand that gave a new feel to this unaccustomed experience. The immediate experience and judgment in such a case is complex and confused. Immediate experience in itself seems to be no criterion of certain know-ledge, either as awareness as such or as judgment in awareness. Therefore faith in the complete reliability of immediate ex-perience seems unjustified.

The next main stage in the pursuit of reliability is the self as the dependable continuum and focus of knowledge. Such a basis for knowledge can be either totally doubted or totally believed. The likelihood is, of course, that just as immediate experience can be neither totally repudiated nor affirmed as the reliable basis of knowledge, even so the self can be neither totally re-jected nor accepted. Immediate experience we found to be in some manner the basis and point of contact with the world to be interpreted, ordered and directed; in some such way also the self seems to be one necessary lead in the attainment of reliable knowledge. Later we shall have to venture some guess both as to the how of knowledge and as to its measures and limitations, particularly as we proceed into the realm of religious knowledge. Such an approach seems to be most suggestive as to the relation between relativity and reliability.

We can doubt, then, that the self is in any way a basis for reliable knowledge. There is no complete identity of experience from moment to moment. Conscious memory, at least, is fallible. There is no way of proving that any self exists as a continuing entity, separate from and independent of the rest of the experienced world. The thoughts of the moment may coalesce into some fragile unity of experience, without necessity of exact continuity or recall. The self seems to have an origin and an end which are both beyond reach of reportable experience. Selves sleep, suffer lapses, and can be radically changed even in the way in which they look at the world they experience. With what right, in such a case, can the self be selected as a basis for reliable knowledge? Experience itself seems mostly dependent upon an outside world and a previously existing way of interpreting what is experienced. Why, then, have any faith in the claims of self to knowledge?

All these considerations count heavily against the opposite stance, namely, that the self is itself the given basis of knowledge and, as such, is the most dependable element in it. The facts mentioned in the preceding paragraph count, of course, most tellingly against any total faith in the self as the reliable basis of knowledge. But, at the same time, in one sense we have no other basis. No-one thinks and reports as a thinker except a self. We know ourselves to be thinking and we experience others who report to us that they share a similar experience. Although we can think with them or against them, we recognize that we all are doing what we call experiencing and reasoning. Neither the continuity nor the unity of the self is perfect, but we have no other original basis from which to proceed than some self.

Therefore to deny that the self is the reliable basis of knowledge in every sense is, like the denial of the reliability of immediate knowledge in every sense, in effect a denial of all experience and reasoning, and is, as such, obviously self-defeating. The main purpose of the analysis right here is not to determine the measure of reliability. It is only to show the need to admit relativity rather than to assert either total denial or total affirmation of reason's reign from any basis and at any point. The recognition of both immediate experience as the general basis of reliable awareness and recognition of the self as experiencing dependable continuity of thinking are nevertheless necessary ingredients in any determination of whatever be the correct proportion between the relativity and reliability of human knowledge.

The next main line of demarcation for questioning the capacity of reason of the finite nature of man concerns man's ability to organize the world or ordinary experience into some total unity. We are not considering here whether this unity contains complete self-consistency within itself. If it did so, in any case, both freedom and sin would thereby be declared non-actual, which is an unenviable position for reason to take. The question is only whether reason can reliably deal with its entire world of experience as one total meaningful candidate for knowledge. Again, the two extreme positions are those of direct denial and of complete affirmation.

For the mood of doubt the question is natural, how can any man, finite as he is, claim to deal with the whole world of experience in one unity of knowledge? There is first of all the lack of comprehensive knowledge. No-one knows the whole world. Perhaps the several sciences can arrive at some theories which are universally applicable. Mathematics and physics can be shared throughout the whole world. The adding machine and the abacus may use differing methods, but operators of both can be judged in a competition because, granting common numbers and stipulated mathematical processes, the results should be the same regardless of means or methods for computing. Perhaps there can be high agreement in the fields of geography and geology, but no one scientist knows all the sciences, let alone all the data that necessarily elude narrowly objective methods. And if any finite knower has extensive knowledge it must be had at the expense of knowledge in depth.

No person lives long enough to cover all fields of knowledge with any appreciable measure of depth. Perhaps an historian spends his life in trying to find the workings and meaning of history in relation to mankind. Does he know equally well prehistory, ecology, and the planetary secrets? Is he equally conversant with the detailed history of all the fields? Specialists, at least, often aver that generalizers sin against much particular evidence of a particular place or time. And is he equally at home in military history and that of the religions of the world? Can he handle anthropological, sociological and psychological considerations with the power of the man who has given a lifetime to a small segment of any of these? It seems that life itself is man's basic problem when it comes to knowledge. It is too short to allow both breadth and depth of knowledge. The study hours are shorter still! Man's finitude is a curse keeping ever beyond reach a reliable interpretation of his total experience. Such, at least, seems the mood and claim of the denial that man can interpret as a reliable unity the totality of his ordinary experience.

Besides, there is the problem of relevance. Even if we pass over, for this section, the question of man's sin and drive to rationalization, is it not true that man cannot help asking his question from the point of view of his interests? The very questions man asks anywhere and at any time are located almost entirely within the narrow parentheses of the questions raised by any age, at least as these are affected by the prevailing emotional patterns and the progress of man's knowledge up to any point of history. Even if a person's own interests should outrun his contemporaries, and if at some possible point his thinking should precede interpretation in general, nevertheless he could not avoid the frame of reference of his own time and of his own personal history and position. No interpreter of experience as a whole can transcend and command experience as a whole as though he were not part of it. He is involved within it, and sees from within it. What he sees has a given angle of vision and an unavoidable personal perspective. In other words, no human being can occupy a universal stance or command a superrelative frame of reference. The total relativity of the situation we have described in these two paragraphs, on the question of man's seeming limitations of reason as a human being, add up to impressions of the world sporadic, shifting and varied. How, then, can anyone claim for himself or for any other human being a stable, synoptic vision of the whole world of experience?

On the other side, there can be faith in reason's capacity to order its total world of experience because it is believed that something universal is implanted in man, as man, which requires that he interpret and understand the world as a whole. Such general experience being a necessary part of man's every equipment in interpreting his world, it is indeed as necessary as experience itself. In other words, to reason as a human being is to deal with universals which apply to all experience, because universality is a matter arrived at not statistically but constitutionally. Wholeness characterizes man's thinking as such and cannot be denied, it is claimed, without the simultaneous denial of reason as such. Whether what reason finds is also true in the world beyond cannot be proved. The world as such cannot be known. It can be known only as it is encountered and interpreted by our minds which contain within themselves a native necessity of wholeness.

In such a case, reason is by all means reliable, for necessity is innate. It is no longer necessary to count noses but only to analyse correctly one authentic human experience. Whatever empirical doubt comes from empirical investigation can be ruled out by ruling out the legitimacy of empirical investigation to establish truth logically inherent in the analysis of experience as such. The operations of cause and effect, for instance, are foundational to reason, the logical pre-supposition of all empirical equivalence, predictability and control, and may not therefore be discounted by any supposed discovery of discrepancies in any concrete instance.

If to live as a human being, moreover, is to be subject to a categorical demand to do right by the very structure of human experience, there can be no use in pointing to the denial of such a drive on the part of concrete human beings. If the experience of beauty, however dim, is part of man's native endowment as man, presupposition of experience as real as experience in general, there can be argument about the concrete nature of beauty, but not about man's experiencing it. If these capacities are universals and universal, and yet also the presuppositional properties of the experience of one person within a unity of consciousness, there can be strong faith in man's capacity to deal with experience as a whole. With such a basis the interpreter can proceed to the more complex problems, for instance, as to the possible presence of a unified purpose within the totality of man's experience.

No matter how thorough and distinguished such an examination of reason in experience may be, however, it cannot avoid the relativity which infects all experience because human nature is itself finite. No aspect of human nature can ensure reliability. Such logical necessity, after all, is only as certain as human experience. Human nature is still the key. To say that categorical necessity is as necessary as experience itself is to say also that in the final analysis it is as finite and unreliable as experience itself. No knowledge can be given the status of necessity as long as it is human knowledge. All human knowledge is finite and that far unreliable. The reliability of knowledge is never a matter of subjectivity and objectivity apart from each other but always a matter of the relation between them. To seek to find certainty in reason by the analysis of the logical presuppositions for human experience is, indeed, first artificially to isolate human experience from the experienced world, and then to bestow on what is experienced some unity from within experience.

Human knowledge is then based on subjectivity in some sense, be it logical presupposition, as in Kant, or decision, as in Kierkegaard. The error is the same in either case. The act of knowledge began with an illegitimate and falsifying abstraction of the self from its world. Or, oppositely, to seek truth outside self in terms of some logical analysis or scientific method as though these could be isolated from the subjectivity and finitude of those who perform the analysis or employ the method, is to err disastrously in the direction of objectivity. Man and his world must be kept together. From the proper analysis of such togetherness we have to find whatever measure of knowledge is open to man, in so far as man can see at all his own situation. There can, of course, be no final guarantee that he can do so. Man's knowledge in any realm is a daring act of faith.

Some have tried to argue from reason to the existence of God. The equation of thought and being has led to an easy implication that perfection necessarily involves existence, and that therefore by the sheer analysis of the meaning of perfection the conclusion follows that God the perfect One must be. Analytically there is much to be said for such a claim. The very definition of the good involves that it ought to be, and consequently analytically perfection ought in a maximum measure to be. If meaning and being are isolated from value, the full nature of the classical doctrine of the ontological argument loses its force. Certainly in Anselm's prayerful analysis 'than whom no better' refers to no value-indifferent meaning. The moral argument is presupposed. God is no being as such, but the best conceivable being. Therefore the ontological argument in its presuppositions is not primarily structured in the implication of idea to being, but in the implication of the idea of the good to being. Such also is the nature of Augustine's deepest intention. The fate of the argument in the hands of Aquinas, Descartes, Hume and Kant is fascinating to follow. Descartes especially introduced a mathematical tone which was much more rationalistic in import. But in his argument from the faithfulness of God to the veridical knowledge of the outside world, the moral nature of the argument is clear even so.

It is difficult, therefore, to deny analytically the turning of the same process from the existence of God to reliable knowledge of God outside experience, or from religious experience to ordinary experience, and endowing this with the unity that is inherent in the ground of thinking. But from the analysis of reason alone we can get to neither the necessity of God nor to necessary universals in ordinary experience. The nature of reason, to be sure, is to crave self-consistency. But reason by itself can bestow necessity neither on God nor on the world. Ontology obviously cannot be dependent on epistemology. Neither God nor the world derives either being or unity from the human mind. Nor can even our knowledge depend entirely upon the mind except as the ability to apprehend and to interpret what is true and real. In such a question the empirical order cannot be bypassed. Reason is an instrument with which to understand the world, not the creator of unity in it, apparent or real. It is no ground for inferential truth apart from the check of empirical fact. Such a check becomes the challenge of faith.

Man's rebellion against his finitude is perhaps best illustrated by his attempt to exempt some part of human nature from finitude. We do not make room for faith by the limiting of reason to certain spheres where it is declared competent, but by the full use of reason within whatever proportion of relativity and reliability actually obtains. Reason in the world of cause and effect, externally testable, can be shown most nearly as reliable with regard to the experienced world. But such reliability is due not to the nature of reason, but to the nature of the world in this realm. Reason in the moral realm cannot be thus predictable because of the nature of freedom and sin. The moral laws are relational and situational at least fully as much as constitutional. To exempt formal moral obligation and to make this category logically necessary for experience is somehow to isolate morality from its full rootage in what is experienced as well as in the experience.

There is no such universally acknowledged or demonstrable experience. No theoretical analysis to the effect that it must be there can be legitimate if one normal, competent, honest person knows that he does not experience such a categorical imperative. Similarly with the aesthetic experience. It can be dim indeed for many people with no real necessity seemingly contained in it at all. The reason we have changed from defining religion as logically presuppositional and thus universally inescapable to our present understanding of it as dependent epistemologically upon its being derived from the total ordering of experience, lies precisely at this point as well as at the insight that religious knowledge must be genuinely free-floating, not coercive even formally. Necessity in religious knowledge is had from within the finding, not for the finding.

How subtly man refuses to accept his finitude! Man makes himself central to knowledge and makes the examination of human reason the criterion of reliability. If there are no necessary connections in the experienced world, man thinks he can supply them from within. He finds a closed world of cause and effect where necessity obtains by the categorical necessity of his theoretical reason. The laws of the starry heavens are then matched by a moral law within, which is equally necessary as some formal categorical imperative. The interpreter then relegates freedom to some realm outside the closed causal order of the actual world, making man autonomous at that. As an amendment to this formal world of moral obligation he adds freedom, soul, and a chance for duty to work out in eternity. Then as an amendment to this amendment he adds God!

The above approach is shot through with genuine insights. At least religious knowledge is not given direct necessity. The position, however, is obviously based on a false separation of experience from what is experienced, of mind from action and affection, and then the whole analysis is reared as a mighty defence against the free flow of analysis through the uninterrupted fullness of experience. It is clear there are different emphases in experience, giving room for different kinds of operations of reason: several semi-autonomous kinds of rational normativeness which must be given their full stress and not submerged under some undifferentiated totality.

That reason can be compartmentalized, however, is a claim that has no standing in the halls of truth. Reason may not legitimately be thus cut and boxed in without critical damage to knowledge. No analysis of human nature can give categorical priorities or any reliability to knowledge that denies the finiteness of man and its unreliability in some real sense in every sphere. If a 'miracle' of physical healing should take place, for instance, the laws of cause and effect of ordinary experience are suspended. If our order of cause and effect is considered to be a matter of categorical necessity (not to be confused with causality as merely some logical presupposition of experience as such) without which experience itself could not be conceived, the witness of such a miracle would be to a supernatural order which then had interfered with and broken into the natural order. Or we should have to suspend judgment altogether and call in question either the claimed event, no matter how well tested, or the original analysis of experience which produced innate necessity in reason.

Possibly the best attitude, however, is to accept the evidence at hand and then to work creatively to establish some comprehensive causal order not categorically closed, and leave it for critical reason to discover whatever ascertainable measure of relativity seems actually to obtain. It seems wisest neither to isolate the order of reliability from nor to equate it with experience as such. Certainly to find necessary order throughout the realm of ordinary experience through some formal analysis of reason, only to fence this realm off from the total interpreting, ordering and directing of human experience, is arbitrary and inadequate.

There are, on the other hand, as we have seen, strong reasons for holding that human nature is too limited to interpret reliably the whole of ordinary experience. No appeal to the innate capacity of man's reason or to the logical presuppositions for thinking can by itself solve this problem. Man's relativity besets the reliability of his use of reason in the interpreting, ordering and directing of experience as a whole. On the other hand, we do have some real reliability. Man's interpretation of the immediate moment presupposes the wholeness of experience which is brought to it as the basis of judgment. Man's interpretation of his individual experience presupposes the social nature of his experience both historically and contemporaneously.

Man lives in family groups. His reason is used reliably for the purposes of the family. He lives in communities, like cities, and his reason can be used collectively to interpret, to order and to direct such communal experience. As a social being he lives also in larger units like the nation, and his reason keeps pace with the growth of his community. Finally he lives also in the whole world, and his reason becomes an instrument on the worldwide scale to interpret, to order and to direct his experience. Such has been the case in many fields such as mathematics and science. We study geography and economics, astronomy and history on a worldwide scale. Right now we are trying to use reason in restraining men from destroying the world and in implementing even politically some way of walking together in creative and constructive peace on a worldwide scale. However much man may have bungled and failed in the past, the fault may have been due more to man himself than to his reason and may have lain more in the sense of immaturity and sin than in the limitations of finitude. Reason is therefore in some respects reliable as well as relative in the ordering of the whole of his ordinary experience.

It may, of course, be objected that we are now dealing with the practical reason and not with the theoretical meaning of the wholeness of experience in this world of time and space. If our previous analysis as a whole has been correct, however, the point exactly is that such separation between practical and theoretical meaning is artificial. The meaning of life is not an extra quantity added to life. The meaning of life is life itself in its wholeness through the interpretation of the whole of experience and its legitimate implications. The meaning of history is history. The meaning of man is man. Therefore an adequate description of life and history in their totality is the only way to deal with these questions. In so far as these questions, moreover, are within the dimensions of ordinary experience they can be dealt with, and are being dealt with, in some proportion of relativity and reliability.

The further question, of course, is whether this wholeness does not involve the religious dimension beyond ordinary experience, whether life and history are not to be seen within a larger context than this world of time and space. In our first section we saw how this religious dimension gives the fullest scope to both the creative and the critical reason in their dynamic interaction. Our problem in this section is whether or not there is some inherent limitation within human reason as part of human nature that precludes man's dealing reliably with what is more and other than ordinary experience. Can the instrument by its own nature be so circumscribed or curtailed that our analysis in the previous section becomes invalid on this account? Is it not the height of presumption for man to try to deal with God, for the finite to deal with the infinite, for the relative to make known or even to try to know the ultimate? Does not human nature make it necessary that theology arrive where many of the greatest theologians have claimed it arrives, either in sheer subjectivity or in fearful or adoring mystery?

On this subject, too, there is the way of total doubt. Man is man. As man, he can know as man, and know whatever pertains to the life of man, but he cannot know beyond that. To claim to know beyond the scope of his own human nature and what is practically relevant to it is to accept for knowledge either idle speculation or prideful presumption. Man may believe and such faith may be of immense value to him. His faith may help him to bear his human lot and even to adjust to the larger reaches of reality whatever they be. But to claim that man knows is subtly to put man on a level beyond the human. As a matter of fact, if God be God and God be real, it is to put man on the level of God. Whether religion be right or wrong in terms of knowledge (from this point of view) should not be the final religious question, but whether man's faith be rightly related to himself and to his relevant environment so as to help him the most to live the life of man.

The opposite side, full faith in reason's capacity to know the eternal, centres in revelation's claim to final knowledge. Religious knowledge, if true, is by nature not relative. Religion deals with the absolute, this view goes on, and therefore religious knowledge is qualitatively different from all other knowledge. Revelation comes from the other side of the gulf between God and man and must consequently be reliable because it is God's self disclosure. Revelation may come in terms of a supernatural person, a supernaturally inspired book, or a supernaturally inspired institution.

Whatever be the method of revelation or of interpreting the revelation, this position holds, it is God's gift and fully reliable. Therefore the answer to human relativity is divine reliability. Such a claim, of course, cannot be denied, for it is not made in the area of human knowledge. It is an undebatable claim of faith. From the point of view of knowledge, all events in human history, personal or impersonal, are in some respect relative. Nothing in human history is unconditioned and devoid of a finite aspect. Then, too, the interpreters and all for whom the interpretations are made are also relative; and therefore such a claim, however real to an uncritical faith, is unreal and irrelevant to all ordinary human knowledge.

Between these two extreme positions, of complete denial and complete acceptance of religious knowledge in the light of human nature, lies another position in which there is no drawing an exact line between reliability and relativity. In answer to the first position—that of total doubt because the finite is incapable of the infinite, or human nature of divine knowledge—I hold that although man is finite he may not be only finite. As a matter of fact, to define man solely in terms of the finite and the relative is a denial of that more and other than ordinary experience which we discovered in our examination of man's interpretation, ordering and directing of his total experience. The very definition of man is thus prejudicial.

If our first analysis is true, man must be defined also on the level of what is more than ordinary experience and, as a matter of fact, what is more than ordinary experience alone affords the fullest perspective for the understanding of man, as man. In such a case man's knowledge of the divine is possible because man is created by the divine and intrinsically related to God as a creature made by him and for him. Man, then, is in some sense finite and in some sense also more than finite. The problem is how to draw the correct proportion between reliability and relativity in religious knowledge, rather than to deny either side of the problem.

Secondly, the manner of arriving at what is more than and other than ordinary experience, we remember, is from within human history and experience. The manner of God's revelation and of man's knowledge is not in terms of some esoteric super-natural formula, but actually in terms of a kind of life and a kind of love which characterize the self-disclosure of God. Faith in God's incoming and self-disclosure is unexceptionally for finite freedom. Thus the revelation of God comes within the finite for the sake of the finite. As such it is accessible. If the question is asked, but how can that be known which will eventually go beyond anything we can now conceive of, 'what eye has not seen nor ear heard', the answer is that faith has no need to know more than is relevant to its present situation. It waits believingly.

If faith has seen a kind of ultimate, a kind of life, a kind of love, and if this be ultimate beyond present human compre-hension, then man can live on meaning which is real and yet essentially surrounded by the illimitable depths of mystery. In such a case man can admit to the densest ignorance and know that he knows only as man in some real sense of relativity, while also being assured in his faith that the centre of his knowledge is reliable. In the case of the kind of religious knowledge that we have found, human nature, therefore, while admitting freely its finitude and consequent relativity, can also know that, being human, it is always related to more than itself, and that it can know the religious realities and powers beyond ordinary experience, not as they are in themselves, but reliably for what they are and in the way in which they affect men.

Besides, even in the knowledge situation man is not alone. He is not trying to know some substantively different, unreachable realm of knowledge, but a personal Spirit who comes to man, identifies himself with him and helps him to know who God is. If God be Love and Love be man's origin and end, the deepest need in man is for love. The love he knows on his own level is a human preparation for the eternal Love which is his ground and goal. Such love participates with man at every stage of his growth. When we are as children, God works with the children. When we become men and put away childish things, God participates in what appears to us a more mature manner.

When human maturity in our earthly life is bypassed, the new knowledge will be reached, as well, not by human capacity and effort alone but also and more importantly by the Spirit who lets himself be known and who participates in the act of knowing. Thus man knows the Eternal even though he is creature, because man is made for God and is more than finite, because God reveals himself on the finite level by 'becoming man', and because God participates on every level of man's growth. Man knows he is spirit by creation and is made to be fulfilled by his growing in right relations both to and within the Spirit.

Such knowledge will always be as creature to Creator. Man never becomes God or knows as God. He knows only as he is known by God. As *personal* spirit, man encounters God, and the realm of God will always be qualitatively distinct from man and unbridgeable. As personal *spirit*, man knows God because of God's presence in him by interpenetration as he will understand and accept God's self-revelation. The more the spirit prevails and man lives in the freedom of fulfilment, the less will there be external judgment and overagainstness in the knowledge of God. The finite will be relative and real, but not frustrating. Eternal life can best be described as that relation between God's transcendence and immanence where all wills and works through love. To stand in knowledge of eternal life, then, means to know in the personal mind and in the whole life of the spirit that creatively right relation, God, self, the community and all creation for which we were made: the fulfilling unity of Love which always abounds in enriching diversity.

In order to clarify possible hidden assumptions throughout our analysis, I am now going to suggest an approach and an attitude to the act of knowledge. Any adequate treatment of it would involve separate volumes, but the central features of it can be suggested in a short span.

Human knowledge in general is mostly the act of God. It cannot be understood basically through the analysis of any human being's act of knowledge, particularly not in terms of his discursive knowledge; nor can the act be conceived of in terms of the understanding of knowledge by any generation; schools or positions, moreover, however old, only stress the richness of the subject. Knowledge, to have depth of meaning, must be considered in terms of the history of life, of the human race and of God's dealing with both.

There is a quality of restless withinness from the beginning of creation, so subtle and so gradual in its push or pull that it is difficult to determine where life begins. The God of the total creation, within all and any of its parts, snailed toward some awareness on the part of the world, particularly on the part of a thin layer at the surface of the earth. By the time an earthworm, according to Darwin's famous experiments, could feel around a leaf to determine the acutest angle for pulling it through its hole into the earth, the process of knowledge was already far advanced in terms of not only identification and discrimination but also definiteness of purpose and the realization of purpose.

The ordering of experience and the directing of it in terms of knowledge had more than begun. The worm exhibits achievement of reason. Reason roots inseparably in the earliest beginnings of life and in whatever power occasioned it. When an animal has a vague 'feel' for abstract numbers—as a squirrel mother apparently half knows the number of her children and yet acts unsure of the exact count when in an emergency she has to move them from one home to another—reason is beginning to triumph in the sphere of abstractions. A dog, of course, will exhibit genuine joy at attainment, and grief at failure or disobedience. However these behaviour patterns relate to human affection and sense of right, or even to conscience, they illustrate authentic evaluation of experience.

Developed animals can even make abstractions sufficiently to enjoy token rewards, like monkeys conditioned to value 'money', and use recall of experience to act with sustained purpose beyond their field of perception, as when a chimpanzee will run for a stick that it recalls being used before, in order to have its help in reaching the proffered banana. No discussion of reason and knowledge that isolates human from animal knowing, indeed from the total life processes and their rootage in the inorganic, can possibly be more than a shallow abstraction. The co-ordinating inner reality of this total process beyond all specific planning within earthly evolution is God. Therefore we said that the act of knowledge must be basically understood in terms of God.

Humanity seems to exhibit a discontinuity in continuity. Obviously there is strong continuity between the ejaculatory communication of animals, as obviously effective at a distance, and even between the signals of insects in their community responses to threats, and the communication of human beings. But the development of speech in propositional form involves a new stage of reasoning and knowledge. A new level of abstraction makes for a qualitatively new kind of experience, continuous with and dependent upon the long history of animal and human life, but never reducible to it. Reason can, of course, be defined in terms of this late top layer, but the fuller definition is truer to its nature.

Human knowledge, in any case, cannot be discussed apart from the relation between the history of thought and the history of speech in their constant interaction. Both of these not only root back but go back into the untold ages. Reasoning is part of life, and knowledge is the result of reasoning as the becoming aware of and responding to the inrushing and on-rushing environment. Knowledge is bodily before it is brain, and bodily-brain long before it becomes mental in any distinct sense, and bodily-brain-mental long before it reaches the higher levels of religious awareness and response. But all through the long process of the development of reason and the achievement of knowledge, the total withinness has been present. We have no right to introduce any level of reality as from an external and foreign source at any time in the process. God was present in the beginning and the Spirit brooded over even the chaos and the void.

Whether we think of God as basically outside or inside is only a matter of spatial symbolism. The point is to recognize the continuity of the Creator and the successive manifestations of creative novelty, however gradually they may have appeared and with whatever relation of continuity to discontinuity. The external symbolism stresses God's transcendence; the internal, his unity with creation. The danger of the former is the tempta-tion to an unrelated supernaturalism; the temptation of the latter is pantheism. I choose to use both in order to combine the respective strengths of both positions and to combat their respective weaknesses.

When the discontinuity of self-conscious, deliberate com-munication first began to take place, we do not know. The likelihood is that even this form of knowledge came earlier and more gradually than we can picture. Then came our recorded history, the learning of various forms of writing, the formal training of children, schools of interpretation, and even printing and libraries. This sudden advance, however, relatively speak-ing, must be seen as the flowering of the wider basis of know-ledge in nature and history on which it rests. To isolate such abstractions of knowledge from the whole act of knowledge is to throw the entire question fatally out of focus. Nature, history, life have as one of their most important ingredients and functions the becoming aware, the discriminating, the ordering and the guiding of experience which we call reasoning, and the results of which we call knowledge.

The child is born into this process and owes the overwhelming part of its knowledge to the past, both in terms of capacity and content. The capacity is an accumulated heritage of sensitivity to the environment and power for interpreting it. The content is the total reservoir of language and accumulated knowledge into which the child is born. The immediate vehicle is the mother's womb in which the child recapitulates the history of the race, and where, through the magnificent wonders of creation, the child internalizes the history of the race. As life overlaps life and shares its priceless heritage in the womb, the greatest achievement of the act of knowledge is accomplished before birth by the child's acquisition of the means of knowledge, its reception of the capacities of reason. Then the child becomes ready and open to as much of the accumulated content of knowledge as it can appropriate. The living continuity of speech and communicable experience and the stored reservoirs of man's interpreted experience challenge the young in so far as they are accessible to them.

What the exact states of discrimination and confusion, or bodily knowledge and conscious understanding, are within the history of the child is exceedingly difficult to ascertain. There may be inherited structures, and even knowledge, as well as dispositional tendencies, beyond what we may guess. The study of the degree of seeming determination in the case histories of identical twins separated at birth suggests that we must be cautious indeed in our stressing the relation of the knower to his environment in isolation from the specific history of the race which operated with him. Even in the animal world we are mystified by the knowledge of fish returning astonishing distances to the spot where they were spawned, or by birds returning by instinct to the same place at distances which sometimes span even continents.

The study of the recall of the subconscious under hypnosis, or of seemingly collective archetypes in the racial subconscious discovered by depth psychology, whatever be the exact form or measure of truth in the findings, suggests the need to keep the act of knowledge in relation to the total 'within' which worked there from the beginning. Thus conscious and formal appropriation of knowledge and the wide reaches of depth conscious and informal assimilation co-operate in the act of knowledge. No study of reason that fails to root fully and solidly in this total milieu can be considered weighty.

God is also the main factor in the act of knowledge if this act, beyond its genetic analysis, be considered systematically. The reason that we can know is that there is interchange between the knower and the world. We now are told that there is not only interchange of energy at close range but that every atom is, so to speak, the infinitesimal centre of the universe. Each atom is related to the universe in its totality. As a matter of fact, the volume of every atom, in one of its aspects, equals the volume of the universe. Thus if the means for magnifying communication are present, every part of any room can receive communication from the whole world, and now even from the interstellar spaces. The mysterious 'within' is not only a matter of discrete entities, but at the same time a total unity. Each entity can appropriate knowledge of the rest according to its inherent capacity for knowing, according to the external means available, and according to the particular scope of relevance for that event in terms of its nature and equipment.

On the most advanced stage of knowing, that equipment is in our day a matter of accumulative, collective capacity for communication dependent upon intricate and complex instruments for communication. We live in the age of technological achievement. But in all cases the principle and power of knowing is the same: the dynamic presence of the creative within of thought and purpose. The power for such knowing is primitive and we cannot fix any boundaries to man's internal capacities to know. The Christian has come to understand that creative within to be love, the manifold presence of God in all diversities, mediating patterned energy and releasing capacities for the act of interpreting, which is the act of knowledge.

Particularly the child, as a unity, learns by response, from the

143

earliest acts and feelings, as its life is overlapped by its mother's. Beginning with such differentiation of life, the process of knowledge builds up through a repetition of response, interpretation and recall. Over and over again the child responds, interprets and recalls. By so doing it develops a continuum of discriminated awareness which lies at the bottom of all knowing. Reasoning is the total process of clarifying the content of this continuum, in terms of facts, functions, ideas and persons. The child does not first of all learn abstractedly, but by the necessity of constant response, interpretation and recall.

Informally there is a constant analysis of experience going on, which, in its accumulative work, resembles, on a shorter and smaller scale, the race's process of accumulative interpretation. Within this continuum certain elements recur with regularity, others are new or occasional. Certain features of the events keep recurring, as well, making it possible for a person to sort his experiences and to learn informally to make certain predictions. Such associations of experience make up the continuum of experience out of which the person responds. This process of response, interpretation and recall is basic to the act of knowledge. The act of knowledge, at bottom, is the analysis of the dynamic continuum of experience which is life itself.

This analysis reveals regularities, which we call 'universals', and discrete events, which we call 'particulars'. Actually, universals and particulars come together in primitive experience and should not be pulled apart except for the purposes of analysis. Then every correct analysis should end by their being together again. We know no universals before or outside concrete experience; nor do we know any particulars before or outside universals. We may not, therefore, go legitimately from the experience of particulars to universals; nor may we proceed from universals to the experience of particulars. Universals and particulars are part of the wholeness of experience. Universals are in experience as transcripts of the world experienced, and particulars are in experience as concrete items in the experienced world. We know no model tree; nor do we encounter discrete trees that do not exemplify the universal characteristics of a tree. Without such characteristics

144

the tree could not be classified as a tree. Universals are classifications of experience, whatever else they may possibly be, and can therefore never be isolated from experience as independent entities devoid of concrete content.

Whatever be the nature of the mysterious 'within' out of which comes concrete creation, its creativity is structured, but the structure is never a matter of quite similar events. Each event is in some real sense unrepeatably unique. No fingerprint or leaf is exactly like another. Thus there is repeated regularity in experience in terms of manifold forms of existences from which abstractions can be made. There is also endless variety within these forms. Sometimes there are borderline cases where experience may easily become confused. A whale is easily taken for a fish! Some men look more like women, particularly when haircut and dress are alike for both sexes. When abstractions develop to the stage of advanced interpretation of large sections of experience, or of experience as a whole, or, especially, of the implications from ordinary experience, the confusion becomes increasingly easy and frequent. But both universals and particulars are in experience as far as they can be directly experienced, and they are there together as neither separate nor fused entities. They are analysed apart within an act of advanced knowledge of a highly abstract character.

Any implications from either particulars or universals must recognize that we never experience either as such. I repeat that we never know any particular by itself; it is always a part of a total continuum containing universals to which it is inevitably related. Nor do we ever meet any universals apart from particulars, nor again do we ever encounter them in a universal sense. The word 'particular' indicates some sense of recognizable discreteness, and the word 'universal' means some measure of dependable regularity or likeness in experience. Any use of either of these facts must hold in mind this primary fact of inseparable relatedness, especially in the examination of whatever implications may be drawn, with some advanced interpretation and even some total ordering of experience as a base.

Some such implications may come from direct experience and

go beyond it. Mathematical calculations of gravitational pulls may lead to the finding of a new planet. Those sensitive to colour can fill in shades in the spectrum without the benefit of direct experience. Similarly, religious implications can lead to predictions of possible experience that for most people can only be experienced in this life as hope in the light of such predictions. Or they can the more readily be had along with the ordinary experience of this life. The faithfulness of God's sovereign love, for one example, should imply a fulfilment for man beyond death which can never be experienced until after death. Or, to illustrate the second assertion, a new understanding of the nature of God can help establish a new relationship in prayer. Such synoptic and synthetic experience is thus creative of new knowledge, eventually or presently, beyond the immediate reach of direct experience. That there can be, and is, such experience is due not to a creative faculty of the mind, but to its creative capacity to receive true reports from beyond present experience. The new planet is found not because the mind has the power to produce such a creative experience, but because the mind can discover and report the implications of experience which can lead to the fuller eventual experience. Nor is the filling in of shades in the spectrum due to the mind's capacity to create colour, but to its ability to recognize colour that is actually there in the spectrum, but not present immediately before the mind. The mind is thus reliable even in its true, creative outreach. Genuine implications are not merely conceptual, but relational to reality. They may not, of course, by their nature be open to present experience, but they are equally a matter of validly implied knowledge.

The mind can also falsify, of course; but false extensions of experience are due to the mind's capacity to create alternate worlds of description and prescription. Such creativity makes freedom both real and significant. The difference between the creativity of reporting and distorting lies in the verifiability in some way of authentic extensions of experience. In the creativity of reporting there is always some eventually ascertainable counterpart, whereas the distorted creation can rightfully never find such confirming report. Artistic creation, moreover, is neither reporting nor distorting, but imaginary outreach and imaginary combinations of form and material for the sake either of sheer creative satisfaction or for the sake of the clarification of experience by abstractive or symbolic relations to it.

The extension of experience by religious implications is neither mere creative reporting nor mere artistic creation. In some sense God and the inner realities are there for the finding. Thus far we have reporting. But the religious realities are not scientific descriptions of objectively existing data alone. They are the personal and spiritual relations that become established in the decision. Therefore to some extent they are created within the commitment itself. In this sense they are more like art than science. Indeed the decisive factors are realities like freedom and sin, or community and love, which are part of personal responses and actually created as well as discovered. They rest on some prior realities, but the relations are not thus until they are made. The God within is at the centre of the relation, but the kind of relation is established in the act. Thus knowledge rests both on an element of description and on an element of creation. Unless this relation between universals and particulars is kept sharply in focus, the nature of religious knowledge cannot be understood.

For this reason we have kept distinguishing faith's knowledge from factual knowledge. Faith's genuine knowledge is neither fiction, or merely created, nor merely fact, or merely discovered. Nor is it merely art as a combination of creativity and discovery by the fashioning imagination. As an act of knowledge it is analytically *sui generis*. Religious knowledge is closely akin to personal knowledge, but personal knowledge is from within the gamut of ordinary knowledge. It is direct encounter, even though the quality of the experience depends supremely on the act itself. Thus personal knowledge is a mutually creative as well as discovering experience.

In religious knowledge, however, there is always a conceptual element which predominates even in whatever direct or immediate experience may be possible. The degree of mediation goes beyond the measure of mediation involved in any direct experience of a human person. In this sense the past must dominate and the conceptual be unusually significant. At this point existentialism as a primary mode of religious knowing reveals its poverty. Only charismatic personalities penetrate beneath and beyond this thick veil, through which most religious experience takes place, to uncover fresh and new content, and thus to enrich the content side of the outreaching implications from the ordering of our total experience.

The problem of reliability and relativity of knowledge lies in the fact that the mind is free to combine reporting and creating, and that universals and particulars are never necessarily related. All knowledge is finding and constructing, from the lowliest sense experience to the most abstract conceptual scheme. There is no experience without the self as context, and without the total past and present as a continuum in some sense, directly or as the assumed background. In such a situation reliability and relativity are always present, contending with each other. The next part of this chapter will try to ascertain whatever criteria are available for judging what the relation may be between reliability and relativity. The following chapter will deal with the far more serious and complex question of the pressure of sin on reason, or the lack of reliability which comes not from the relativity due to finitude, but to rationalization or depth-driven attempts to hide from the truth. But first I shall make a mere comment on the total situation for knowing.

Some start with the self as the given datum and seek to know from the self outward how the world can be known. Others start with the givenness of the world and wonder how legitimately to allow for the self or for subjectivity, unless, indeed, they dissolve the self altogether or ignore its part in the act of knowing. Others still, start with the self and with the world in encounter, seeking by this means to overcome the onesidedness of the other two approaches.

None of these approaches will do. Obviously, to start with either the self or the world is to court disaster by giving illegitimate priority to either side and to accept a partial perspective to begin with that can then never yield plenary knowledge, unless, of course, it is in effect abandoned for a fuller approach. But even to start with the self and the world in encounter is also to abstract two artificial entities and then to worry about how to unite two falsely separated realities or else to keep them apart unnaturally. There is no self that is not also the world, and there is no world known apart from some knower. The world includes the knower, and, in some sense, the knower includes the world.

Then can we start merely with the whole? No, to do so is to accept some false unity which does not exist. The self and the world are both together and in some sense apart. Somehow the act of knowledge must register initially this foundational fact. The self can control itself in a way it cannot control others or the world, while, at the same time, the self is also affected by and partly under the control of the world of which it is a part.

Therefore the act of knowledge must be both analytical and constructional. Either approach by itself as a start and a procedure prejudices the outcome. The act of knowledge must include discrimination among countless universals and particulars within the background unity of the total field of knowledge, but it must also view these together and with regard to whatever implications attend such construction. To remember such dynamic duality as essential for the understanding of the act of knowledge may at least help to deliver the interpreter from all kinds of theories of knowledge that artificially choose separate aspects of the knowledge function or situation, and then labour arbitrarily to put together what is never known except in some sense as together, or, contrariwise, labour to keep separate elements which in a basic sense are inseparably one.

The first assumption of knowledge, in any case, must be that there is authentic knowledge. Therefore a primary assumption of knowledge must also be the general reliability of reason. Without such acceptance, call it faith, presupposition, givenness, or what not, knowledge itself is unaccepted. After that, the examination can begin as to how far knowledge and the means to it, reason, must also be considered unreliable because of relativity and sin. Before turning to the question of knowledge and sin I shall suggest some considerations that bear on the relation between the reliability and the relativity of knowledge.

There are five central considerations as to the question of the relation between the reliability and relativity of religious knowledge. These considerations pertain to the general problem of knowledge, but apply with special insistence in the area of religious knowledge. The first is the question as to the frame of reference. We recall how we found that we can learn to distinguish frames of reference in many general cases like that of the two trains, one of which begins to move. To what extent, then, can man claim reliable religious knowledge, since God alone can have the full focus of ultimate truth? Is not God's the only frame of reference that can be granted the status of knowledge? Is not the claim to religious knowledge, therefore, in the end, presumptuous?

Suppose we imagine two theologians with differing views waking up on the other side of death and both being utterly astonished at their own previous naïveté! A radically altered frame of reference might throw all knowledge into a different cast. The context might basically alter the meaning of the same content. There can be no question, for this reason, that religious knowledge is highly relative. The wide variations in the interpreting and ordering of experience on the subject demand that this relative nature of religious knowledge be heavily underscored. Certainly no human being can know as God knows, or speak directly as though he knew full well the mind of God. Even when revelation is accepted as authentic, the interpreter is not the revelation, and consequently receives a finite view of the revelation. Even if God discloses himself in a person as personal Spirit, he is yet Love within love, he is eternal within time, God within man, so that even in such a case the religious knowledge imparted is highly relative.

The fact is, however, that religious knowledge can nevertheless be reliable. Within the diversity there can be, and are, approximations to the truth. Some form of religious knowledge can be highly reliable amid the myriad false, distorted, or even misleading partial forms. If God is love, as I believe we have found, we can know that he is dependable concern and therefore we can trust him in life and beyond life without knowing him as he knows himself and without knowing as he knows. We know dependably, nevertheless, that he is love, i.e. faithful. Subjectively, we can have our spirits held steady within his Spirit and know the inner assurance of his presence, beyond our capacity to know or to explain the experience ontologically or psychologically.

Objectively, on the other hand, we can find that the more true Love is had—universal concern, full acceptance, creative adventure, co-operative community, faith in freedom and responsible faithfulness—the more persons and people can both be fulfilled. We can know that mental problems caused by anxiety, that crimes bred by uncontrolled lust, that political corruption fostered by greed, that social pains engendered by invidiousness, that frustrations occasioned by lack of acceptance, that meaninglessness due to lack of compelling convictions can be met head on and worsted by faith's finding the reality of love. We can also overcome the burden of moralism, the emptiness of legalism, the pressures of narrow conformism, and the fear of death by the trusting of a Love at the beginning of every undertaking, as the companion on every lonely road, and as the greeter at every destination.

How God will come, we cannot know; what his form will be, is beyond our ken; what he will show us, we cannot imagine; but we can learn in the ordinary living the reliability of a Presence both on the heights of life and in the valley of death. The relativity can be rich beyond measure with creative diversity, but the reliability can nevertheless be qualitatively dependable to faith's discerning vision.

What if such faith cannot be falsified because, whatever happens, this, too, is taken to be the work of a faithful God? The God who could be falsified in such terms must himself be false. Only the finite can be falsified. Faith fares ill when it turns its eyes to the finite as the final test of its truth. Faith feeds on the creative, meeting life and death in the flexible attitude of humble trust. The frame of reference of the fullest faith is the infinite, not the unconditioned mathematical or metaphysical abstraction from living reality, but the ultimate Concern who is the ground and goal of our lives, and the constant companion of those who make the rights of all others their own. Such a frame of reference will always baffle the finite. Man will never become God or know as God knows. But man can share that Love in the Spirit, and find that truth at the centre is no intellectual formula nor any scientific demonstration but a way of living, a kind of love and a kind of community. Such a frame of reference can provide both the inner security of steady walking and the unfolding satisfaction of eternal finding.

A second consideration with regard to the relation between reliability and relativity of religious knowledge in face of man's finitude, is the accessibility of the field of knowledge. Obviously, in this case, too, religious knowledge is peculiarly touched with relativity. How can man mount up to heaven to bring God down to be tested in his laboratory? Who can fetch the Spirit and bind him for the sketching? Who can run around eternity to draw its lines? Who can sort the saints by sociological statistics or pry into their psychological states at prayer? And such subjects for investigation cover only a corner of the field of religious knowledge. The field of religion covers all of life; nothing can be left out of final count from the focus of eternity on the whole of creation. The field of religion occupies, in terms of its accessibility, the height of subjectivity. It is centrally an 'I-thou' field, where objective data are the corpse left behind from the living relationship. Therefore not to stress the exceptionally high relativity of religious knowledge is to deny central evidence.

But there is also the other side of the question. If human nature is the most subjective and therefore, at the least, a highly relative subject for knowledge, especially in its relation to God, human nature is also the only directly accessible field for knowledge. There can be a click of inner conviction based on experience in the religious field that cannot be had in the case of any external knowing. What we know the best, the most intimately, the most persistently is ourselves as we live with ourselves. Sometimes we may be mistaken in this knowing, but we cannot let go of it except at the risk of our own self-being, if not sanity. Therefore we can undertake peculiarly to find for ourselves the truth of any religious claim.

Inner experience, if highly relative as knowledge, is also uniquely accessible for knowledge where it counts, for decision in ordering and directing life. The Christian religion at its highest, and perhaps all religions at their truest pointing, claim that only by full trust and love can God become real. Such knowledge requires as a prerequisite the unequivocal living for his will for the common good. He who is ambitious cannot know God. He who is conformist cannot know God. Neither self nor others can dominate life without excluding God from view. He who centres in self cannot know God. He who fears life cannot know God. He who does not want fully to forgive all others at the depth sources of his life cannot know God. He who shrinks from total, constant concern for all others cannot know God.

Anyone can try to make this decision as the unequivocal decision of his whole life, dare to be tried by God, and then find whether or not, after patient waiting, he will not have such experience of encounter, of pattern of living, and of a revolutionary concern for the true welfare of the world that he soon begins to doubt far more the depth sincerity and depth simplicity of his commitment than he doubts the reality of the Way of the Spirit.

Thus the field of religious knowledge is both highly relative and highly accessible to reliable knowledge for life. Such knowledge can be communicated in confession. Consensus will not be the test in a world so far from even the rudiments of religious attainment, but those who have climbed the mountain and have seen the ocean in the far distance know, when they confer with each other, that the others, too, can witness aright to an experience they cannot deny. More and more, then, God becomes known as reliable and the self as relative. Human nature can thus witness to both reliability and relativity in whatever proportion it has experienced religious reality and to whatever extent vision has become consummated.

If such religious knowledge should prove personally and communally reliable, would it not, nevertheless, be entirely subjective? Can religious knowledge ever be more than existential, more than personal knowledge within the choices of life? Human nature being the primary field for investigation, there is no escaping the fact that religious knowledge at its centre must be self-knowledge and personal experience of a kind not accessible to rigid external testing. From the point of view of testable objective knowledge affording a high order of consensus, religious knowledge is definitely unreliable. Religion simply is not physics or mathematics.

Our third consideration, therefore, is exactly the question of objective testing or measurability. There is no possibility for exact and demonstrable testing of religious knowledge. Even the endeavour of parapsychology to deal with objective evidence, if this subject is accepted as a candidate for scientific standing, is too relative because of the private and personal nature of man's communion with God. If prayer can be reduced to measurable response in relation to measurable stimuli, it is not the invocation of a personal will on the part of real freedom, but some manipulation of objective forces available to psychic influence. If spirits can be bidden to appear at the will of some human medium, there is no spiritual freedom or privacy beyond death. The nature of the field of religious knowledge is far too personal, private and subject to spontaneity to be regularized into any pattern open to parapsychological tests, even should we admit the reliability of this discipline. Thus human nature at this point, as well, reserves for itself an immeasurable degree of relativity with regard to the reliability of religious knowledge.

Nevertheless, there can be a measure of objective observation of the fruit of the Spirit, like love, joy, peace and righteousness. If religion is both true and real, it must satisfy man's deepest needs at their central drives. If man needs love centrally and the kind of love that he needs is not forthcoming in the religious experience, there can be no claim to religious knowledge, however high the personal certitude or the confessional assurance, within the closed community of believers. If true religion ministers to man's need for faith to meet his inner crisis with steady sanity and creative satisfaction, if the religious life lacks such qualities there can be no religious knowledge as objective observation, however insistent its claim to inner experience or communicative vision.

If man's community does not reach a dimension of fulfilment

at least incipiently consistent with the claim made to inner experience of such community, there can be no legitimate claim to objective knowledge in the field of religion. 'By their fruits ye shall know them' is the counterpart to 'whosoever wills to do my Father's will shall know of the doctrine'. Although the objective counterpart is not primary but resultative, without at least general results in line with the subjective confession to religious experience, religious knowledge suffers in its claim to reliability. In this sense, life is language deeper than words.

There must be vision for open and universal society, and some genuine sense in which power is exhibited to all honest and open viewers of the life of the religious devotee. True religion is known from within in the making, but the making must be knowable as fruit of the Spirit to those outside the community. Christian claims to ultimate truth stand radically questionable and, for many, hopelessly discredited because of the failure of the Christian community to establish a dynamic, creative, co-operative spirit among its members and to cope with problems of critical importance for man, like war, property and crime.

There is no exact way to deal with the field of love as productive of objective knowledge within the experience itself, and no way to measure with exactness the results in personal and social living of such love. But there should be objective results for observation sufficiently convincing for those who look with open concern for the kind of truth that life itself can find at its centre. The only objective confirmation of religion is the kind of life lived and the kind of social results produced by such living.

Two more considerations remain with regard to the relation between reliability and relativity of religious knowledge in the light of the finitude of human nature. One of them is the kind of equipment or competence the religious reporter commands. This competence must be of two kinds: first-hand experience and vision, and training. Without possession of first-hand experience no man can deal competently with the question. The interpreter must at least have tried with honest commitment to enter into the central claim and experience of the religious knowledge to be tested. But beyond such attempt, the interpreter must also be trained in the meaning and standards of knowledge. If the religious interpreter claims historic basis for his faith as far as knowledge is concerned, he must be trained in historic methodologies and have proved himself competent in the field. Obviously, as an historian he cannot be subjected to external tests of competence in terms of alien metaphysical assumptions. If historians rule out the historic importance of Jesus or of the Christian message on the ground of its being mainly religious, they prove themselves prejudiced metaphysically and methodologically. If a person, on manuscript evidence, believes that the Resurrection has genuine historic foundation, he cannot on metaphysical grounds be ruled out as incompetent as an historian.

If, again, the religious interpreter makes metaphysical claims to knowledge, he must be in a position to be tested as competent in philosophy. Certainly such competence does not depend upon belonging to any prevailing tendency in philosophy, but rather upon the possession of knowledge of the historic positions and of alternative contemporary interpretations, and upon the open and critical philosophic attitude. Whatever the inner religious experience may be, if it is to be accepted as more than data to be interpreted, the interpreter must show general intellectual reliability as to his total experience or as to what he sees in the total ordering of his experience.

Even then, religious knowledge is far too relative to be objectively coercive. As a matter of fact, the line between convictional language and assertive language is fine. Religious knowledge must be more than convictional in the subjective sense, and less than assertive in the objective sense. It can only commend itself to the serious seeker for the kind of truth which confronts and results from religious convictions and decisions: subjective enough to allow genuine freedom in finding; objective enough, like the conspiracy of creation, to allow the free spirit to find some structured confirmation.

The fifth and final consideration as to the relation between reliability and relativity in religious knowledge due to man's finitude, is the character of the witness. Competence must be assumed for the formal interpreter. Such interpretation for knowledge means powers of knowledge to deal with a subject according to the nature of approach, and to communicate both meaningfully and convincingly to others who are competent in the field and flexible both to faith and fact. But religious reality does not depend upon formal training or even intellectual brilliance. Sincerity is not enough, either. The religious witness must be simple in the sense of unselfconscious integrity. The best witness is 'transparent' to religious reality. Some have called these people religious geniuses; some have called them sports in religious evolution; some have called them charismatic personalities. They had best be called exceptionally real, genuine, or authentic. They live and breathe their faith, and their faith produces results in other lives.

The religious instinct to make Jesus Christ central to the Christian faith is more than idolatry wherein something in human history is substituted for God. The more real Jesus was religiously, the more he mediates the knowledge of God to others. Judaism has its Moses; Islam, its Mohammed; Buddhism, its Gautama. These personalities function as criteria for the reality of the religious knowledge claimed in their respective faiths. Or great interpreters like Paul, Hosea, Al Ghazzali, or Amida focus attention on the personal nature of religious knowledge. In the modern world Gandhi stands out for countless liberals, for instance, as a person who lived deep mysticism and whose life had practical effect, in the social sphere, to break down caste, and, in the political, to set his people free. As a matter of fact, his life signifies a systematic approach to the ways of love among collectives, the method of non-violent resistance, and persistence toward a socially desirable goal. In such witnesses, inner experience and outer results at least converge.

The character of the witness brings to attention the relativity of religious knowledge. How can people come so close to religious reality as did these and yet not agree as to what they saw? If God is one and if there be unity in the world-ground for world ethics, why should not those who are great in life and insight within the field of religion report the same vision

157

and the same experience? In the final section of this book we shall deal precisely with this question at some length, but for now we can say that if God is the source of integrity and concern, of faith and wholehearted devotion, these leaders exhibited such lives. If they are taken at their common best and delivered from the conditionedness of their respective backgrounds, there are exceptionally large areas of common testimony in their lives and teachings.

The men who both lived deep faith and influenced history for better days, such as Socrates, were both open to truth and willing to die for it, be it respect for law or respect for people. Therefore there is reliability in the kind of religious knowledge that lays central stress on the believing life, the open mind, and the compassionate heart. The interpretations vary, often sharply, but such relativity of reported knowledge gives way to the central reliability of the kind of life they led and the rightful implications which can be drawn from their lives. Thus in the cases of Socrates, Jesus and Buddha, for instance, interpretations of reality, centring in their kind of life and in the implications of their lives, become dominant aspects of religious faith. Integrity and concern join in witness within and beyond high-grade religious experience.

Lives are ways of walking; they indicate central attitudes toward life; they give the basis not only for ordering, but for directing life. Therefore true discernment would find in the character of the witnesses the kind of reliability and relativity that enriches life with the necessity of personal and social choice with regard to ultimate meaning and stance for living. The only final judge in this respect, however, is the man who can view with integrity his own finding and lacking, who can make his own considered choice for living, and, in his own integrity and concern, can help to indicate by the way in which he steers his life in what direction ultimate truth lies. Religious knowledge is mostly a matter of creative faith subject to critical thinking; some of this can be formal and systematic. Most critical thinking, however, will have to be personal and informal as faith confronts each person: the faith which shapes his life and judges its worth.

If we can summarize our findings, they are that religious knowledge is the kind of personal knowledge where human finitude matters profoundly. Religious knowledge is necessarily highly relative and incapable of exact objective testing; it is through and through subjective and exceedingly varied in its approach. Therefore religious knowledge has a small measure of reliability in the objective sense, except for certain areas of cosmic history—which involve the arrival of new dimensions of creation that provide more data for objective knowledge—and the meeting of human need, as such need reflects beyond man the objective reality in which he lives; and even in such cases the evidence is more suggestive than conclusive. The relativity of religious knowledge makes it by nature non-coercive. It is more convictional and confessional than assertive and coercive in any argumentative sense. Not to recognize this fact is to distort the nature of religious knowledge.

On the other hand, religious knowledge is in a sphere more intimate than any other, what each self can find real in his own seeking and findings as to the meaning and call of life in their deepest dimension and longest reach. The truth of integrity and love can be known only from within, and can come to be known at such depths of the knowing self, in its deepest needs and fullest powers, that the self speaks more of realities and powers of which he is unworthy, and which he serves best when he is grasped by them instead of in control of them.

The whole frame of religious reference, the accessibility of the field, the kind of measurement of religious knowledge, and the equipment and character of the religious interpreter come together in a meaning so receding into mystery, and a mystery at that so fraught with meaning, that before them both he stammers and stutters. Yet in such failure of speech he may know, at his deepest, that he has uttered the most profound truth open to man.

Chapter XII

Sin, Sainthood and Sanity

The two main factors in human nature that call reason into question are finitude and sin. We have just discussed the problems raised by finitude. An even more serious indictment of the reliability of reason in religion comes from the dominance of sin in the life of man. Is such indictment genuine or only a false charge? If the indictment stands, how serious is it? Is man corrupt at the centre of his life, and does his nature involve reason so intimately and thoroughly that he can but rationalize in matters religious? Does the power of sin in man's life preclude reliable reasoning with regard to God?

Or is man sufficiently independent of his reasoning in such a way and to such an extent that he can both have his reason under the influence of sin and also be sufficiently aware of the fact to criticize it, to some extent transcend it, and find ways to reinforce reason in its struggle with rationalization? Can sin, in other words, be offset by sainthood? Can sainthood, perhaps, become enough of an actual power in man to make reasoning rather than rationalization the dominant fact of reason, even in religion? If so, to what extent can man command reason in its search for religious truth? Are there any reliable criteria for judging whether man is reasoning or rationalizing in matters of faith?

Is the most dependable standard perhaps sanity? But if it is, how can what sanity is be established? If man is generally sinful with a captive reason, sanity obviously cannot be judged by normality. If this is so, can right reasoning in religion escape the charge of special pleading? Or is there enough sanity in man generally for him to recognize religious truth as real at the depth of his life, and even if he tries to evade or distort it, will he not, or perhaps can he not, entirely hide such religious reality from himself? Is religious reason a matter of nearly constant conflict, with a number of people fighting the light with demonic intensity and shrewdness, with another number representing the religious claim with real power and wisdom, while the innumerable masses of people just live their ordinary lives for the most part hardly aware of the intense cosmic drama that is taking place?

Do any of the actors or agents, for that matter, know or even imagine what the total struggle is, and how they are, or let themselves be, used within this struggle? Is there any hope that man generally will become actively concerned about ultimate matters, or is and will religion remain the battlefield of those few who are intensely interested either to destroy or to strengthen the realities and powers of religion in the life of man? These are the questions we must treat in this chapter.

The charge of finitude is that human nature is unable to know religious reality; the charge of sinfulness is that man *will* not know it. Man is dominantly sinful, reads the indictment, and therefore his reasoning powers are corrupted by self-drive to the point of evading or resisting the saving truth. Reasoning man, driven by sin, perverts his thinking into rationalization. Sinful man does not seek, but loathes authentic religious knowledge. He does not search for, but hides from God.

Will such an indictment, if tried by an honest and competent jury, be upheld or dismissed? First of all, is man dominantly sinful? For this claim it can be shown that man's most natural drives are self-centred. Man is situationally self-centred. He cannot escape living, thinking, feeling, and acting from within the self. This self-stance is a matter not only of seeking satisfaction but of assuming responsibility as well. Self-centricity is central both to desire and to duty. Self-centredness of the situational kind, however, is not culpable. It is unavoidable, and if life is good, such self-centricity is not only acceptable but meritorious within its proper bounds.

But the self also approves being central in more than a situational sense. He chooses primacy and power over others. He fortifies situational self-centricity by approving and abetting self-centredness. He lets himself become centrally self-con-

161

cerned by caring for his own interests at the expense of equal concern for others, and even by willing them evil to enhance his own standing or attainment. Man becomes invidious and ambitious for self. Situational self-centricity degenerates into spiritual self-centredness.

The way in which we know such sin to be dominant is through honest self-knowledge. We do not naturally rejoice when others excel, and we like to win, that is to be superior at the expense of others. We know the power of sin best by knowing ourselves. Those who work with people, however, also come to have a subtle sense that when a few deserve special recognition or privilege, the rest are not naturally going to rejoice at their advancement or reward. We know almost instinctively that it is natural for people to be selfish. We sense and deal with sin without calling it by name!

To these general observations, which demand common acceptance as true, can be added the grievous list of human crimes and of mental illness due to uncontrolled self-drive. The self or society at least no longer faces and heeds the standards and demands of physical, moral or social reality. We shall, of course, consider mitigating circumstances and proper qualifications, but right now we point to main facts.

These facts the jury must weigh. Some manifestations of sin are fear, pride, anger, doubt, and indifference. Whatever else may cause or occasion these defects, sin is there. Fear is in large measure due to faithlessness. Man lacks faith mostly because of self-concern and self-importance. Adequate self-acceptance requires willingness to accept the total good and self-fulfilment only within such allegiance, without primary regard to the fate or fortune of self. If sin, at least symptomatically, is basically partiality for self, and if this drive shuts out man's will and ability to trust, the prevalence of fear in man's life is a witness to his sinfulness.

Similarly man puffs up his own ego. He wants to be central and to have all relevant activity swing around him. He courts praise. He generally dislikes even constructive criticism. He compares his attainment not so much with objective tasks as with the achievements of others, and then tries to be better or do better than they, or to make himself and others think that he is or does better than is actually so. He fashions an inner image of himself which is ideal rather than real. Few people are without pretence, and pretence is a witness to pride. Man wants to think of himself as right, and he is pained at having to admit being wrong. He craves recognition, and if he refuses it, he is often secretly proud over his very humility. Pride crouches at the door of every man, but most men invite it into their lives whether openly or shamefacedly. The presence of pride in the life of man is a witness to his sinfulness. And it is easier to build around the ego than simply to live genuinely in one's own house.

Anger (not righteous indignation) is another sign of sin. It is the indication of the frustration of false self-drive. Anger is the opposite response to acceptance. Acceptance need not mean acquiescence. It can mean acceptance of a situation as the challenge to its transformation, or some deeper acceptance of it beyond self-help. Anger is due to the crossing of self-interest and the lack of inner acceptance to handle or to endure the frustration.

Anger is the explosion of hate. Hate comes from either a defensive or an aggressive self-concern. What stands in our way or threatens us we hate. Hate generates anger. Hate is, of course, a category all its own that shows the prevalence and power of sin in the life of man. Hate is inner response and may lead, beyond anger, to harmful deeds. Anger, however, is an open and obvious sign of sin. The more natural response to frustration than the cherishing of an opportunity for growth or for helping others is anger, and the naturalness of this response shows the power of sin in the life of man.

Doubt, moreover, can be attributable to lack of evidence and need not indicate man's sinfulness. Much doubt, however, is due to rationalization. The challenge of truth is hard to bear and man prefers to consider reality as less demanding than it is. Therefore man questions truth with malice aforethought, and, having forced it into distortion, kills it. He finds reasons to doubt a requiring reality, and further reasons to accept the more palatable interpretation. If it were not for this deep drive

163

in man, false prophets and propaganda would not be effective. Man now suffers, for instance, from the terror of peace and the terror of plenty, not because on the whole they embody the cause of terror, but because it is easier and seemingly more profitable to acquiesce in political and economic arrangements that seem threatened by them. Scepticism is always endemic because it relieves man of otherwise plain responsibility. Man subtly suspects that he shall show the truth that not only makes him free but also makes him work and suffer for others, and therefore he creates mists to spare him from seeing the sharp outlines of truth. Within such a mist for seeing he doubts. Such doubt is a sign of sin.

Another sign of sin is indifference. Indifference implies that life makes no difference. Life seems to make no difference when the self is starved and frustrated at the centre of its will to self, when the fever of life has gutted inner receptivity, when the consequences of one's actions are felt to be external because the self is not genuinely involved beyond itself. There can, of course, be physical causes for lassitude. But when laziness seems constitutional it is often because of a drugged inner condition where social stimuli no longer enliven interests or provide zest for living. False activism, of course, can be equally the result of sin, but for our present purpose we mention indifference as a common experience to present before our dependable jury.

We have now mentioned a few signs of sin. None of these is due to sin alone. Each is occasioned circumstantially as well. We have mentioned both major and minor forms of sin, and have even referred to hate under anger for the sake of showing that we are presenting samples suggestively for the thoughtful jury to use according to its own experience and insight. The prevalence and power of sin, in any case, are beyond dispute. Most people, it seems, would readily agree that fear, pride, anger, indifference and doubt, for instance, as response to people and problems, come more easily than faith and love, or concern and humility. Many would hesitate, unable to decide. For them man simply is good and bad beyond any dependable assessment. Others would admit the prevalence and power of

164

these drives in their misuse and abuse, but would insist that man is not dominated by sin, but only hurt and hampered by it. What kind of evidence, then, is there for the other side?

The indictment is made and passed on for jury trial, we recall, that man is sinful to the point that his reason, corrupted by his nature, is incompetent to have religious knowledge. There are no exact evidences as to ways of establishing precise criteria, and therefore we must necessarily suggest a kind of case that can persuade the jurors from within their own experience. The case of the defence of human reason, we believe, can take the following line: Reason obviously is affected by sin; otherwise there would be no such fact as rationalization. But reason is not damaged beyond repair, because man is not basically corrupt. If he were, he very likely would neither admit the fact nor try to escape from it. Even if the easiest way for man to respond is in self-centredness, due to situational self-centricity and due to emotional drives for self-protection and self-promotion, man is not only not totally self-centred, but not even essentially or basically so.

First of all, man's ideal of himself is that he should be genuine not only as a man among others, taking and giving as his lot may be, but also a helpful and generous individual. Man's ideal of himself depicts his deepest nature, his inmost drive. He likes to be right and hates to be wrong, precisely because he identifies himself with what is good and right rather than with what is evil and wrong. Nor is such identification merely deceit or presumption. Man actually strives to better himself, regrets his falling short and his misdeeds, and works to alter or to outgrow his sinful drives. As a matter of fact—and here we appeal to the honesty and competency of the jury—man even feels, deep down, that what is called sin does not really belong to his true self. He feels at the depths that his true self, the self that is real and right in all relationships, is the one he genuinely craves to become. Somehow in his deepest searchings he feels that he most essentially is what he most inmost craves to become.

Nor can it be shown conclusively (and very likely it is not the case, either) that the main drive of man most of the time is sinful. Whatever the prevailing opinion about man may be, the combination of pressure to self from within and from without, as a power within and on man's acceptance of the will to self at the expense of others, is hard indeed to assess. How frail and precarious life is! How hard it is to cope with its complex problems! How very much inner physical depletions or social pulls toward dejection affect the spirit of man! How hurt man can become from competition, both fair and unfair, unless he does attend diligently to self, letting others care for the welfare that is most relevant to them! How misunderstandings harm, sometimes even quite natural and unavoidable; and how misfortunes hurt!

Within such inner deficiencies as befall man and such dangers and damages as threaten him from without, who can say how much self-centricity is less intended wickedness or even depth-overagainstness, than the kind of self-protection and self-promotion that the self has found necessary to tolerable existence? Who can genuinely draw the line between finitude and sin, between creaturehood and culpability? Who has the right and the knowledge to judge man with regard to the proportion of finitude and sin, in their interactions within reasoning and rationalization?

As for overt acts, they can hardly be appraised more dependably than can inner experience. But if failure of social relations are adduced as evidence of man's corruption, the contrary fact bears weighing that there are more men who escape being criminals than who become participants in crime; that there are more people who stay married than break up the relation; that, collectively speaking, there are longer periods of peace than of war, and, individually speaking, that there are more people who withstand the temptation to commit suicide than who do not. In spite of myriad temptations to greed, power and hardness of heart in our kind of world, there is enough decency of life to make social relations possible and continuous. Impurity and promiscuity may be rampant, especially in deteriorating societies, but there are also countless people who try to carry on lives of moral integrity and faithfulness.

Periods of history, conditions of civilization, kinds of mores and morals affect every appraisal. From within a rapidly changing culture and from within disintegrating eras of history, the assessment is peculiarly difficult, but the jury should at least be self-reflectively aware of the complexity and ambiguity of the charge. Certainly no verdict can be rendered without reasonable doubt. To say that man is exceedingly sinful is one thing; to charge that he is sold in sin and therefore impotent for religious reasoning, is definitely another.

The general verdict, I believe, is to the effect that man is sinful dangerously but not disastrously. Possibly he rationalizes more than he reasons in the areas where his personal and social interests are at stake. But he reasons enough to keep living personally and socially. Man is sinful, not merely in terms of some set religion, but with regard to his capacities for personal and social facing of reality and adjustment to the conditions of life, but such sinfulness is no final fact. Man both distorts his interpretations self-protectingly and self-promotingly and also labours to remove the distortions. Man is in conflict within himself and within society both to flee and to find the truth, or, oppositely, both to hide from it and to uncover it.

Is such the case, however, specifically with regard to his religious response? Man's ordinary problems and even human powers are one thing; the religious dimension, being ultimate, is quite another. Can man by reason find out God? Can man endure the shock of divine self-disclosure, or will he insulate himself from the divine impact? Is not man's dread of eternity too deeply hidden even from himself to bear essential exposure? Must man fabricate religions in order to protect himself from a burden of demand from a revelation he dare not face?

Granted that religion deals with the ultimate dimension and with powers and realities that are more and other than ordinary experience, is religious knowledge in a class all by itself? Is religious knowledge so qualitatively distinct from other knowledge that man's sinfulness precludes categorically his reason's dealing with it dependably? What of the individual and what of society in their relation to the knowledge of God? Does sin debar them from it? If it does, is the shutting-out total or partial? If partial, to what extent is man thus shut out by sin from the knowledge of God? And if he is kept from it by his sinful nature, is there a remedy for his condition enabling him to change sufficiently to obtain it?

On the side of man's inability to know God because of his sinful nature it can be pointed out that for most people in their natural state in this world, the God of universal love and righteousness is not real, even when they know of his nature. The idea of God may be held as a tenet taught from childhood or as a truth generally accepted. But most of life is not lived, it seems safe to say, with God as the all-pervasive and all-influencing centre. If God is real to experience he can be no less than such a centre. When he is not real, life-changing prayer is lacking. There may be much perfunctory prayer, that is to say prayer on a low enough level to be self-protective and self-promotive rather than delivering from the narrow confines of self to the overarching concern of God for the common good. Lack of life-changing prayer indicates that God is simply not there for people in an effective manner and measure. Sin does block the experience of God. For those who live mostly in and for themselves, God cannot be experienced as real. Such a confrontation would break their whole stance of life and their consequent use of reason. Or God may be feared and fled. Many people do not want to stop to think about life, and they resent being reminded of death. They are lifted by little or no transcendent meaning, but are mostly driven by the mundane setting of their lives in terms of duty and of companionship.

Or, fearing God, men seek to placate him. They long to buy him off. Afraid of God, men are frustrated by the kind of life he offers. Fearing God and frustrated by him, they hate him. The God of all the earth is an enemy to their provincial selves and partial interests. The God of the open, universal community judges their limited loyalties and circumscribed communities. Inasmuch as the mind is peculiarly capable of ingenious rationalizations, the true God is consequently dismissed as sentimental or idealistic, while the god of low and limited human emotions, corresponding to the state of the natural man, is elevated into the holy God before whose wrath man must

168

tremble. The sinful man is clever enough to block his knowledge of God by means of an impoverished confession of him.

Perhaps religions are partially man's collective attempt to hide from the true God by allowing just enough of truth in some combination of idealism and of judgment to fool himself into thinking that he is open to, and dealing with, God himself. If man is dangerously sinful, the religions he creates are also dangerously false. Deep and saving truth is cleverly mixed with offsetting qualifications or distortions in order to blunt the judgment of and curtail the salvation from the man-created God. Even small adjustments of a ship's rudder can keep the ship from reaching its destination. Small changes of doctrine can likewise radically alter the nature of any religion. Must we not grant readily, in view of the facts, that man's sinfulness engenders false religions? It occasions the rise to profitable acceptance of false prophets who perform the alterations or distortions, additions or subtractions, that both change the nature of the revelation and redo the conditions and results of religious confession and practice. The rigorous radicalism of the universal God who offers and demands the open, inclusive society, can easily be blunted and obscured by man's sinful drive to protect himself from the nearly impossible, high vision thus offered.

Religions are conscious relations to God. However slowly and indirectly they may come into human history, or with whatever sudden and startling power, religions are man's deliberate seeking for right relations with God, but as such, in view of man's sinfulness, they are also man's chosen vehicles for thinning out and for obscuring the revelation of God. Therefore, in so far as the worst is the perversion of the best, religions offer man both the best and the worst ideals, realities and hopes.

A more subtle way for men, using their sinful reason, to flee collectively from God, however, is to use their interpretation of ordinary knowledge religiously without naming it so. Thus man's conception of the State and his allegiance to it can be matters of ultimate ideals and loyalties even unto death, which are religious in nature. Man substitutes for genuine religion realities and powers out of ordinary experience more to his liking or more suited to the development of his nature and experience.

Or an economic interpretation of history can in effect become the organizing centre of a world view by serving as a religion, focusing man's highest expectations and defining his chief enemies. The State or the System can represent man's collective selfishness as well as his collective idealism, and be raised to the level of religious substitutes, not through formal acknowledgment, but through the depth sorting and organizing of life drives that indicate man's ultimate understandings and hopes. Man can use these life drives religiously, not knowing what he is doing in any formal sense, yet knowing all too well at the depth level of his choices that he is actually shutting out from consideration the true God by means of his construction and acceptance of a religious substitute from ordinary life.

Possibly the most subtle way in which man in his sinfulness can use reason for self-deception in the realm of religion, a way that is half genuine and half known in the deeper layers of the self, is the employment of his ordinary knowledge as substitute for religious knowledge. Sometimes man's philosophy can perform such dubious service; in other ages psychology may become considered the final measure of man's mind and the best basis for making ultimate commitments. Or scientific facts can be given a context of ultimate and unexceptional mechanism, not because the facts necessarily demand such an interpretation, but because man flees half subconsciously from the freedom he has before God. Thus man in purporting to describe nature can actually work most subtly to shut out God from man's life. Or the question of ultimates beyond man's ordinary knowledge can be declared to be a no-man's land of meaninglessness. Thus religious knowledge is declared impossible, and God is effectively banished from his world. Or scientific facts of probability can be combined with some all-or-none logic to deny the presence of any real order beyond immediate analysable data for physics, so that physics in effect becomes metaphysically competent to deny metaphysics!

Such subtle attempts to deal with religious knowledge are not on as crude a level as using rockets to find God in the skies, in order then to declare him non-existent according to actual empirical evidence, but they are equally illegitimate and misplaced. Thus man's knowledge can be used falsely to indicate conclusions that cannot be had in such manner, while man deceives himself into half believing and half thinking that he now knows the objective falsity of the religious claim. The power and the problem of such subtle self-deception by means of man's knowledge become compounded when ordinary people, who have learned to trust these disciplines in their own proper field, now mostly innocently and yet half in relief accept their illegitimate findings as veridical knowledge.

Most people, in such a case, can hardly know that they are not honest but only deceived when they bow to such a substitute for religious knowledge. As a matter of fact, a perspective of knowledge long operative and commonly accepted generates an atmosphere of truth that penetrates and colours even the depth feelings of experts, who theoretically may barely see the falsity and who therefore are dominated more by custom than by sinful evasiveness or rebellion. How much easier, then, it is for people in general, especially for students used to trust their teachers, to assume the rightness of the substitution. Especially difficult becomes the personal situation for those who want to 'belong' and 'get ahead' within an atmosphere subtly sustained as well as generated by man's depth desire to flee from the God whom one part of his nature hates and dreads. And how easy is the continuation of the power of this pattern of interpretation by all those who want not to trust and not to serve the living God! Sin in man is exceedingly subtle.

The greatest problem of the sinfulness of man, in its bearing on his use of reason in the field of religion, comes in this sphere of the depth combination of the subjective and the objective collective, where divided responsibility is generationally deep and world wide. Sinful man, fearing and fleeing God, neither dares nor wants to defy him openly and directly. Although personal distortions have their place and power in the life of man, they are far too near the surface of interpretation to offer the depth of self-deception that man needs in order to be able to choose with his eyes nearly open, and still hardly see. Man finds reason most subtly usable to escape God when it seems to be bravely open to the truth. He flees truth behind a facade of honesty.

Man has two choices for thus fleeing God while seemingly seeking courageously for him. One choice being urged on us is somehow to use religious categories and language in such a way, perhaps symbolically, that the heart of the religious intention (supposedly!) is vigorously affirmed while the threatening content is somehow removed, buried or misdirected. Man's surest way of avoiding God and tempting others away from him has always been the capture and the transvaluation of religions. Another way, perhaps more obvious, yet possibly even more subtle in its ablest forms, is the use of man's ordinary knowledge and loyalties as idealistic religious content for the organizing centre of man's life and thought in the place of the erstwhile professed religion, so that man can then even pride himself upon his honesty and maturity in his discard of the superstitions of religion and particularly of religious knowledge.

This kind of religious subtlety of substitution may have been made depth-consciously by those who charge that religious reason is constitutionally incapable of reaching religious reality. The deepest root of such rationalization is sin in genetic depths and contemporary complexity, beyond all possible probing, and yet evident in the totality of the stance. But in this case, too, is there not another side to the story? Is not reason used within man's whole response precisely to fight and to offset such rationalization?

Are we, perhaps, looking at a relative historic situation in terms of some all-or-none capacity? Historic understanding, development and acceptance are relative; light, therefore, must be conceived of in relevant terms. Is it not both natural and right that religious construction should be proportionate to religious maturity? If sudden light startles the worshippers and dazzles them, is not the attempt to ward off and do away with such light altogether understandable? Does not each age need constructively to reinterpret its symbols, however much pain man may have to suffer in the process, and however many mistakes he may make? Perhaps religious knowledge must keep pace with general development and somehow be proportionate to man's general measure of intellectual attainment.

Does not man fight religious retrogression as well as progress? To some extent, the sudden bringer of startling light, the prophet and the seer, is persecuted because he calls in question and undermines the tried truth which men have long lived by and supported. The new knowledge comes as a threat to the old, and may not seem relevant to the worshippers at the time of the revelation. To say only that men flee and fight God when they contend for the faith they have lived by, even against a faith which to us is more true, is not to take into consideration the question of habituation of loyalty and relevance of understanding.

Secondly there is much power of reason in man for realities and ideals beyond private or collective interest. Just as there is much good in ordinary man outside of any direct religious confession, even to the point of dying for others, so there is much religious longing, acceptance, appreciation and practice among men in general. All peoples have been religious at all times of history, the claim goes. Not all of such religion has been merely defensive or aggressive. Most of it, at its inner heart and drive, represents some self- and group-transcendence that opens up to realities and powers beyond ordinary experience, that go beyond self-centricity. Such is the case among the vast mass of general religious devotees, as well as among people who make no direct confession but who, in integrity and openness, transcend in religious quality and dimension their substitute religions. The reason that there can be integrity in religious transformation and growth is that man's nature is sufficiently open to truth genuinely to weigh, and authentically to choose, the fuller and better revelation. Therefore, granting freely the fact that man's nature and reason are dangerously corrupt and incapacitated in their dealing with religious reality and knowledge, nevertheless, neither is disastrously curtailed in its capacity for religion. Thus relevance of religious knowledge and generality of religious capacity combine to insist that religious finding and decision are genuine acts on the part of responsible selves in society.

173

Nothing we have said in support of religious capacity for knowing, of course, should lessen our stress on the naturalness with which man fights or flees God, at whatever stage God threatens his self-centredness, personally and collectively. The negative side, or reason's corruptibility by sin, is strong beyond most comprehension, but is never apart from the positive side of man's religious longing and attainment in some part. We should also remember that there are saints and seers who release and help to make real and relevant more light. If the sinfulness of man should be remembered in our assessment of the capacity and the willingness of man to know religious truth, the power of the saints to find and to support religious truth ought equally to be kept in mind. Sainthood and growth in religious knowledge are the opposite side of the coin of man's sinfulness. At this point we turn constructively from man's defective reason, due to sin, to his effective reason, due to saintliness. To what extent can reason be made effective for religious knowledge by its deliverance from sin and its finding the eyes of faith, the eyes of the creative reason?

If we grant that man is sinful with a strongly captive reason—remembering, of course, at the same time, that he is a creature beset by finitude and within partial attainment of maturity according to his stage in the creative process, and keeping in mind also that men vary considerably in their actual capacities to transcend self and their in-group societies—can such generally dominant sinfulness as affects man's reason be done away or offset? Can man's sinfulness be conquered by his saintliness? If reason is pressured by sin toward rationalization, does not the forgiven and mature self affect reason toward the finding of reality? If sin leads to falsity, does not sainthood lead to truth? If self-centricity occasions rationalization, does not the God-centred life make for genuine reasoning? If sin frequently underlies insanity, does not the release from the power of sin provide the basis of sanity?

The problem is basically whether human nature can be changed. If human nature affects reason, as is altogether obvious both to cursory and careful inspection, can religion concretely effect a different human nature? Terms can confuse.

'Converted', or 'saved' have been common words in Christian circles, but these terms have been damaged by their connection with stereotyped conformism without general actual change in human nature. 'Maturation' is a good term, but, again, it has all too often been used against a psychological background that has not, or at least has seldom, come to grips with man's genuine sinfulness. Usually man's sinfulness has been ignored, or it has been conceived of apart from any adequate religious orientation. The approach to human nature has therefore been some shallow development or superficial self-realization.

To pose the problem in terms of socialization is no help in the light of the actual sinfulness of society. The problem is how to break through the power of sin over reason, both personally and collectively. The Bible uses such terms as a new creation, a new creature, or a new being, but it lacks an explicit, appropriate, positive epistemology. Several religions think of human nature in terms of the false self that rationalizes, but there has been little understanding, within distinctive religious source material, of the fact that the true or essential self is freed for reason.

Perhaps it will be best simply to think of the converted or matured self as the forgiven and developed self and consequently as the self free of the pressures of sin, or at least for some essential part sufficiently freed from sin to allow genuine reasoning even in the hotbed of religion. Since, according to our analysis, such freedom results from faith as the right relation to reality, we can say that the faithful self is the free self, and that the free self is the saint. If we may also use words freely without fear of historic or pious coloration, we may say that the saint is the free soul. Can a soul, then, become sufficiently free from sin to allow his reason to look straight at truth even in the religious realm? Can sainthood produce the kind of sanity in all dimensions of life that can squarely face reality and authentically interpret it?

The first observation crying to be made is that we should make no false claims. The witness to religious reality is never helped by overstatement. Padded accounts do not add up, and disillusion the honest seeker who alone can elicit long range credibility. An insecure person can try to make himself believe something which might seem necessary to himself and socially laudable as well. But blown-up testimony, although it may fool and seemingly even help many, will be punctured and emptied by the honest and competent inquirer. No inner experience can testify convincingly to a change of human nature except it be seen in the kind of life which cannot be hid to those in full position to know. Nor can in-group conspiracy among believers fortify a false confession to newness of life. Often in-groups assume a superiority which is not at all apparent to those on the outside. However unconscious such conspiracy may be, it can constrain no strong power for conviction, inside or outside.

Often persons and groups will treat such change of human nature within the group as presuppositional. The change is tested as real by virtue of the confession itself. The group is constituted confessionally in terms of such new natures or such new kind of life. But presuppositions can blind adherents to actual situations, or at least half blind them and paralyse the other half into a rationalized dishonesty. A sect that claims sinlessness as its peculiar norm for association, for instance, when informed that some of its leaders had committed moral misdeeds, refused to vote to reprimand those culpable, or even to acknowledge the situation, inasmuch as the group was pre-suppositionally beyond such sinfulness, especially among its leaders. The pretence of this particular group was obvious both to outsiders and to some of the more honest insiders who reported the decision, but subtle sham characterizes a good deal of religious witness to newness of life.

Not only is there such false witness to contend with, but there is also a strong tendency on the part of religious in-groups not to acknowledge genuine attainment outside their own pre-scribed way of salvation. Thus Christians, for a relevant example, often find it both difficult and disagreeable to acknowledge any height of religious attainment and any breadth of religious objectivity outside the Christian confession. Socrates, they say, must have read Moses! Gandhi reached his stance of love only because he read the New Testament! Secularists

176

sometimes seem to be both highly moral and fair, but they must have hidden lacks or rebelliousness!

In our seeking for truth in this book, we want definitely to make no false claims for any kind of religion or for religion itself. If religion is real, as I believe we have found, and if man can be genuinely free from religion by God's own humble choice, we want to accept this perspective as the directive for our investigation from now on, even though this perspective, of course, should not be allowed if it does not square genuinely with the facts to be observed. Furthermore, even from within this perspective, we should expect that God's universal reign is sufficiently indirect and long-range to include all men within common human nature, within a common general environment, within common conditions for history, and with relation to some genuine, general religious insight and attainment. Our final main section in this volume will be devoted to this question, but even in this connection it is necessary both to show and to stress our intention and endeavour to make no false claims with regard to man's overcoming the pressure of sin on his reasoning.

Similarly, we may not isolate individual man from his concrete past in cosmic process and in human history. We may not define human nature in terms of product apart from process. We have no right to judge sainthood in terms of some absolute demand or some normative ideal for man, in such a way that we uproot man from his place in time. All religious demands in terms of eternity at the expense of time are destructively one-sided. To look at man merely as he is, of course, is to forfeit the religious perspective altogether. Therefore neither eternity nor time will do as the focus on man's sinfulness and sainthood. The dialectical confrontation of actual man in process with the result of the proposed product of this process is the only adequate way to assess either man's sinfulness or his sainthood.

The same is the case, of course, with regard to man's relation to society and to nature. Neither the social nor the natural situation excuses man for his sinfulness nor accounts for his sainthood, but they are inseverably involved. What we have to probe, therefore, is rather the extent to which man can be raised from the general attainment at a particular stage of history to find freedom beyond it and power to change it. Can sainthood be obtained to the point where man reaches new depths of reality in vision and power to challenge his actual corruption of life and distortion of seeing? The most that we can accomplish by our analysis is to provide for view the framework for obtaining such freedom, and secondly to suggest that such experience has actually been obtained, in surprising measure, on the part of a few, and, in lesser power within a larger number who know both some vividness of occasional attainment and much dullness and conflict of ordinary failure. The best we can do, I repeat, is by honest testimony and suggestive analysis to try to strike the chord of reality in the reader, who will have to be on the jury that passes final judgment on this work.

According to our analysis in the first section, right religion centres in truth and love objectively, and in integrity and concern subjectively. God is the Father of all men and the power and reality over and through all things. Or to use different language in the attempt to transcend spatialization, God is the inmost reality whose rightness and goodness extend to the thinnest edge of objectification or materialization. The opposite frameworks just used should make clear that the question of direction is not important. The Holy Spirit is thus the Spirit of rightness and integrity everywhere, or under all conditions. Instead of using 'upward' or 'inward' we can use such a term as 'spiritward'. Such Spirit judges man as sinful both objectively and subjectively, or to use traditional language, both materially and formally. Is such Spirit also available to man for his reorientation and remotivation? If such is the standard and such the judgment on the sinfulness of man that distorts his reason into rationalization, can man obtain the right spirit with sufficient power to rid his reason of the pressures of sin and obtain the power for right seeing?

Within our total approach there can, of course, be no dogmatic answer to this question. There can be, however, a suggestive confrontation of it. Man seems to have not only a sense of right universally, but also a 'feel' for truth. The sense of right involves man's generally wanting to feel that he is doing the right. Some sense of duty works within man, making it natural for him to try to justify his actions. This sense of duty seems to go deeper than mere self-defence or expediency. In a general way, it goes beyond even group rules and loyalties. Many men suffer for what they feel to be right, and some even die for their convictions, even in the absence of the approval of others. Jesus and Socrates are examples.

Similarly, there seems to be some sense of truth and a longing for men to know it even when it is unpleasant. There have been martyrs for truth as well as for right. Generally, even though the two converge or even merge, there are differences in feel and stress. Men in general know these internal longings and drives. The whole feel for self-consistency in man's experience is more than prudence and more than stubbornness. Reason is part of man's total self that demands its own kind of satisfaction, which is truth for truth's sake.

Within the Christian perspective, this deepest drive for right and truth within man has been attributed to man's being created in God's image. The voice of right and truth in man, accordingly, is the voice of reality. To accept the challenge of this voice is to face reality. Beyond private conscience and beyond social convention works this insistent prodding in man for truth and right. The Holy Spirit of God has as his counterpart in man the holy spirit of integrity and concern at the very foundations of human nature. Therefore human nature cannot be characterized by sinfulness alone, without regard for the depth drive to sainthood. Man is potentially and actually both sinner and saint.

Such a description seems to some extent truly to characterize all men in varying measures. Man potentially is made to mature in truth and goodness, and, although all men pervert and fall short of their potentiality, no man fails entirely of being human. Man can be changed to a saint, it seems, because he is made for sainthood. Sinning is perversion of human nature. Rationalization is distortion of reason. Sainthood is the attainment of human nature as the proper product of process. Analytically, therefore, man can become a new being, a free soul, because by nature he is made for such newness, and the nature of his deepest environment, as we shall see later, makes for it as well.

In order to reason, man needs to be motivated by openness to truth as well as by access to information. Human nature can fail reason by finitude or by sinfulness. We have discussed the possibilities for religious knowledge in our first main section, and the problems of finitude in the foregoing chapter. Of reason's two inhibitors sinfulness offers the more severe threat. But man is made to overcome sinfulness. His deepest drive, with which he identifies himself and which seems persistent through all generations, is his being made for truth and right. When man sins against these, he violates his inmost nature and therefore experiences guilt. This sense of guilt generally pervades man's total consciousness in a vague sense of something being wrong, but in particular it blows up a storm of fear within him, driving him to fear the truth and the right. Thus what he most needs and most desires at the depth of his nature becomes his occasion for deep dread.

Nothing tempts man to distort reason more than his sense of guilt. In general, this sense leads him to a dread of truth and love. In particular, man is the most unfair toward and feels the most strongly against those whom he has treated unfairly. When he has wronged someone he has a harder time to be objective about that person than if he had been wronged himself. This is a common experience of human nature. Deep down, man knows that he should be open to universal truth and concern, while all the time he wants to put himself first or to get pleasure out of some in-group loyalty that can let him experience overagainstness. Moral equivalents for hatred and fear are almost impossible to find because man is guilt-ridden and rationalizes his loyalties. Thus truth and right come to be identified with limited loyalties and objectives. The fuller truth and right threaten these partial loyalties and perspectives far more than do smaller loyalties and perspectives, in terms of which man could actually feel not only good but superior.

Because of the presence of such guilt accumulatively, personally and in society, man rationalizes rather than reasons, to the point where he can be self-protective and self-promotive. The way to get rid of the power of sin is to stop more than just specific sinning. Man must get rid of the load of guilt which burdens him as a person and as a society. The only real cure for guilt is forgiveness. But man cannot forgive himself. This fact he recognizes at the depth of his life. Neither will specific acts of forgiveness by others avail. Man feels a general sense of guilt, due to his deepest sense of reality as truth and right. Man, deep down, knows himself to be up against the ultimate, the absolute, the unconditional, the final standard— that is, against God. His guilt lies far below all conscious levels of conscience within the depths of his violated image of God.

This deep sense of wrongness and of guilt is an actual state of man known subjectively from within and objectively by those who counsel men in their deepest needs and relations. Such guilt cannot be talked away or reasoned into oblivion. Specific facts in the past can be faced and rationalized, but the deeper sense of wrongness and the drive to rationalization remain. Therefore forgiveness by God is needed. The only final transfer of the sin-sick patient by the counsellor or the priest is to God. And God, as we saw from our analysis, wants to forgive and to remake man; but he cannot and will not do so until man is willing to open up to the fullest truth and to the widest kind of community he can see. Forgiveness presupposes the fact of freedom.

Acknowledgment of man's situation, therefore, willingness to face it, and readiness to be forgiven and remade are the prerequisites for getting rid of the power of sin over reason, and obtaining instead the power for genuine reasoning in terms of truth and concern. In this sense, man is one, and truth for truth's sake, in ultimate and personally involved matters cannot be separated from the universal concern which is openness to the wider right as well as truth. The fact that there has been such facing of reality on the part of human beings, such acceptance of the will of God for the good of all, is a matter of sincere testimony. If God is faithful and man is honest in such commitment, at least there is such a reality as reorientation and remotivation in the decisional and intentional life of man. In this sense, at least, human nature can be changed. Can there also, however, be effective implementation of such experience in terms of God's bestowal of help and of man's growth?

Such reorientation and remotivation, at least in depth intention, are facts of experience. Naturally, the content of the experience differs. Some people focus mostly on God, and fail to include the full scope of human concern. Others focus mostly on man, and fall short of intensive focus on God. What matters, however, is the inclusive fullness of God and man, and even of nature. Otherwise there can be escape in one from the other. The religious gift and responsibility involve all there is in acceptance and obligation. Only the fully intensive and extensive appropriation and commitment are fully religious. Thus man's actual experience is heavily conditioned by his external circumstance of time, by the nature of the religion to which he subscribes and by his own development religiously. Most people never even see the outlines of the scope involved in basic religious reorientation and commitment, or sense how radically their lives must be changed if they are to accept and to live the will of God for the all-inclusive and fully open community of total concern.

The reason that for almost all people the concrete involvements of the full religious reality are hidden is the presence in man of finitude and sin. Man is a creature at a particular stage in cosmic and social process, and only certain ranges of conviction are relevant. The fact that man does not see more, except possibly theoretically to the point of irrelevance, is because of his legitimate finitude, but the fact that man does not see and accept the highest range of religiously relevant light is due to sin. Actually these two factors in human nature combine to make one man, a creature sinner or a sinful creature, who can and will bear and dare the light only up to a certain point. Even reorientation and remotivation, or what is traditionally called conversion, are subject to such concrete combinations of finitude and sin.

The negative side of this picture, however, must not crowd out the positive, which is the dominant fact. Man is not only driven but also drawn toward the light. This longing for orientation and positive motivation for self-fulfilment is not apart from some basic conceiving and acceptance of the nature of the reality in which the self finds itself. Personally and socially man strives for meaning, not only theoretically, but much more deeply with regard to the depth destiny of life. Thus every stage of reorientation and remotivation is a costly acceptance and a sacred achievement. When charismatic personalities threaten this concrete attainment, they not only convict men of pride and faithlessness but make them defensively conscious of deep loyalties to a holy heritage won at countless cost.

It is necessary that the fuller light come both in human history in general and in personal histories; but we must be willing to understand that resistance to such light is not only due to failure of faith or to moral intransigence, but even more powerfully to a natural clinging to the kind of securities which have been tried. The religious status quo represents both the fighting for and the fighting against the light. Or prophets are crucified, to see the other emphasis, not only out of fear of the light but also out of love for the light. Only within such a setting can the meaning of reorientation and remotivation become clear. Only thus can we understand why change for the better often elicits not only the joy of new insights and commitment but also a sense of guilt and shame at the betrayal of accepted standards of faith and conduct.

Full response to the will of God for the universal good is such a radical demand on any self that when it makes a decision for the universal good the drives fight it and affect the reason. Rationalization is therefore involved both in the decision itself and in the consequent implementation of the intention. Can there be growth in objectivity in view of this fact? Can the self learn to reason as an act of a new nature, rather than to rationalize in the fiery realm of religion? Does sin effectively preclude religious knowledge?

The decision itself shows that man can transcend the central drive to self even in the perspectives and powers of religious reality. Such transcendence may seem momentary and ineffectual with regard to man's use of reason. But it could not come about at all except for a long period of preparation. Thus reason has its depth allies in human nature, and its contacts over against rationalization. Growth toward the inclusive goal was taking place right along, whether gradually or abruptly,

N   183

whether accepted or fought. For this reason, all pious affirmations of God's sudden confrontation and drastic changing of man, apart from man's growth and decision, are false. God works at the depths of human nature and along with man's deepest drives against the inhibiting factors in his nature. Any conscious decision is therefore mostly a clarification and consummation of relationships. The call of God is better understood, as well as more deeply felt, than before; and man in a sudden decision enters into the new relationship mostly in terms of a deliberate acceptance of the will of God, for which there had been patient preparation.

Sometimes men are converted away from God by a similar process of preparation and decision. Often the decision for or against God covers so long a time and so wide a range of experience that people are not conscious of having made any decision at a pinpoint of time. They just know that somehow they have entered into a new relationship, that their minds have been reoriented and that their emotional set has been genuinely altered. Some dramatic conversions are due to particular psychological and sociological conditionings. The converts have been led to expect such experiences as prerequisite for right relations with God (or for denying the relationship) and having internalized, finally externalize the expectations. Many cases, however, seem genuine in their cataclysmic decisiveness, not only as felt, but as these dramatic decisions affect the converts consequently. In all cases, however, there was preparation of both knowledge and attitudes. Such preparation was mostly the focusing of man's drive to be meaningfully related to his whole universe, often in terms of some central focus, the reality of which is the living God of ultimate concern for all.

Growth, however, not only comes before such facing up to the central reality of God, at whatever stage and with whatever content, but also can persist after the culminating experience. Such growth is not automatic or merely natural. It must be sought and sustained. The experience of acceptance can even become the excuse for further growth and lessen the demand on the worshipper. It can be interpreted as making the person right once for all, and thus stand in the way of religious growth.

Such interpretation, of course, in the last analysis, is sin's rationalization. Man under the power of sin is subtle in the way in which he allows himself willingly to deceive himself in an aura of holiness. The power of sin seems almost personal, making legitimate a reification of the word 'sin', so intimate becomes its reality within the life of man.

Whenever growth continues, three main factors are at work. The first and central of these is faith. Faith means trust in, and openness toward, the source of all love. God becomes the main subject of the life of faith. God's presence as Spirit never does away with his also being separate personally beyond man. Faith stands judged and trusting under the personal God, allowing God as Spirit to become the reorienting and re-motivating power of life.

Faith lives in prayer and meditation. Meditation we shall treat under the third factor: study. Prayer, however, is the baring of self to be judged and changed by God with regard to his will, for the sake of finding the true nature of self and the fullest possible constructive relationships to all men. True prayer is the fullest possible transcendence of self, wherein the self becomes accepted within a new view and a new reality. Prayer is, therefore, continuous relationship with God, making for fuller reorientation and remotivation. Prayer is a central means for the growth in the kind of objectivity which is the sign of maturity. Prayer, when real, is central power actually available for the getting free of the drives to rationalization, and for finding the inner strength for reasoning. Through prayer the self learns the inner disciplines wherein function can change emotional structure to get beyond immediate recourse to self-justification or self-condemnation. The self in prayer learns to face reality rather than first naturally to excuse or to accuse itself. The way of true prayer is the way to central emotional maturity where the self finds not only release but genuine satisfaction in the common good under God.

The second factor in the growth of the self along the lines of reasoning rather than rationalization is commitment. There can be no deliverance from the individualistic and in-group reasoning which is a sign of sin as well as of finitude, apart

185

from identification with concrete causes that open horizons and make real larger fields for emotional attachment and growth. Prayer apart from deed is pietistic escape. Prayer apart from identification with others not only emotionally but in action, is flight from reality. When God offers grace it is free, but never cheap. The acceptance by God cannot be earned, but the free gift of God involves the acceptance also of the costs of the cross of the common good. Many people never find God real and never find power to combat the power of sin over reason because they are not genuine in their identification with God's will.

Only those can come to know the breaking of the power of sin over reason who will consistently, in faith and a power not their own, let themselves and what they have and can do, become part of the common lot of man. Only an authentic living of the universal, open community of faith and concern can find increasingly some genuine breaking of the power of sin over reason, in the way in which the new self more and more responds naturally in terms of the satisfactions within the common good. To find reason flowing without clog, from God's will to the common good to the full measure of concrete interests consistent with its realization, is a late flowering of maturity which is seldom an authentic experience. But if sin as well as finitude is to be broken in basic principle and power, such victory comes only within the coincidence of the will of God and the will of man in the life of faith and commitment. Only in the Spirit can finitude and sin become basically transcended.

The third factor, which is a prerequisite of the kind of growth in grace that releases reason from the power of sin, is studying. Mere acquisition of facts cannot help the religious life. Dependence on learning can be a way of false self-sufficiency and self-security. But the person who has found God's will for the common good to work genuinely within his life, craves to know more about both God and man. Love craves to know for the sake of being with and for appreciating the beloved, as well as for the sake of helping. Truth for truth's sake is not inconsistent with truth for love's sake. Genuine concern spurns false knowledge. It cannot abide what is spurious, for the sake of both knowing and helping. If prayer or work gets in the way of study, prayer and work are not the full fruit of faith. Faith as openness to God and to all there is involves an uninhibited thirst to know.

Religious knowledge, however, comes mostly through meditation. Meditation means the chance to find the deeper meaning that mere facts or discursive reasoning cannot provide. Meditation means the identification of the total self at the depth of his life with God and man. Meditation involves the going to the root of reality as far as this can be found. Facts must be had both for knowing and for helping. Concrete ways of entering more deeply into relationship and service must be explored. But such search must always head up in the inner identification with truth and help. In meditation, faith, prayer and work are enriched as well as centrally directed. Study becomes integrally related to life, and a wholeness of relationship results that is impossible apart from some time and some ways of meditation. The drive of sin in us, therefore, always fights meditation. We are tempted to pray or to work, to study or to sleep, instead of being quite still and open to the transcendent reality that can make us whole and set us into right relationships.

Just how much meditation can achieve I cannot say. We know that lives like those of Jesus, Saint Francis and Gandhi affected human life profoundly because in them became expressive for men the deeper and fuller community of God's concern for all men. The fact seems to be that there is no lack of medicine for sin's power over reason, but that there are few willing to take it in healing doses. Perhaps man's present attainment in religion reflects more by far the power of sin over reason than the power of love, but many saints there have been, and many more, by far, have been touched by sainthood. These lives have been the leaven allowing for the further spreading of the universal love of God as the full reality within which alone reason can come to full acceptance of truth. They work not to rationalize self and group interests, whether for self-protection or for self-promotion, but to find the reality that alone can set men free. If sin is an actuality in human life,

187

making reason impotent in the life of religion, so is sainthood, as well, making potent and real the findings of the religious reason. Both sin and sainthood are there and at work. In the saints reason defies rationalization.

If our analysis is right, faith in the God of love seen in Jesus' life is the prescription for sanity; false faith, for insanity. Obviously such analysis is merely directional and proportional. But the more man finds true faith, the more he finds total focus, the more he faces reality as it is with meaning and with power. The more his faith is false, the more he approaches life from a distorted and a misleading point of view, and the more he therefore also flees from reality by means of rationalization. Sin, consequently, is deep down, a cause of insanity, while sainthood is the approach of sanity.

I have suggested that religious reality resides in the powers beyond ordinary experience that further the interests of life rather than destroy them, that fulfil rather than frustrate man's deepest need. When man finds faith, he finds the resources for meeting his need for love. When man finds faith, he finds the resting-place of truth, amid its changing, dynamic and creative manifestations. When man finds faith, he finds the meaning that can bind his life into a whole that matters. When man finds faith, he enters into the relationships that alone can satisfy his deepest drives. True faith is the prescription for sanity.

Faith is the inclusive acceptance of social relationships anchored in the social Reality. The social fulfilments of true religious faith have no endings, being as they are within the creative eternity of God. They are not cut off within small overagainst in-groups, which cause splits and splinters. Even when the smaller loyalties reject, and perhaps persecute, the larger love, that love knows the nourishment that can ever keep the deepest social self from starving. On the social as well as on the religious plane faith, therefore, makes for sanity. In the moral realm, faith means rectitude. Faith is not moralism, oppressing the self by futile striving to satisfy an impossible law. It is not legalism, substituting abstractions of law and justice for life and people. It is not a matter of do's and dont's, making life miserable with moral frettings. Faith is a matter of making the tree good and of bearing good fruit. Morality finds meaning and motivation. It finds context in the community of concern, and yet also concrete directives based on insight and experience. Faith in God, the ultimate concern for each and all, gives both moral freedom and free motivation. Attainment is real, while failure is not condemnatory. Obligation is serious and concrete, without being a burden beyond fulfilment. The life of faith is therefore the prescription for sanity.

Faith also accepts the physical life as real and right. Creation is from God and not to be fought, except for its abuse. Man can thus accept the physical self and enjoy the material life. And yet these cannot, on the other hand, become the occasion for his hiding from the spiritual, moral and social life, nor for his self-centricity in material accumulation. Centred in God, man is relieved of the insecurity and anxiety which attend the material life even as a proximate end. To whatever extent true faith has been attained with regard to the material life, therefore, it makes for sanity.

As a whole, when real and full, faith is integrative life, within focused sources of strength, clarified directives of concern and a quiet resting in love. Such faith clears reason and empowers it. The more faith, as central and unconditional facing reality, is had, the more reason escapes the rationalizations which are related to the false life of insanity and discovers instead the strength and steadiness of the life of sanity. On the contrary, false faith leads to avoidance and distortion of reality, to moralism, legalism, and the anxiety-ridden conscience, the guilt-laden reason and the severance of social ties. False faith leads to the self-punishing avoidance of the natural world or else to a spurious delight in it which dreads its being taken away. Sin is the seemingly easy way of self-concern and of lack of faith which lead toward the distortions of insanity, a symptom of which is rationalization, while sainthood is the narrow way, even seemingly disadvantageous, that at cost of self nevertheless leads to the finding of self and the fulfilments of sanity.

As far as human nature and its relation to reason in religion goes, man lives constantly within the pressures of sin and sainthood, both from within and from without. The outstanding examples of each drive live at the edge of man's experience. Most men, however, live in the central field, neither notorious sinners, fighting God openly and persistently, nor saints of God touched by the beatific vision of his will for the common good. Just where mankind is now in this struggle is beyond our judgment. The religious problem is, rather, prescription beyond description, that is, how to reach the middle masses with divine discontent as to their use of reason in rationalizing rather than in finding religious truth. 'Sinners' seem easier to reach, for at least they have a conscious struggle with the fundamental problems.

How can we touch with religious dissatisfaction in an effective manner those who seem mostly to vegetate their lives away within the status quo? How can we give them the positive vision of religious reality and the stimulus of the actual satisfactions of sainthood? For most people, sin or sameness seem most attractive. The struggle for the better life and for the new world seems to them either boring or too costly. How can we communicate dependably, whether for acceptance or rejection, the fact that meaning is the more desirable the wider its concern? This fact is learned only by experience, but is sufficiently prefigured and prefelt, within the larger preparations in experience for religious truth and reality, to make meaningful the attempt to have people in general find the fuller satisfaction of religious knowledge and reality.

The final question for us is how to cut through the drive of sin which makes credulity seem hard realism, and which makes creativity seem vain idealism. Sin creates a false mirror for the self in which it sees all things in the distorted light of self-advantage or of fear's loss. Thus the drive of sin creates its own canons of critical and creative reason. Sin's critical reason defends fear's citadel and creates illusions for self-protection and self-promotion. These illusions become socially acceptable and registered as realism by the spirit of the times. The illusions, however, are not mere fabrications, but only distortions and changes so slight in stress as to seem real and right even to the discerning self.

Faith's critical reason, on the contrary, tears down both strongholds and subtleties, causing panic within the army of fear, creating instead such relations in reality as are basically discoveries of what God offers to man. Human nature wavers within finitude and sin. Today such wavering is on the edge of civilization's disintegration from within and destruction from without. It is no false preaching of truth for the sake of salvation rather than for its own sake to say that mankind's best hope resides in its general willingness to open up to God's will for the common good, which is both the surest antidote for sin's power to rationalize and the truest power for finding the truth of religion within the proper use of reason.

PART III

Reason in History and Nature

Chapter XIII

Can Reason Find Meaning in History?

A most complex but urgent question is that of God's relation to the world. If both God and the world are real, there can be no doubt that some relation must hold between them. How, then, is religious reality related to the created order, and how much of this relation can reason know?

False ways of stating the problem preclude clear thinking on the subject. One such is the way of the Great Negation. Within this approach, God is first defined as infinite. Thereupon it is declared to be analytical truth that every assertion about God makes him finite, and therefore refers no longer authentically to God. Consequently in this view it is impossible to make positive statements concerning God. To discuss him is to limit him, whereas the infinite is the illimitable. Whatever we affirm about God must accordingly be taken, not as reliable indication of his nature, but strictly as our attempt to express the inexpressible reality. To designate God as 'living' or 'personal' is, in fact, in this view, no different from calling him 'red' or 'green', except that as human beings, having to use meaningful language, such classifications as 'living' and 'personal' are categories decidedly meaningful to us. After such an assertion, naturally, there is no point to seek for any knowledge of God, nor does the attempt to experience his presence have meaning. Therefore to the Great Negation is added the Great Refusal to try to know God either by reason or in experience.

No determinate reality, from the point of view of the Great Negation, can be ascribed to God. To define him as the sum total of finite events is also to limit him. God is therefore the inexpressible reality that can never be defined, and consequently can never be related by reason to the created or the finite world. What this adds up to, if every assertion is trying to catch God

195

in some net of words that cannot confine him, is complete agnosticism with respect to reliable ultimates. As far as knowledge is concerned, whether through reason or experience, we are left with the negative way to God; a total *via negativa* amounts to agnosticism. In any case, inasmuch as God cannot, strictly speaking, be known at all, we cannot discuss reliably his relation to history and nature.

Especially misleading, according to this point of view, is the use of the indefinite article in connection with deity. To speak of God as 'a' being implies that he belongs to a class, in which case he is obviously finite; but God by definition, according to this point of view, cannot be finite in any manner. Nor is the definite article much better. By implication the article must be used to distinguish God as 'the' being and therefore as comparable to finite existences. Such an implication, we have seen, is considered to be a contradiction of the definition of God. Sometimes the term 'unconditioned' is used, as in Kant, to indicate divine reality. The unconditioned cannot be related to the created world without becoming conditioned, and therefore by definition no longer God. Or, again, God as the absolute cannot be related without becoming relative. Whatever the term used, the same Great Negation leads to the Great Refusal.

We have already called attention to the illegitimacy of such procedure in discussing God. Let us recall the analysis now as we turn to discuss his relation to the world. Such defining of God can be a depth-consciously motivated, escapist verbal trick. Sinful man at his depth may see that thus to define God involves God's not being. Such an infinite, in any case, not only cannot be known, but cannot even be. We know as human beings who are finite. The finite is given by the analysis itself. If God cannot be related to the finite, or referred to in finite terms, he cannot, of course, be known by us.

But such a denial is only the first step. More severe negations are implied. To claim, for instance, that although God cannot be known in any way, yet he must be presupposed, is either to know something in some way or else to say nothing. If God is reliably known at all, even as a necessary implication or presupposition, he is in some real sense known. If he is not implied or presupposed by the interpretation of experience, he is not known in any way.

Even such a denial, however, is not all that is implied in the use of the Illicit Infinite. As a matter of fact, the God who cannot be related to the finite without losing his infinity cannot even be, unless we deny the finite. The infinite, ontologically considered, that is unrelated to anything is not infinite.[1] If God is not related to the world in any way, he is not infinite. He is not all-inclusive either extensively or intensively (interpenetratively). Therefore the implication of the illicit definition of the infinite is that God cannot be known precisely because it can be known that he is not! Such a way to define the infinite is analytically to preclude its being ultimate. In these terms there can be no Supreme Being. We can know that God is not. Theism is eliminated as a choice for reason.

Given the finite, the unrelated, or the unconditioned, infinite is certainly fiction. Such is a true example of mythological language in the fictitious sense. The use of such language may be due to lack of analytical competence, although the reason for its employment may rather be fear's need to exorcise God behind the purported competent use of reason. There is no way we can know how much of this kind of thinking is reason's constructive guarding against idolatry, and how much is the rationalizing of man's fleeing from God. Some of it is, of course, simply lack of clear and deep seeing. Before trying to ascertain to what extent we can know God's relation to the world by reason, it seems wise, in any case, for our purposes here, to suggest as far as we can in bare outline the nature of the ultimate religious reality in its authentic relation to the world.

Granting that, since we are finite, we cannot know the infinite infinitely, or the infinite as such, and granting, too, that the theoretical infinite has its proper uses, but never in theology, where we must start and work with reality as known through the fullness of experience; and without repeating our previous analysis of the relation between finitude, sin and theological knowledge, I want to indicate in brief compass the nature of

[1] Observe that we are not discussing mathematics.

God's relation to the world in terms of ultimates in order to provide the setting for our fuller dealing with the relation of reason in religion to history and nature.

God, we recall, is basically to be conceived of in terms of spirit, as the widest category, and of love, as the highest. The third term 'the personal', bridges the two basic constitutive concepts. Spirit can be conceived of in terms of energy—all pervasive and all-flexible. There is no place or condition where God as spirit is not present in some form, just as we know no actuality where energy is absent. No vacuum can be known except in relation to energy. Whatever 'emptiness' can mean, it cannot be known except in relation to actuality, which in turn is always in some way the manifestation of energy. God as spirit, we recall, is the fount and generator of all energy, or the source and creator of all existence. The fact that he is source and creator of all there is does not involve his being or becoming less than ultimate by the presence and power of finite events.

God includes relatedness within his ultimacy. Not to include finite events would be to be bounded by them. Nothing is external to God, and in this sense independent of him. We can speak of God as infinite only in the sense that he is ultimate reality, and the source, container, and ultimate controller of existence. In such terms, God is the only being beyond compare and cannot be known as infinite within the finite.

Such an affirmation in no way describes the nature of God within himself or as known by himself. God as the personal Spirit of Love is no more bounded by any outside reality than is an ultimately undiscriminate or undifferentiated Unity. To say that God is personal Spirit who in love creates and works in creation is more realistic and intellectually more easily conceivable than to say that God is ultimate Unity who cannot as such be related to any finite existence. The totally unrelated is totally irrelevant.

Can we say that God is not literally, but yet authentically known in, or with relation to, the finite? In some sense he must be literally known to be authentically known. He is not literally known in finitude, of course, with respect to his infinitude. The

198

infinite, indeed, cannot be a matter of human knowledge, but is a faith stance. Reason in religion is concerned not with a theoretical infinite but with an all-controlling and all-embracing reality. God as such reality can be trusted completely. The religious reason works only with the implications of such fundamental faith judgments. In this way, God may be called infinite, but the question itself is far more a matter of man's pretension than it is a true problem of reason in religion. If literal knowledge of God means knowledge of God as infinite, such knowledge is obviously impossible both by means of, and for, the finite.

On the other hand, the infinite can be known only as present in and for the finite. Without ever being reducible to the finite, God comes to man, and man knows him by participation. The eternal Spirit witnesses to finite spirits. God is finally known only by self-revelation and self-authentication. Such knowledge, God being love, can come from the observation of a life of love or a community of concern in history when such vision is joined from within the knower by a personal experience of such love in the Spirit.

The God who is known as personal is indeed finite, in the sense of not all-inclusive, as we have seen; therefore he is known in finitude, in *incarnation*, but within the participation on the part of the believer in the reality and power of the infinite Spirit.

Thus God is both literally and not literally known. He is known by faith within the totality of experience, by presence and by participation, and therefore literally; but known not literally but nevertheless authentically as One who, as he is in himself, within his infinity, is always inexhaustibly beyond, more and other than the experienced presence. God the infinite remains infinite in and with the finite, but is also capable of particularized or individualized attentions and relations. God is Love, at the same time the infinite, unbounded Spirit and the finite, personal Spirit. The infinite, that is, is not primarily a theoretical problem, but the exhaustless Concern and Power for concretion. If we start with true religious ultimates instead of with frustrating and obfuscating abstractions, there is no

o

true problem as to whether God can be related to the world and still remain infinite.

The question is, rather, *how* is God related to the world; how is the ultimate related to the created order? If God is the Spirit of Love everywhere present in some sense, he is the God of freedom who does not in his own ultimate unity of Love need to have all finite existences in line with his being. The creation of free finite beings and of the conditions of finitude can be so consistent with God as love as to be includable within him. When the ultimate is defined, moreover, as a holiness that cannot include sin or the conditions that make sin possible, then, of course, sinful creation contradicts the reality of God's ultimacy. When God is defined as the personal Spirit of Love, however, who creates in freedom for the sake of sharing his love in and for freedom, then the sins and failures within creation can be treated within the pedagogical wisdom and humility of God. He has planned this kind of world, and plans beyond it the kinds of existences that can increasingly reveal the unsearchable heights of the Love who contemplated as his work for us a freedom real and ample enough to begin at depths so low and slow that we can now hardly hold together the heights and the depths.

There is nothing in our ultimate which precludes our searching to know its relation to the world. The problem is, rather, the poor measure of our knowledge. Without pretending to have anything but a genuine clue to God's eternal Purpose in the kind of love that Jesus lived and taught and without trying to settle within the fugitive fragments of earthly existence the fuller meaning of God's way with creation, we turn now to examine history and nature with a view to ascertaining how much of God's purpose in creation can be authentically seen in these realms. Unless God's presence can be seen there in some real way, or unless there is another interpretation that more fully accounts for the way in which history and nature operate in relation to man's meanings, we have no right, in terms of reason, to hold the creative faith we do. Here is where the creative faith of religion must humbly let its own reports be examined by the critical reason.

Full knowing is by the nature of the case impossible; we are not God. No knowing, on the other hand, dooms faith. Faith lives in the vast stretches between full knowing and no knowing. Its only appeal is to such seeing as can inform and direct experience where no more adequate interpretation is available. So to see in integrity and humility is faith's only confidence. Whatever central light may be the heart of faith, the mind of faith must have as much universal applicability as possible. Such seeing, however, is always in part and on trial.

How, then, can reason find religious meaning in history and nature? Positively, there is purpose, and negatively, there is evil. Such evil, I believe, can best be understood as the frustration of purpose. Therefore both the positive and the negative side of the meaning we find in history and nature are at bottom of the same kind. Purpose, moreover, is best understood in terms of the highest and the most inclusive meaning that we have discussed as the heart of religion. The basic finding of this section is going to be that the religious meaning we experience in history and nature depends on the use of our freedom. There is no inclusive purpose which is continually and inclusively predictable. God is no adding machine cranking out answers. There is only a basic need, a basic drive, a basic way to fulfilment, the denial of which is frustration. Such is our theme. Now to the more detailed discussion of it, the first part of which will deal with history.

The choices for seeing meaning in history as a whole are as follows:

(i) There is no meaning.
(ii) Historical man participates in partial meanings.
(iii) He partakes of ultimate meaning.
(iv) History as a whole exemplifies religious meaning.
(v) History is the means of producing eternal enrichment and accumulation of personal and social meaning.

We shall consider each one in turn. When I use the phrase, 'history as a whole', I mean the order of history as such. We are not discussing personal meanings or social meanings which are merely local, temporary and relative. We are concerned with meanings that pertain to the warp and woof of historic existence, as such, on whatever level or in whatever stage of development. The meanings to be found in history can then be discussed as partial or as plenary, and man's relation to these meanings can vary, but they are in fact meanings *of* history rather than merely *in* history.

By meaning, for our purposes, we are intending fulfilments of personal and social natures and aspirations which are organic or superorganic to persons and obtainable only through the means of historic existence. History itself, on our definition, must be the means and medium through which people not only find such meaning, but also attain such meaning. By history we mean human living with nature in terms of choices and the continuation of choices whereby the stuff of both people and nature gradually becomes uncovered. We mean the course of man's life as a social being in the natural world. The structure of our discussion will have to be a moving between the affirmations of creative faith as we have found them, on the one hand, namely that the ultimate order is one of totally inclusive and creatively concerned Love, and the cautions of the critical reason, on the other, to the effect that faith must test its offerings in the light of our actual world. The religious pole can supply context, but this context is always subject to tests in terms of the concrete content of human history.

(i)

The first choice to consider is that there is no meaning at all in history as a whole. In support of this choice it can be said that no person can ever glimpse, let alone grasp, the whole course of history. It can also be said that if definite people do not see or feel themselves part of historic meaning their witness precludes further discussion. History as a whole is all-inclusive. All that is needed to refute the claim that history as a whole is meaningful or contains meaning, consequently, is a single negative instance. It can be contended, furthermore, that since all people die and are removed from history, none ever experiences history as a whole; therefore there can be no meaning for human beings of history as a whole. Besides, the meanings of history change decisively from major epoch to major epoch. How, then, can we legitimately speak of meaning on the part of history as a whole?

To these charges there are also answers. We can know history as a whole without knowing all of history, as we can know God without knowing all of God. We can know the law of gravitation, as a whole, we have said, without knowing it in all its manifestations. Again, even if some people do not experience knowingly the meaning of history, history as a whole can have meaning, even as religion can be meaningful in its totality without all persons being aware of its meaning. Awareness involves both knowledge and will, as well as level of experience. The meaning of history is not predictable in the way that gravitation is, but is a matter of long-range conspiracy depending upon freedom. It cannot, consequently, be demonstrated like the working of a natural law. It certainly cannot be proved. Forcible conviction of historic meaning can be lacking, however, even while historic meaning can be real and communicable.

The meaning, moreover, which history exhibits may be larger than any personal experience and destiny. The fact that all people die and leave history does not mean that the order of history, as such, cannot be the carrier of meaning from generation to generation. The content may vary, the scenes of history may shift; but the constant meaning may remain. Therefore although people die away from history and although there are basic changes in history as to the kinds of decisions or the kinds of concrete life that can be lived, there can yet be some genuine constant throughout the entire historic order. There can, for instance, be a purpose perceivable in history as an order, which has the same meaning underneath different stages of development.

As a matter of fact, meaning in human time here on earth may even be continued beyond this life and still have the same basic import. If God is creator and sustainer of nature and the author of history, meaning should be found in the order he has made possible. Unless we find such meaning, our critical reason must rule our creative reason wrong in its choice of ultimates. If God is supreme love and wisdom, a meaningless order of history is in fact a denial of his nature. No merely formal reason for denial of meaning, therefore, is enough, provided that we can show that some positive meaning can be found. Therefore we pass on from the completely negative choice that no meaning can be found in human history as a whole.

(ii)

The next stance offers only a limited meaning of history in the sense that man participates in its partial meanings, either as less than total meanings or as total meanings unavailable in history. We have already dismissed as irrelevant to our discussion merely relative or personal meanings. Our concern is not with meanings of any kind found in history, but with historic meaning. History itself must, in the point at issue, be characterized by some order of meaning, partial or plenary. When people live to impress their name or deed on history for as long as possible, history is meaningful to them.

Some believe that immortality means being remembered as well and as long as possible either in the hearts of family and friends or, for example, by means of some memorial endowment carrying their name. Sometimes a survivor tries to make the one he loved thus live. Or a man may live for causes that give meaning to his life, but which, beyond his life, have their own locus in history. He may die, but his cause goes on and is helped. The soldier's death is meaningful if the cause of the country is thereby served. Such meanings are ingrained in historic existence. They do not span the total meaning in history, but history as an order allows for such partial meanings. History as a total order is characterized by capacity for the creation of such partial meanings in terms of which men can live with purpose.

There can be and should be no denying of such meanings. Such purpose for life is coeval with man. The life that is not touched by such immediate meanings can hardly find the fuller meanings except as substitutes for the partial meanings which he lacks. The acceptance of self and family, of local loyalties and identifications, should be the first experience of growth in meaning. Except as these frustrate growth and become substitutes for the fuller meaning of history, these more intimate reasons for living should simply be acknowledged and accepted. Such meaning history surely does exhibit.

Or, in the second place, historic man can participate in eternal meanings in history as the result of historic existence, even while history itself never can attain or produce such meaning. Such meanings qualify within our definition even though they are only partial. There may be paths of discipline within historic life that can lead man to transcend historic existence in mystic ecstasy. Then history is left behind, for history cannot contain eternity. All anthropomorphic experience is given up for total identification with the ground of being. The self of history is merged with universal meaning and delivered through such identification from the fever and falsehood of self. History is then seen as the outgoing of the Ultimate into objectification, for the pleasure of diversity or through love for the concrete, but as having its deepest meaning in the joy of returning to the eternal ocean of harmony and rest.

History is then like contented people in a happy home who for the sake of a change undertake the inconvenience of travel, but who enjoy nothing on the trip so much as the anticipation and the joy of the return. Thus all history is driven out from the Fullness only to long for it back. History is, in such an instance as this, incapable of expressing the eternal meaning, but it can afford the disciplines and experiences that allow man to view from afar the harmony and the rest of the Goal. The struggles of the journey are not too great a price for the joy of returning and the harmony and rest of the Return. Thus self is not without eternal meaning in history, even while neither self nor history can exhibit such meaning.

History as an order affords man partial meanings. In this way, historic man participates in partial meanings in some sense made possible by the historic order. The meanings cannot be part of the historic order in itself. They find no at-homeness there. But apart from man's nature as a creature of history, he could not experience such meaning. Therefore we grant partial status to such claims for the meaningfulness of history.

We do not deny that eternal meaning can be experienced in history. Certainly, too, inasmuch as our history is not only imperfect but characterized by much evil, we do not claim that history, as such, can be qualitatively characterized by the fullness of eternal meaning. Granted any perfection of meaning, and granted the evils of history, there must be some truth in this second contention, that man merely participates in eternal meaning. Just as we cannot deny that there are local and partially fulfilling meanings of history, so we must not deny this second insistence that no meaning in history can contain the fullness of the eternal meaning characterized by high religion.

From the point of view of the Ultimate that we have advanced, however, the objection to the former view is that historic meanings are not limited to these partial meanings of history, while the objection to the latter view is that the relation between the Ultimate and history may be more positively fulfilling than the second view holds. In line with the former view we take the actual meanings of history more seriously, while in line with the latter view we refuse to accept the charge that historic meaning is limited to our participating in it in this life. My own positive view, then, in order to prove adequate, will have to contain a fulfilment of the deepest positive intention of these two views, finding, in fact, that constructive historic meaning rests and is realized in the eternal order of meaning. Such a finding, if I can competently suggest it, is, of course, in line with the nature of the Ultimate which our analysis has already disclosed.

(iii)

Historical man, in the third place, beyond participating in historic meaning, may actually partake of it. He may do so, again, either basically in the historic order or beyond the historic order. Historic causes may be considered as giving purpose to man's life, or life may be seen as part of the purpose itself. In one case, the emphasis is mostly subjective: What can give meaning to my life? In the other, the stress is largely objective: How can my life be given over to the historic meaning which transcends it? In the former instance, man tries to make himself or his friends as immortal as possible. In the latter instance, he tries to change the historic order itself by his self-offering. Man becomes fulfilled by being lost in the historic cause to which he devotes himself. The cause may be the same, but in the latter case, there are not only higher motivation but also more intrinsic relation between history and the cause and between the cause and the person.

History, for instance, may be conceived of as a struggle of neutral forces where historic powers are created for good and ill. Each life and each people play their part. Life is thus felt to have crucial importance and to be urgent with present meaning. Or God may be thought of as limited in his historic power by man's freedom, or, for that matter, by something in himself or in the nature of things, in which case man's freedom matters profoundly to God. Thus man not only participates in some meaning that gives purpose to his life, but actually partakes within his very choices in the nature of things in such a way that his life matters definitely to history. History is therefore meaningful, and its meaning penetrates beyond man's own choices and experiences of purpose into the very objective destinies of man. His own cause or that of his people may not be identifiable with the totality of history, but history as a whole provides the means for life's critical meaningfulness according to the place and proportion of a man's life and circumstance.

Or man may partake of history's meaningfulness by actually contributing through history to the eternal order of things. God may so have created, or in any case be dependent on, man's freedom that man by his living can produce new creative possibilities even for God's eternal order. Because man has lived creatively and compassionately, God may receive into his eternal vision, or into the power for his eternal vision, new possibilities for historic choices. We may perish, but what we have been and done may provide more than historic immortality in some secondary objective sense; it may provide objective immortality in God's possibilities for further creations or for his further creative guidance of mankind. In any case, according to this view, our lives at least give joy or pain to the Eternal even though we ourselves are mortal. Therefore we can live for God's will and way for the world, with unrestrained abandon and genuine joy, knowing that our work is not 'in vain in the Lord'. The meaning of our lives in history goes beyond our lives, while also fulfilling our lives as they affect either the historic order or the eternal order by our becoming part of either, or of both. Man, therefore, in such a case, more than participates in some meaning of history; he is part of it. He veritably partakes of that meaning.

How adequate are these views in the light of our ultimate? Naturally, both of them contain significant truth. In the former, history itself is affected by lives by being constituted of them, not only in the present but in a dimension transcending all present tenses. History itself is made by choices coming together into an historic order. The whole meaning and satisfaction of history, therefore, depends upon man and his kind of living. And these choices have results that enter into future realities. Man thus does not live for himself or for his times alone, but is a responsible member of the transgenerational community. He himself is a debtor to the past, suffering from its guilt, and he himself is now providing the kind of life that will be possible for his children and children's children. When these choices are considered in the light of the ultimate order of things, they become religiously significant. History, in such a case, is seen as the carrier of meanings that have ultimate significance even though not necessarily ultimate survival value. The limited contributors of these values disappear, leaving room for other lives in the seemingly endless procession of historic change.

In the case of the second position, man's life enters into the eternal order of things. Man thus partakes of ultimate significance by virtue of sharing in this order, if not as a person, at least by the result of his life as a person. In this case, man's historic existence has not only religious significance, whether for God or man, but importance of eternal meaning. Man is lifted from the heaviness of the historic treadmill to the open road of lasting significance. Man leaves behind the fragility of fugitiveness. Man's life lasts in God. He may die, but that with which he has identified his life does not. He may be captured by death, but death can never destroy even the personal value of his life as possibility for other lives in the future, either perpetuated in the ocean richness of the personal God, or safeguarded by the God who stores within his transpersonal safety vault whatever personal value life has achieved.

If these are the positive aspects to these two ways in which man in history contributes meaning beyond himself, what are the negative aspects? In the former case, no matter how real and rich life may be, and no matter what wealth it may leave as a deposit for the future of history, fulfilment is still subject to the ravages of actual history as we know it, and can always be frustrated by man's freedom. Although man's immediate struggle in history matters to him, history thus offering meaningfulness, nevertheless from the perspective of the infinite Spirit who is all-capable Love, historic meaning is both too fragile and fugitive, as well as too partial, to satisfy God's purpose in creation. If history can exhibit no meaning more real and rich than such value-producing partaking of struggle in history, even under God, it cannot be the creation and the continuous ordering of the God our creative reason has envisaged.

In the case of the second view, history has meaning in and for God. Thus it is neither fragile nor fleeting. It is religious in its depth dimension. Nevertheless the view is from man up, not from God down. It is continuous with creation, and not with the Creator. It is history viewed not ultimately, but proximately. The God who loves all and can save all would not let all perish, and he would surely have succeeded further in eternity with history, if accumulative and improving meaning is limited to earthly history. Such a view gives man real meaning in history, but fails in its view of God.

If no fuller view of the meaning of history can be had, we must accept with honesty and good grace the fact that while, from the point of view of man's deepest need and highest fulfilment, God as universal Love affords our best understanding of the ultimate, from the point of view of the meaning of history, such a view is not indicated. Obviously, man as a personal and social being could be ahead of the historic order as such, or the historic order might not reflect directly the more personal and social meaning of man, or the analysis of the highest in history in the light of cosmic creation may be a fuller indication of the nature of reality than that offered by the historic order. If, however, there is a view of history that truly indicates a general meaningfulness which is not only consistent with, but even confirmatory of, our view of the ultimate, we have to say accordingly that however much truth both of these positions of man's partaking of ultimate meaning in history may offer, nevertheless they must be seen as partial and pre-liminary to the fuller meaning which more adequately accounts for the facts of our historical existence.

(iv)

Or, in the fourth place, history as a whole may exemplify religious meaning. Such a position involves a vital problem of classification: Religious meaning of history is more difficult to ascertain on our definition of religion as 'that which is more and other than ordinary experience with the power to help and harm man' than on the more widely open definition of religion as 'any sought-after ultimate or religious concern in its ultimate dimension'. The history that affords choice for eternal salvation, for instance, has definite religious significance in our view, however little organically integrated with history as such it may be, while other theories in which life and history are far more organically interrelated may, on our terms, be less definitely religious.

History may exemplify meaning in its totality, for instance, by exhibiting an inner drive toward the classless society. Nature and history may combine organically, according to such an interpretation, to exhibit what is taken to be a scientifically ascertainable development toward the full freedom of man when plenty is provided and when the state itself has withered away. Obviously, if one is persuaded that such is the meaning of history, and if one becomes an ardent advocate and partisan of such a determined destiny, one finds in history definite and humanly fulfilling meaning. Countless persons have died for such a faith. In a way, too, such an interpretation of history is

210

supposed to be grounded in the very nature of things and there-fore to have the force of religion in its more general sense. Whatever the toughness of the means, the end is humanly high and all-embracing, while nature itself serves relentlessly the cause that finally cannot lose. Nevertheless, on our definition of religion, such a view does not exhibit religious meaning of history.

Or history may exemplify historic meaning if religious belief holds that man's total experience in history is to work out the consequences of his choices in the light of transmundane reality. History may not have permanent meaning of religious signifi-cance in terms of some other world which is organically operative in this world, either partially or in a plenary manner, but all of history may nevertheless exemplify orders having an ontological status beyond ordinary experience. The order of karma, for instance, may both transcend and comprise all human history as the conjunct of all human choices finding their proper consequences at their proper time. The karmic order may be presuppositional for history as well as descriptive of it.

Such an order, moreover, may be part of religious faith, which some accept as grounded in the ultimate nature of things, while others scorn it as an order of ignorance and unreality. To this interpretation of history we can add the dimension of consequences beyond man in terms of transmigration into non-human forms of life or promotion into non-earthly planes of existence. In this latter case, we have a definite religious dimension even from our more strict point of view. Historic life, in such a case, may be the burden of a feared continuous reincarnation or the opportunity to get into the higher stages of life's possibilities. In any case, the meaning of history is tied up with religious faith, and even though the historic order, as such, may have no ultimate meaning, history exhibits meaning for man as the medium within which he must work out in-escapably his destiny.

Or history may exhibit meaning as challenge and response. Such challenge and response may not lead to any eternal destiny, and may not cover the life of all peoples, but may nevertheless exhibit meaning on the part of history as a whole.

211

The challenges may vary. They may vary in different kalpas or cosmic epochs beyond all possible ken. Or they may vary from historic kairoi to historic kairoi. Each historic kairos may have its own specific kind of total meaning that is non-transferable to any other kairos. There may even be some normative kind of kairos for history as a whole which is yet inapplicable rationally to any other kairos. Thus history may be said to have a central meaning which can best exemplify the ultimate order of things. Both challenge and response theories and kairic interpretations exemplify historic meaning.

The problem with all such views, however, is that they may have no clearly defined positive content for the religious ultimate. In such a case, they can hardly be called religious in our full sense of the term. Men may hold them, however, along with varying agnostic views of the ultimate: some may in fact presuppose total agnosticism, while others may affirm agnosticism only with respect to the relationship between any ultimate order and history, or only, indeed, with respect to our knowledge of such a relationship. Therefore it is hard to say that these views of history have no religious meaning. The emphasis, in any case, is overwhelmingly on the order of history rather than on the nature of ultimate reality beyond history. The weakest part in these theories of history seems usually to be the nature of religion in its bearing on the historic order.

As a matter of fact, some even define God as the God of history, envisioning neither a God beyond history nor a fulfilling destiny for man beyond history. God is precisely, in this view, the God of history. As such they call him the living God, even the living God of the Bible. An existentialist view of history conceives of it as the historic order of choice, of which God is the ground, providing only proximate goals. Thus there is no 'supernatural' or transmundane Creator, nor an eternal destiny as fulfilment beyond human history. There is only the God of lively choices and of the communities of choice. These interpreters dismiss cosmic history as itself not being a historic question because it is not open to human choice.

The kind of analysis that we carried out in the first part of this book, for example, they reject as speculative and historically irrelevant. The meaning of history for them is precisely freedom. The Christian meaning of history many hold to be the freedom of love in a community of creative co-operation. According to this point of view, the question of the meaning of history is itself falsely posed. History has no one or no central meaning in terms of a chronological goal. Rather, the whole order of history exhibits the meaning of freedom. Religion is the understanding of freedom as rooted beyond man in the God of history who is conceived of so dynamically that even to discuss his nature is to be guilty of substantive rather than historic thinking.

History, moreover, has been considered to be the process of human progress. God, in this view, has worked in history to effect a finally perfect human race as the end result of creation. With the advent of science and education, particularly with the advent of some of their amazing powers, many have felt that the goal is obtainable, and have worked with self-sacrifice and religious fervour to help bring about the meaning of history. The view of progress or of social evolution, however, has generally fallen on evil days. Nevertheless for some time in human history it has given urgent meaningfulness to numberless believers who have seen in God's coming day for man the meaning of history as a whole. These believers have deemed individual sacrifice worth while in the light of the perfection of man's final destiny.

In our day there have been minor attempts to understand history as perfectable by modern medicine, as, for instance, when man can manufacture life, control genetic inheritance, banish all illness, and make himself immortal by his skill in continually replacing outworn parts of the human organism. Or theories of education have proposed that some drive toward mature education started with man at his creation as man, a million years ago and more, which nothing can now stop, no matter what slowdowns or digressions there may be on the way. History as an order, in such cases, may exemplify meaning in the light of nature or of the totality of things, and may consequently be considered as having religious meaning, however tenuous such meaning may then be in terms of religion.

In the light of our religious ultimate, God as unlimited and totally concerned creativity, these theories must be judged for their adequacy of meaning. They all exhibit meaning on the part of history, as such, and, therefore, whether we want to use the term or not, they classify as having meaning *of* history. But none of them adequately combines a view of the ultimate with a view that can serve to utilize our knowledge of cosmic history, within which human history must be seen with its own specific meaning. There is thus discrepancy between the broader and the shorter perspectives. Generally speaking, this kind of discrepancy, which is exhibited by all the views in this group, tends to discredit them as the highest ranking candidates for the understanding of the meaning of history in relation to our knowledge of ultimates. No doubt all of them contain their specific though partial truth, but none exhibits meaning in history organically expressive of the infinite Spirit of Love. None of them is thus adequate to the ever-expanding horizons of such an ultimate. The view of history of all these theories is too narrow and too short.

History as the means to achieve the classless society, to return to this view, no doubt signifies the coming of the age of the common man. It also declares the shortcomings of capitalist theory. As the feudal order had its day and was surpassed by the industrial, even so capitalist ideology seems to give way to socialist systems of thought and organization. We must interpret man more intimately in relation to his technological history. Knowledge itself must undergo examination and re-interpretation in terms of its sociological determinants. This dynamic view of history as leading to the freedom of man within abundance of things offers truth and power, but lacks the central reality of God the Creator and of love as the dynamic of life and society.

Similarly the karmic interpretation of history as the out-working of deed and consequence contains undeniable truth. This view is particularly impressive when it proceeds to show that since we are born unequal, there must have been a life before this, and that since we have to keep facing the consequences of our deeds there must also be some kind of continuity in lives beyond. Such a position demands both freedom and justice, not mostly as man's choice, but as grounded in the very nature of things. What deep religious drive may underlie such a view of history! How it uncovers the superficial thinking in any position that holds that this life settles man's fate, or that man is frozen at death in whatever mould he has chosen for himself in this life. Furthermore, such a view of human life in history takes the problem of evil with utmost seriousness. Such willingness to face up to the problem of evil in its depth dimension characterizes high religion. In the view of our own ultimate of God as Love, however, the karmic view is both too individualistic to represent God's work in history, and also lacks organic relation to any purpose of God for history consistent with his nature. We therefore still seek for fuller meaning for history as such.

We have really evaluated the challenge-and-response point of view in the way we originally discussed it. We found that unless it is connected with some definite religious ultimate it does not even qualify for discussion within our ultimate perspective. Whatever truth the position contains (and I believe it to be based on profound meaning of history), we shall discuss in connection with my own point of view, which incorporates the truth of this stance within a definite religious position.

The existentialist viewpoint, moreover, cannot be answered from within its own assumptions. The reply to its claim involves the whole analysis of our first section. Reason in religion arrives at an ultimate that is more and other than ordinary experience in terms of which to interpret the meaning of history as a whole. We have the perspective. The truth of existentialism is that freedom is an indispensable aspect of the order of history. Freedom of choice is inseparably part of full freedom, but full freedom is not obtainable apart from freedom as the fulfilment of life, and apart from the conditions in nature and history within which such freedom can be attained.

Freedom is never apart, moreover, from the directives from past experience and from the structures which underlie the future. Apart from some degree of predictable results, freedom would be meaningless, and predictable relations are due to stability in the nature of things. Existentialism's stress on

P

freedom is therefore welcome, but, again, it is partial. It does not even stand for full freedom, let alone that fuller life within which freedom itself finds its meaning. The God of history, moreover, is the God of order as well as of creative newness. He is the God of continuation as well as of choice. Existentialism underlines the meaning of freedom as part of history, and that far, but only that far, it is true.

The view of social immortality, furthermore, expresses accumulative meaning in history. Without some such development we are not going to find the meaning of history that characterizes it as a whole in the light of our ultimate, but social immortality has too small and too callous a god. The god who cannot create the end without such large and long waste is not the sovereign God, and the god who makes use of countless generations in pain and death in order to produce one final perfect result is not the Spirit of Love. Thus such thinking may result partially from the fuller and truer claim that is derived from our ultimate, namely that history has a goal that fulfils man, but it lacks both the power and the goodness to be adequately religious. It is a combination of an optimistic and an insensitive, creative faith apart from the control of critical reason.

(v)

We come, then, to the fifth and final point of view as to religious meaning in history. My own point of view will serve as an example of it. This view finds that history is the means of producing eternal enrichment and accumulation of personal and social meaning.

To write positively about the meaning of history requires both courage and care. Here if ever the creative and the critical reasons need to be combined. Our thesis illustrates the nature of ultimate reality as found by our analysis. God's work is seen in human history, but the meaning of God's labouring to produce persons in community cannot find full context within human history itself, but only within eternity. We are therefore proposing not a philosophy, but a theology of history. At no point, however, may the danger of misinterpretation be more threatening. At no point perhaps must we distinguish with greater care between the faith stance for interpretation and the factual content. As far as is humanly possible, context and content must not be blurred. We must be determined not to let our faith stance alter or add any fact to our analysis of history. Such use of faith is illicit. All faith can do is to provide a clarifying context for interpreting the facts of history.

Nor can history prove the nature of the ultimate. The proximate, according to our analysis, should be generally in line with the ultimate; otherwise it disproves it. Or perhaps we had better say that the deepest understanding of the proximate should bear testimony to the truth of the ultimate. It should confirm the ultimate according to its deepest meaning and the measure of its importance. Between the two, however, may be immense distances and differences. God may be Love so unimaginably from the perspective of human history that, in it, we see only the least snatches of a beginning. The faith stance, consequently, cannot be used as fact nor to produce new fact, but only to organize fact. At the same time, if our perspective is legitimate, in proper proportion and power we should see human history more meaningfully in this light than in any other. Such caution the critical reason requires of the creative.

If freedom is the key to history, moreover (since our ultimate assumption is that God in love creates freedom through history), we should not expect any fixed result from history. What we should look for are evidences that human history is in fact, at its core, the scene of freedom and the conditions of freedom. But beyond such freedom and conditions for freedom there should also be some purposive structuring of freedom through the conditions for freedom that would help create community without destruction of freedom. If God as love is in charge of history, human freedom should be neither irresponsible nor forced. It should be genuine and riskful, possibly within some general external control of it by the Creator, but mostly charted inwardly in such a manner that man through history can begin to feel for, and find, freedom both through frustration and through fulfilment.

If God is love, such freedom finds fulfilment only in com-

217

munity. Human history should therefore afford the opportunity to learn love in freedom, or to find fulfilment in community. Within our definition of religion, and from the concrete findings of our analysis, it is obvious that no consummation of human history can be expected in this life. If God is love and human history is ultimate under his creative care, earthly life can only indicate the nature of God's purpose. It cannot demonstrate its consummation. Without flinching we have to keep in mind the power and prevalence of sin. So overwhelming is the fact of man's being burdened by sin, and so primitive are his beginnings generally, throughout earthly history with respect to the life of the open and universal community of creative faith and outgoing concern, that there seems slight relation between man's general attainment and the kind of life and love we see in Jesus.

The temptation, therefore, is to downgrade the exceptional in favour of the general. It is to deny the deepest meaning offered for history by means of the most general data. Unless human history is understood eschatologically, therefore, it is a travesty of truth to make any Christian claim for it. Unless earthly time is seen in the light of eternity, our time is full of trouble and frustration, where even the best lives are the victims of man's cruelty and resistance to love. But increasingly my conviction grows that only from the perspective of the highest in history can history as a whole be understood. The creative faith offers the critical reason the choice of frustration or of taking a flight high enough to a point from which the human maze is finally seen as a whole. Having had such a view it can choose between remaining frustrated in the maze or believing in the final opening which cannot be seen from within the maze. Life seems to offer no other choice. Our decisive choice is between no adequate meaning of history and a full-fledged theology of history. History, I believe, receives full meaning only in the light of God.

In such a spirit I offer the following analysis of the nature of history. It should appeal to no fact not generally ascertainable nor should it distort the meaning of fact.

The meaning of human history is to create community. It is

to make man in community. Such making has length and breadth. It accumulates with the generations and the centuries; and it keeps extending to the ends of the world. This meaning cannot be made or appropriated except in freedom. It can also be set back, distorted and corrupted by freedom. The meaning of history is variously created and understood from the minimum social relations, inward or outward, of the recluse to the maximum community of a universal, open society realized at least within the vision of faith working through love.

No neat division can be made in man or in community. Nor can the conditions of community be divided into isolable categories. But the main channels can be located, no matter how much the water may move in eddies or counter-eddies in between. In general, man grows into the experience of community by means of what I have called 'the push of process' and 'the pull of purpose'. We might say that he grows, as we shall see, between his needs as a physical creature and his need for love. Or we might say that he grows between his need to control the conditions making community possible and his need for the community itself. As we come to analyse these categories, we need to remember vividly that man is one, with aspects of his being reaching out in diverse manners, sometimes co-operatively and sometimes in conflict, and that man's community is similarly a matter of wholeness, but with aspects of it that help to enrich its growth or become the occasion for struggle.

The push of process whereby man is driven by his creaturely needs has made for widening modes of community. The pull of purpose, on the other hand, whereby man is drawn toward unity and freedom because he was made for love, has led to intensive modes of community. Again, we repeat that no full line of demarcation can be drawn between these two modes, but that they nevertheless have relevant, analytical distinctness. Man's creaturely needs may be classified as physical, social and spiritual, but the pull of purpose operates on these same levels. In man and community as a whole these divergent aspects interpenetrate and overlap, even while they afford genuine ground for analytical distinctions as directives in human history. The important consideration to remember is that the extensive modes of community are in themselves neither good nor bad. They are morally neutral, except as extensive depth may increase intensive quality. The fact that man has wider relations in history or that his consciousness has expanded in reach does not in itself determine, in any way, what the nature or quality of that relation or that consciousness may be.

Man may be better or worse off because of the new relation or new breadth of consciousness, but the new dimension or measure in no way makes the relation or the consciousness better or worse. Nevertheless man confronts a new situation because of such growth in terms of which he must relate himself differently. He now has to respond to history in a new way. Neutrality in the moral sense on the part of the extensive modes thus in no way involves absence of choice or of responsibility. As a matter of fact, the moral neutrality of the modes calls for some concrete response that is always morally committed. The context of community grows but the content has to be determined by man's choice. The container is larger, but the size of the container does not determine what is put into it.

That such growth in the extensive modes of man's togetherness has taken place in human history is plain fact. Even though it does not pertain to all individuals, and even though history passes away from all individuals, nevertheless the fact of the growth as a form of history remains. People are born into different human histories because of this fact. It makes no difference whether man began as an isolated individual hunting food or as gregarious groups hunting food. Man in human history has passed from narrowly circumscribed near-animal existence to his present world consciousness and mastery of nature.

This growth in the extensive measure of man's community has come mostly in connection with nature. Man's physical needs have driven him to utilize nature. Or more accurately, they have been the occasion for his utilization of nature's resources. Man has created neither his needs nor nature. They are both given. But man, being man, has changed both. Man cannot be considered merely an animal who has met the drives of his needs. Man has the endowment with which to meet them, nature has the resources, and man has made increased utilization possible by means of the development of his understanding of nature, and the techniques by means of which he can take advantage of what nature has to offer. Nor has physical need in a narrow sense been the mother of all inventions. Rubber tyres were first invented to ease the suffering of the sick.

Man's extensive modes of community grew at the push of process mostly through and along with his history of technology. To be sure, when man domesticated cattle his increasing herds called for larger pasture space, but it was really the invention of tools that made manufacture possible, and the fuller use of both lands and animals as well. The history of man's expanding modes of community has generally kept pace with the history of his means of production. Manufacture led to trade and trade to specialization of production. With property came the need for its protection. Man also became settled in fixed locations. Thus arose the need for government, the rise of law, and the institution of sanctions. The police symbolized and exercised power. As centres of property and production grew stronger the arm of the police reached longer. Conflict between concentrations of power resulted in war. Standing armies arose.

There is no need for us to describe, but only to suggest this process of expansion of man's modes of community. Technology led to an ever more diversified and complex system of production requiring complicated ways of business and highly divided manners of labour. And this ever-growing utilization of nature's resources for the fuller meeting of man's needs became reflected in more complex government and wider reaches of trade. Thus came into man's consciousness wider and wider boundaries of interest. With trade came travel, and, with wider interests, travel became also something valued for itself. No human being and no groups of human beings deliberately charted the development of history. Man's modes of togetherness grew as he was driven by his needs; and as his population expanded he was the more driven to understand and to use nature the better.

As some people became liberated from narrow bondage to

nature, they began to have and to crave things for convenience, pleasure and display. Today much manufacturing is not for subsistence needs, and much tilling of the soil is for such purposes as tobacco and intoxicating beverages. But even if our age should be passing in large part into an era of material abundance and inbuilt waste, there seems to have been no time when time and material was not spent on pleasure and play beyond mere need. Thus we have to consider man, the total human being, and not merely the economic man in the use of goods as well as in travel.

However this process of expansion has taken place, there are many factors besides physical need that enter into it. One is man's social nature. Man is not only physical, needing food and shelter. He needs more than tools with which to utilize nature. He needs community and to communicate. Man's expanding horizons have both been due to and also given rise to speech. Man developed language. Not only did he learn how to abstract from experience and to communicate about things not at hand, but he learned to write and to send his writing instead of coming in person. Man's capacity to write and to record agreements led to the development of public life and to expanding modes of consciousness.

To a great extent, speech and writing were generated within the milieu of man's growing community in dependence on nature. His writing was the use of nature to extend his tongue and to help his memory. This process received vivid and vigorous help when, beyond the creation of alphabets and writing, man learned how to multiply his writing inexpensively through the printing press. Before this time man's growing modes of community had received help from schools and religious orders in the dissemination of knowledge. With the invention of printing, however, education in the sense of general reading at least became an increasing reality.

To describe in any detail the modern revolution in communication is useless. The telephone and the telegraph are now taken for granted. The radio and the television bring the whole world potentially into every home. An assassination in Japan, for instance, is shown on a news film, first just as it happened, and then repeated in slow motion in such a way that children in the United States, seeing it in every gruesome detail, know far more about the event than the people who were actually present at the assassination. History displays man's majestic mastery of nature in the realm of communication. We have not described, nor need to, other modes of communication that have brought men together all over the world: the wheel, the compass, the steam engine, the jet plane. As far as modes of communication go, the world is potentially a neighbourhood; we can even say that it is already virtually a neighbourhood. The extensive modes of man's togetherness have grown incredibly. The swiftness of advance is beyond all responsible predictions of the past. The future advance, possibly into interplanetary dimensions, had better not even be mentioned. We know little in comparison to what may come to be and be taken for granted.

Who can deny that our sketch is factual reporting? Is not our description, even in its impressionistic conciseness, speaking of the real facts of one side of history? Is this growth of man's extensive modes of togetherness meaningless, or does its staggering reality point to some purpose? Something has happened of enormous consequence in history as a whole. Multitudes, of course, have been largely untouched by what has taken place, and all have had to leave the course of history. This is not the place to discuss the problems connected with the passing of people from history by death in relation to the trans-generational accumulations of potentialities in history which remain and make further development possible. We are not discussing human progress and we are not claiming this growth in man's expanding horizons to be good. What we are pointing out is that there has been undeniably a stretching in man's extensive modes of community, both in relation to the production of property and in relation to man's need to create community and to communicate within ever more extended areas of community. The same process has also taken place in the spiritual life of man as we are now about to consider.

There is no exact equating of religious growth with the extensive modes of man's community. To be sure, there is no precise way of determining or delineating even the external measure of man's togetherness. The organizational aspects of it, like government, trade relations, and means and manners of communication, to some extent are fixed entities, and yet they also vary according to man's response to them within the consciousness of men. Nor has progress, even technically, always been gradual or inclusive of all stages of development, as archaeologists find, for instance, in the use of stone in building.

Nonetheless we have the basic facts of the conspiracy of history to bring about the increasing widening and interrelation of man's manner of living, including the growing complexity of life both technologically and in terms of the division of labour. We have, for example, in the spiritual realm the fact that today the religions of the world face each other self-consciously as never before. Just as the United Nations symbolizes the need for man's vision and world responsibility, even so the local nature of religions is coming under increasing pressure in today's world. As a matter of fact, there may come a general defection from religions among the thoughtful throughout the whole world, and among all religions, for the very reason that no religion may seem fully universal and adequate to the expanding modes of man's politico-social community.

The facts of the extensive growth of religions, however, are not reducible to any neat, systematic arrangement. Religions have grown, to be sure, in relation to man's need to adjust himself to his world as indicated by the push of process. As man has answered the push of his need in relation to nature and in relation to the human community in terms of expanding contents of togetherness, even so he has interpreted the realities and powers which are more real and other than nature and history in terms relevant to his concrete needs as a historic creature. History seems to be starkly particular. But since man is a creative being, responding as a whole, and not a pre-fabricated thinking machine giving automatic answers according to the data and correct mathematical and mechanical procedures, interpretation has never been proportionate to need or circumstance. Thus, in some periods, need outruns interpretation, while at other times the prophetic seer becomes irrelevant for being ahead of the push of the process. The response, too, as we shall see in some real sense, is made in freedom and appropriated in freedom by the community. Therefore the growth in man's religious extensive modes of community vary sharply, not only from age to age, but within any age and within every community.

Nevertheless there is some truth in a process of expanding religious interpretation. Animism, animatism, totemism, family gods, tribal deities, nationalism in religion, and universal religions, at least in their extensive intention, may be stages that overlap and that follow no common pattern invariably. There is no development in religion, however, that does not participate in some way in an over-all pattern. There may have been some kind and measure of monotheism behind all hylozoisms and henotheisms. The intention and concrete content of the religious consciousness may vary, depending upon the nature and reason for the interpretation. Seeming universalism, for example, may be mostly lack of knowledge or lack of sensitivity to what lies beyond the confines of the religion held to be ultimate. Religions, too, depend peculiarly upon unusually receptive and creative personalities through whom the interpretation is given to the people and received variously according to both general relevance and concreteness of personal and community response. As a whole, in any case, we cannot authentically gainsay that the external modes of man's religious interpretation have been not only affected but significantly conditioned by the push of process. The extensive modes of man's historic situation have been one determinant ingredient affecting the interpretation of religion, whatever be the driving motivation in terms of fear, duty and love working through faith in their proportions of invariant togetherness in the life of man.

Besides this push of process in terms of man's needs, physically, socially and spiritually, there seems to have operated in human history a pull of purpose far more than any single or collective human purposing. The pull of purpose involves man's longing for fulfilment in history and the possibilities and powers offered for such attainment in history. Human history has offered ways of living and acting that lead either to basic frustration or to basic fulfilment. Certain ways of behaving involve defeat of life, while others provide more release of life. Our thesis is that man has never chosen his extensive modes of community.

Whatever creative freedom has entered into the making of the historic process, the historic results have been contained within and confined to external modes of community, for the extensive modes are neutral to good and evil and to satisfactory or unsatisfactory living. The extensive modes are conditions for community, not community as such. These modes have resulted from man's interrelation with nature because of a certain kind of nature fit for man's use and a certain kind of human nature needing nature's resources. But even though man's extensive modes of community are not due to direct choice, but given to man when and where he is born, at least in overwhelming measure, his intensive modes of community are the result of his choices. Every external event, in terms of the extensive modes of community due to the push of process, awaits man's forced choice as to the way he is going to respond to the pull of purpose for that event. Each event, as well as each age, has possibilities for living and acting which are peculiarly relevant to itself. Man's choice makes the difference.

The meaning of history is the way in which man, caught in the push of process, answers his situation with regard to the relevant pull of purpose for the situation. History is a matter of concrete decisions of a given nature at a particular time. Obviously, most of history is living. It is the reaping of the results of previous decisions which are being lived out in various kinds of community. But living is the sustaining of decisions within a pattern of new decisions that flow into history. The religious meaning of history is the manner in which and the measure to which man answers the needs of his particular historic situation in terms of his ultimate concern.

The ultimate concern is conditioned by man's interpretation of religion and the response he makes within it. The thesis of this inquiry is that the meaning of history, seen in the light of God, is the finding of the fullest possible open and inclusive

226

community within the right relationship to God, in trust and right living. Right religion is the fullest possible directing and empowerment toward fulfilment of community, where each individual finds his own creative fulfilment as a person, and his own social fulfilment as spirit, within the fullest possible creative acceptance of, and intelligent allegiance to, the total community.

Our thesis runs further that community is the more satisfactory the more it is characterized by open and inclusive relations. Since God is love, man trusts him increasingly the more he accepts the concerned and co-operative society. Since man needs love, the more he is open to others and the more concerned creatively with them, the more he is fulfilled as a human being. The more, too, man lives in creative faith and in co-operative community the more fully he can make use of nature, and the better use he can make of it.

When, on the contrary, man refuses to be outgoing and responsibly concerned, he develops destructive tensions within himself and within his community. When groups, through lack of trust and care, become invidious within themselves and antagonistic outside themselves, they develop internal frustrations and external conflicts. In a world where man is dependent upon nature and competitively involved in its employment, fear and hostility become indigenous to human history. History accumulates patterns of fear and hostility, reflected supremely in war as an institution, from family blood feuds to tribal warfare to international carnage. The more, however, man can recognize with realism his historic heritage, with all its structures of antagonisms and all its accumulated associations of hostility, and also with all the complex behaviour motivations and behaviours of invidiousness and overagainstness even within so-called normal and even friendly associations, the more he can seek out and avail himself of the relevant kind of religion that seeks to destroy, or at least to tame and harness, these drives and to provide instead patterns and powers for creative and co-operative living. Religion both reflects and offers to change man's kind of community. The truest religion is at the least the one that most fully understands and acknowledges man's actual nature and historic situation, and provides the most relevant form for finding the kind of relation to reality that helps man the most both to cope with his drives and historic situation and to experience the creative release that comes from the fulfilment of faith within genuineness of community. With this analysis as our thesis, and remembering the complexity of both human history and human nature, we shall advance to discuss the pull of purpose.

The pull of purpose in human history operates in all dimensions of life, with some accuracy classified as physical, social and spiritual. Within both the total and the specific historic matrices these distinguishable dimensions coincide in one basic reality. But just as plurality of numbers is more than mere appearance, even so diversity of manifestation is more than appearance of function. Thus, for instance, we may use the family as our concrete occasion for discussing the pull of purpose on the physical level, while obviously the family participates in all the other levels of historic life as well. Even the pull of purpose as a whole in its unifying and universalizing operation cannot be sharply and definitely separated from the push of process based on need. Man's deepest need as creature is for God, and God, being love, exerts unifying and universalizing attraction. Need from below and from above, or from behind and from before, or from without in and from within out, are basically the same in the ultimate purpose and at one within the person and the community in their serving the same final purpose of fulfilment. The family illustrates signally this fact of unity in diversity where both are real and significant.

The family is a good example of the pull of purpose in its intimate relation to the push of process. From one side of its nature, the family depends upon the physical drive of sex. It exists to perpetuate the race. It is also an economic unit wherein through most of man's history women and children have been provided for. Similarly it illustrates man's need-driven gregariousness on the social level, as well as his need-drawn opportunity for love on the self-giving level. Certainly, too, family religion has within it varying proportions of exclusiveness and invidiousness, as well as the power to transcend the limited and the local. But when these facts pertaining to man's natural filling of the extensive modes with what is less and other than the pull of purpose as regards family life have been duly recognized, there can be no question, in any case, that family life exhibits the most intensive forms generally of human togetherness. The provision of these forms may, for the most part, be within the extensive modes of the push of process, but the filling of them, in any case, is by definition within the intensive forms, and offers exceptional opportunity for love to arise. No matter how basically need-driven the family as a unit may be, in other words, it is peculiarly open to the lure of love. Leaving out romantic ideals of marriage as prevalent in the West, the fact remains that family life not only calls for, but engenders, the love that leads beyond self whether to mate or to child, whether to parents or to siblings.

Mother love may not be inevitable but it is natural. Father love may often be neglected, distorted or frustrated, but out-going, self-giving father love is a genuine experience. Brothers and sisters may be envious and quarrel, but both within and above such relations genuine affection and concern flourish, rooting not primarily in the satisfaction of self but in the needs of the other. Whatever the subconscious struggles may be and however cynical the interpreter, those who have experienced such love as recipients, bestowers, or intimate observers cannot deny the facts. Driven together within the needs of human nature, too primitive and racial to be reduced to rational motivation, historic man nevertheless begins to experience something of the outgoing love of God at the mother's breast and in the father's arms. The family circle, to be historically effective, must provide love as well as bread. When family life is undermined, social life in all dimensions suffers.

When religion is strong it has a hearth in family life. In their depth conscious as well as in their social habits, children, in the over-all picture, are strongly affected by their original family experience. The promptings of love may possibly become frustrated or fulfilled, far beyond usual estimation long before the child awakens to explicit rational or moral choices. Besides the push of sex and of the economic-social arrangement in family life, is the pull of love, of longing for wholeness of life as unity and as inclusiveness, and of the urge to give and to forgive, to sacrifice and to help. When the push is accepted and authentically lived within a love received and reinforced from the Source and Standard of family life, the intensive and intimate modes of family life can both exhibit exceptionally the pull of purpose and become effective in the generation of the unity and inclusiveness which society in general needs.

The pull of purpose we have illustrated on the physical level by means of the family, where drives of sex and economic and social needs can be transformed by the common pull of co-operative concern, to the point where the most concrete aspects of the physical push can become the most concrete examples of the pull of purpose. Certainly society, as a whole, illustrates peculiarly the hard facts of competition and destructive conflict. Are not most social and economic arrangements the minimum necessities for social life, rather than the expression of any outgoing good-will? Have we not considered selfishness so flagrant and obvious in so-called secular social and political life that to use this dimension of historic existence as an example of the pull of purpose seems sheer idealism? Nevertheless we do so because social life could not go on at all if it rested entirely or even basically on selfishness. The bare negative cannot carry such a load. All the negative facts of corruption and crime, of deception and lust, of distortion and evasion, as well as the successful contention through law and sanctions with such evils, are possible only because we take man's positive nature for granted. Man not only needs society and responds to this need in terms of gregarious behaviour; man is also a social creature with an innate feeling for humanity at the depths of his drives. At the primitive level of self-assertion and group push there is also a still more primitive reality of social cohesiveness and feeling for solidarity.

Herd morality roots not only in common need for protection or aggression. It roots even more in what is common to the human herd: human nature. Man is made in God's image, which is never individualistic, but basically corporate. Conscience is based on more than convenience. Its urge to right is God's claim on man, which is always a call to community. Thus man's expanding extensive modes, due to the push of process, have always been matched by an inner longing for wholeness, which expresses his corporate nature as man. Individual man is real in time and space, and groups have their actuality in history, but both individuals and groups owe their deepest nature to their being part of all humanity, and members together of the whole historic process. It seems to be within the will of God for the common and eventual good that persons become genuinely themselves, and that community be effected through long struggle and conflict as well as through co-operation and experience of unifying and universalizing community.

Through all the depths and lengths of the historic process we see man driven by the push of process, urged on to possess nature and to conquer whatever stands in his way, including his fellowman, but offered also within this struggle relevant pulls of purpose. All human communities have been the outcome of the way in which men, caught in concrete pushes of the process, have answered the relevant pull of purpose in terms of conflict or co-operation, of destructive struggle or fulfilling community. The choices have been ambiguous, both because of man's previous history in which he is caught, what some call the reality of 'original sin', and because of man's sinful as well as finite nature. The actual choices offered in nature have also often made constructive solution well nigh impossible. Therefore history is what it is. It must be pictured in its gruesome actuality beyond and below most people's capacity to imagine.

From descriptive history can come no direct evidence for God as sovereign love. The God of history, as seen up to this point, is not worthy of worship, whatever power may be ascribed to him as dynamic force of life. But history stands, and up to now goes on, including new levels of development, especially in general inclusiveness as well as preposterously creative technological advance. The reason is that man, deep down, has a tough endowment of corporate humanity and that within the wide stretches of ordinary history there are the commonplace planes of constructive community living. The pull of man's humanity is God's long-range purpose, which, if it is true, can only be seen as beckoning historic man with the measureless future of God's intention in creation, in this life and beyond it. No mere philosophy of history will do. It will necessarily cut off the guiding threads and stand shorn of effective perspective. Only a theology of history, engendered by creative faith, can afford to submit its vision of history to the critical reason. The critical reason, in turn, can only criticize the consistency of the interpretation and its correspondence, as a beginning and in transit, to the facts of history in its crudest incipient forms of life and formulation. We turn, therefore, to the pull of purpose as it is best exhibited on its own distinctive level, the spiritual.

Religious interpretations vary. The nature of spirit is to make for unity and universality. Therefore the permanent problem of religion is the struggle with self. Perennially the self, moved from within, strives to get beyond self, even to lose self. Religions may modify, or be the expression of, group needs. But the restless selves cannot rest within religions. Prophets within the group reach beyond it, drawn by the spirit. Created spirit may become demonic and frustrate outreach; but since, at innermost, it is related to God as Spirit, when it is distorted, spirit fails to fulfil. Instead it becomes destructive within and without.

In high religion, on the contrary, the pull of purpose has led to the aspiration to universality. The universality may be the Creator God of Second Isaiah. It may be the Sovereign Love of Christianity. It may be the inscrutable will of Allah. It may be the impersonal absolute of Brahman. It may be the absolutely unknown not of this world, negatively or positively, of primitive Buddhism. The pull of purpose refuses to heed, as finally real and right, the push of the process. For every situation within the process the pull of purpose offers some relevant ideal, which is felt to be judgment from within the pressures and fears of man's response within the extensive modes. Man is inclined to previous ways of looking at the situation and of choosing concerning it. But the pull counters with ever fuller measures of unity and universality. It calls for co-operative modes of behaviour, and for concern instead of conflict and general group-centredness.

232

'The fullness of time', to use a Christian phrase, shows the meaning of history, namely to find the creatively unified and universal community. The centre of history is the open and universal community where all are concerned with each one and each one with all, at least in inner attitude and relevant outer action. Christ is then the centre of history, not as some pious phrase or some limited symbol for in-group loyalty, but as the symbol, at least conclusively expressed in human history, of the maximum kind of love which is the power for the fullest possible community. The pull of purpose, at its end expansion, is the will of God for the maximum good of all men. In history such a pull could not be seen concretely except as a quality of life and a kind of teaching. With reference to groups, it could be seen only as an ideal and as a partial actualization within the ambiguities of historic existence. But the eventual and inner history of man could thus be clarified and anticipated. This pull could then work as the standard for God's will, applicable by creative faith to the varying concrete events of history.

Different ages have different choices. In our present day, perhaps, the question of transcending nationalism and finding worldwide co-operation is man's most pressing choice. The push of process carries emotional attachments to nations far beyond effective national and moral control. Hence fear and hate blind men to true vision and bind them to a destructive past. Man's extensive modes of community in trade and government, in travel and education, have gained world-wide dimensions. The obvious call now, accordingly, is for some form of world law and world rule. Man needs to tame the destructive powers which have gained world-wide effectiveness. His situation is admittedly critical. The pull of purpose is always for a corporate community commensurate with the extensive modes. To advocate such proposal for world community, for instance, which alone is true wisdom, wherein man chooses concerning the pull of purpose with respect to the concrete push of the process, seems dangerous idealism and treacherous lack of patriotism.

But the way man chooses between the push of the process and the pull of God's purpose determines his destiny. Religion is thus sheer realism at its authentic best. The universality and the unity of the spirit of man at its corporate depths in God are man's best guide, aid and hope. Since fear is best relaxed and conquered by love, and since trust is the surest motivation of concern, the meaning of satisfactory historic existence centres in the genuineness and sufficiency of man's religion. Reason in religion is no mere abstract discussion of meaning, or of testing meaning by fact. It is the confronting of a concrete situation with the evaluative use of reason in the wholeness of interpretation of man's experience. Reason in religion involves existential choices. Reason in religion can generate courage and hope. Rightly used, it can make saving fact; wrongly used, it can find a destructive destiny for man.

In the same way, man has to decide concerning property. The crisis of our age is the crisis of the distribution of property. The masses have risen to self-consciousness during the last few decades as never before, demanding their share of the world's material good. The powerful rich can no longer take main monopoly for granted. Similarly, the underdeveloped nations of the world are waking to a strong drive to possess their lands and to find the level of living of the more advanced nations. Along with distribution and the releasing of the fullest possible consumers' power, looms the problem of releasing artificial checks on the economic systems and of freeing them from the production of an undue measure of negative goods, like production for war.

Perhaps our central problems are how to combine freedom with security—political, social and economic—within any actual or proposed economic order. The push of process has inescapably set the problem before mankind on a worldwide scale. How man answers this inescapable push in terms of the pull of purpose, which calls for the fullest concern and freedom for all, determines, more than we can imagine, man's actual future history. Co-operative and concerned living is no formula for church community alone. It is God's creative call to man in all dimensions of togetherness.

Race, too, is an area where the pull of purpose calls far down to man's subconscious depths of heritage. Past patterns and prejudices persist within the racial drives, as deep as man's un-fathomable mouldings in the crucible of historic existence. The factors entering in are countless and intermixed beyond separa-tion. Only idealism takes the problem lightly. But the extensive modes of togetherness and man's past response to them in terms of fear and hate are accessible to his basic corporateness as a human being. The power of the pull of purpose when it becomes livingly relevant through a religious prophet by means of religious community is beyond calculation. Law and economic need, plus intelligent education, can combine to hold back the drives for division in outer society, but, for the creative fulfilment of community, the whole man and the com-munity in their dimension of depth are needed. The problem of race is increasingly a world problem.

Thus the extensive modes of community expanded by the push of process play a fuller part than if the problem lacked this more far-reaching proportion. The universality and the unity of the pull of purpose, the inclusive and open community under God, are both necessary conditions for the successful solution of the racial problem. Man stands in a new urgency of decision beyond mere rational and moral resolves. He stands in need of the empowerment of the inner resources of religion in their full interrelation with the realities and powers more than ordinary experience that can help and harm man. Man finds meaning in history basically in the kind of community for which he decides. The meaning created by his decisions is possible because satisfactory community comes by discovery of man's genuine nature as he finds the full dimensions of his own being.

Chapter XIV

Nature and the Problem of Evil

History is the confluence of man's decisions within his natural development. To discuss history without nature is deleterious abstraction. Nature is the womb of history. History takes its rise from within the developments of nature. When history is born, nature becomes its body. It is as easy to understand man without a body as to understand history without nature. Nature helps to give birth to history, but when history is born the relationship becomes like spirit and body in human life. History depends upon the push of the process, the progress in technological and organizational matters engendering expanding modes of human community, while history also uses nature according to man's decisions concerning the pull of purpose. Thus history and nature belong together inextricably in earthly life, just as do body and spirit in man. We have already discussed the role history plays in this collaboration. We turn now to the part taken by nature in the same drama. We shall discuss nature's role in history under four headings: development, dependence, destruction and death.

Development characterizes one part that nature plays in its role of supporting history. It is wrong to cut the history of nature from the history of man. Even before man was created on earth, however long ago and however gradually, nature was developing the conditions for life. Inorganic and organic evolution are presupposed by human life, both for its coming to be and for its continuance. To discuss human history apart from the total process of nature, is like discussing fish without water. The development of fish can be understood only in terms of and with regard to the properties of water. The development of man can be interpreted only with reference to its formation in the womb of nature. The existence of man throughout history is possible only because man is made, carried and sustained with the natural processes of the body. The long ages of human growth, particularly before civilization began, are presuppositional for human history.

Humanity is a process and a product. The process of creation became in one area the product of human beings. But that product, although independently real, is not independent of the process. Man still participates in the natural processes out of which he came, not only through embryological recapitulation, but also through continuous dependence on the processes of nature which constitute the continuum of his life. From the point of view of the Christian tradition, this fact of man's being both product and process in the present as well as the product of process in the past can be summarized and symbolized by the statements that God made man from the dust of the earth, but did so on the last day of creation. Man is the culmination of both the natural and animal creation, and remains part of it. Therefore neither historic good nor evil can be properly understood except in close relation to natural good and evil, while conversely natural good and evil find their meaning only with reference to history. Development characterizes both nature and history, but development and history alike begin in nature, and nature always remains to undergird all historic development.

Nature in this sense of development constitutes the condition for history. History is a matter of human living requiring decisions, either of taking new directions or of continuing chosen courses. Nature is the condition for human freedom. Man can make choices which are truly his own and which are nonetheless responsible. When decisions are made, they refer to man's life in the body and in nature, personally and socially. Thus man uses his freedom within the conditions of nature and receives answer from nature according to the use of his freedom. He uses or abuses his body. Nature answers. He utilizes to good ends, or wastes or uses to wrong ends, nature's resources, and nature gives its proper reply. Both memory and ink are part of nature; memory has more than mere nature to it, while ink can preserve quite objectively man's past decisions. The weakest ink may outlast the strongest memory and a calculating machine is more accurate than a person. Thus nature undergirds history. Nature works in all instances, making response to man's freedom. The present meets the past through nature. Therefore man can learn with a real degree of freedom. Through memory and judgment man can know that he made a decision and that he is responsible for the result. He can therefore learn self-objectification, and through such self-objectification can learn maturity.

Through development in nature God has made human history possible. Nature is the condition for human history. Human history depends upon natural history, past and present. It is product and process, coming from the prehuman past as process and product. Nature, by making man face the consequences of his own choices, is the condition for freedom. Freedom is the prerequisite for genuine self-being. Freedom is the pre-supposition for community. Nature is thus the womb and nourisher of human freedom. The development of man in nature is the development of human freedom. To be human is to be free. To be human is to be responsible for freedom. To be human is to learn through freedom.

To be human is therefore to develop through freedom. Often interpreters have classified man's life in nature as the life of bondage, and man's life in history as the life of freedom. Such interpretations cut athwart the basic fact of the interrelation between nature and history. The purpose of the total continuum, in accordance with our main perspective, is the development of community. But community presupposes real persons. Persons become real through freedom. Freedom is real only on account of man's opportunity to learn from the consequences of his choices. The chance thus to learn is provided by nature. Therefore nature is the condition for human history abetting human freedom. Freedom finds its main locus in history, but the tangible results of choices become objectified in nature, posing for man always the problem of the consequences of his choices and the further and correct use of his freedom.

God wants man to be free. Freedom is not real apart from serious choice. Risk alone makes freedom vital. Particularly is this true of the use of freedom within learning. Not only by observing externally but by becoming existentially involved in the pleasures and pains of the consequences of his choices does man learn by living. Man is made for satisfaction. His deepest nature calls for fulfilment. Man suffers from frustration. Thus man learns from pain and opposition not only in the physical world, the world of nature, but also from inner frustration of purpose, the world of history. By the necessity of choosing, man learns that choice matters. By the meaning of his choices as reflected in their consequences, physical and social, does he learn to seek the life that fulfils. Learning through freedom is long and difficult, but real and vital. Man fears and flees freedom but is caught in it as a creature in nature and a participant in human history. Man also welcomes freedom as the opportunity for becoming a real self and for developing creative community. But fearing or welcoming man is forced to be free. The deepest urge of life is for fulfilment of freedom, which can come only through the community of concerned and inclusive love. God wants man to be free to become free. He has created him in nature that he might perfect history.

Freedom in nature is for the sake of providing man with an indirect relation to God. Nature is not only the condition for freedom; it is also the condition for God's control of freedom. If God controlled man directly man would not be free. Such would be the case even though God could induce in man the inner feeling of approval of his control of man's life. By whatever name, direct control is not freedom. But by providing man with the opportunity of making real choices and taking the consequences, God has given man the chance to learn for himself what kind of freedom he most deeply craves. Man's choices are real and he can and often does choose against his own real good. Choices would not be real unless they were risky. They would otherwise not really matter to man. They would lack vital meaning. Therefore God made man a creature in nature with limited hindsight and limited foresight. No man can see the total balance of his past choices. Man is no machine who can add up exact evaluations of past uses of freedom. Therefore he lacks in the powers of prediction for future conduct.

Emotionally as well as intellectually involved in his own past, he never in this life frees himself totally from his bondage to past evaluations of situations, while he also tends, for the sake of self-justification and needed self-esteem, to approve of what he has done in the past. Therefore man's vision from the past is not only finite but sinful.

Similarly man cannot see the total future. His vision of it is necessarily limited. The future, too, depends a great deal upon the choices of other people. In addition to these factors, man's own prejudices enter into his viewing the future to distort it. He is free, therefore, partly because of his ignorance. If man could always see correctly and with some degree of fullness what he has done in the past, and if he could always predict with accuracy the result of his future choices, he would choose only what is best for him. His very enlightened self-centricity would incline him toward the best possible choice. He would also see perfectly the penalty of his sin at the time of choosing, and his evil choices would thereby lose much of the attractiveness that comes from one's projecting a false evaluation into the future, or from concealing the gravity of the results from oneself at the time of choosing. While sin is not reducible to ignorance nor ignorance to sin, nevertheless man's freedom is incalculably dependent upon his ignorance of consequences because of both finitude and sin. Thus man's place in nature makes freedom real, and, through freedom, makes man real.

Nature is the condition for man's freedom, but it is also the condition for God's control of freedom. Controlled freedom, we have said, is no freedom if that control is direct. In so far as freedom is directly controlled it cannot be free. But indirectly controlled, freedom can yet be real. God can appeal to our reason and to our experience. By endowing us in the first place with a basic drive to fulfilment and making such fulfilment possible only within a community of love, God can appeal to our experience as we evaluate it through reason within our deepest drive toward fulfilment within a community of love. When we reach pain and frustration in our search for freedom within false fulfilments, we seek new and better goals. Thus as we keep experiencing frustrations and fulfilments, we can

240

choose among them and form our own conclusions as to what we fundamentally seek.

Pain and frustrations within certain kinds of experiences have different meanings and different evaluative responses. We can come to find that even pain and frustration within the search for, and partial findings of, open and concerned community can leave us more truly satisfied than the attaining of success and pleasure along lines less basic to our natures. Thus God poses the choices for us responsibly, where our natures are given, and where the conditions of freedom in nature and history are given. By certain free choices we may surrender freedom; by others we obtain it. Our evaluation in the depth response of our total reason can distinguish to some real extent between true and false frustration and true and false fulfilment. And always our nature drives us on, while another part of it draws us on toward fulfilment. Thus both with regard to man's nature and the nature of the environment, God has created set conditions for freedom, in terms of which he exercises indirect control of it. God has set man's freedom within responsible limits in accordance with what is good for man. Full freedom can be obtained only within free choices based on concrete experience of the community of creative concern, nourished by faith in the Source of freedom, which alone can satisfy man's nature as it is created by God.

Inasmuch as in this life there is only partial finding of such freedom, more by some and less by others, history cannot exhibit any conclusive demonstration of the purpose of God in creation. From the point of view of history, God is a failure. If sovereign love has created nature as the condition for man's finding freely through history the community for which he is made, that love has had only slight success. We can see the need for community; we can see how nature and history conspire toward community. But we can also see conflict and failure. Mostly we see mixed results where man finds only partial and partially satisfying community.

Such data confront us with a basic choice. We can use our creative reason to extend the scene of God's teaching process, or we can stop with whatever measure of meaning we do see.

To stop here is in effect to deny that our data is dynamic process wherein something of importance has happened up to now, and of late with incredibly accelerated speed. It is reasonable, in one way, not to go beyond the evidence at hand, but not to do so is to leave out of effective account the nature of the primary data. Or we can let creative faith extend the scene of God's work beyond this world and beyond this life. In this case, all the loose ends of history in its transgenerational accumulation of both meaning and problems reach out to find their meaning and solution within a fulfilling context which makes what we see ever more meaningful and urgent with hope.

Neither stopping with present partial meaning in process nor fulfilling it within its projection in God's total purpose gives us a probable conclusion. Reason cannot rest in either position. From one point of view, the carrying through of the indications of history demands faith far beyond vindication by the critical reason, but at least such reasoning is in line with the positive facts and through and through for man's good. Stopping the process where we are, merely to recognize its partial meaning and its staggering lack of success up to this point, demands less creative faith and is more in line with the critical reason on its negative side. On the positive side, however, even the critical reason will have to own that such stopping is arbitrarily abrupt, lacking in power of explanation for the powers of process and the workings of nature and history that we do see, and failing man as well in his need to make constructive choices for his life with regard to the meaning of nature and history. With this fact in mind, we turn now to discuss, beyond nature's part in the development of life and freedom, the way in which nature enters into man's development of community through his dependence and interdependence upon it.

Through man's common dependence on nature he develops community. Dependence on nature develops creative members of community. In order to live and to live better, man becomes resourceful in his use of nature. He takes initiative as he learns that the results of his work in it can be foreseen. Man becomes inventive. Not only necessity but concern for community can mother invention. Pressed by need and lured by luxury, man becomes more and more independent of nature the more and better he appropriates its resources. He also learns responsibility as he comes to understand that his own fortune and the welfare of the community depend upon his utilizing of nature. Thus, as we have seen in connection with the discussion of history, man's modes of community have grown in relation to his technological advance. God's use of nature in history, here too, is thus indirect as he prepares through it creative and responsible members of community.

God creates the community itself through its dependence on nature. Men have learned to co-operate as they have had need to learn skills from each other, to use each others' tools, to share each others' crops or products. Men come to need each others' help as they plan together against common dangers in nature, like storms and floods. When disaster strikes, they share each others' burdens and resources. In order to wring more good from nature they learn to plan creatively together. Men learn, as we have seen, to protect property, which is nature, by hiring special help for this purpose. The more complex civilization becomes, the greater also the division of labour. The greater the division of labour, the more men depend upon each other in order to keep going a society that is built increasingly on indirect relations to nature and on an ever refined interrelation among men. The more proficient man becomes in his mastery of nature through increased specializations of work, the less dependent on nature he feels, even though actually the more dependent he becomes.

Individuals may feel no direct dependence on nature, but the whole life of man is increasingly dependent upon its refined and intensified cultivation. Therefore the dependence becomes increasingly a matter of the community of man as a whole. As a matter of fact, the more nature is developed by community, the more man becomes dependent upon both nature and the total community of man. The lack of awareness of this fact in no way does away with its serious reality. In an atomic or post-atomic age, the dependence may become more remote, but all the more critical, since with staggering population increase, made possible through new ways of harnessing and releasing the energies of nature, the load nature has to carry is multiplied, and since, too, that load depends increasingly upon human responsibility and competence. When small bits of nature like neutron bombs may destroy man's life in nature, it is obvious that man is increasingly dependent upon those responsible for the use of nature. Nature can be used to set man free for creative community, or it can be used to set man back in conflict, destruction and want. The kind of community that man develops in nature because of his common dependence upon it therefore becomes of increasing importance.

We have thus discussed the part nature plays in history in terms of development and dependence. The two terms are not exclusive but correlative. Nevertheless each term stands for a distinctive emphasis. History depends upon the development of the conditions for and of life in nature that made the creation of humanity possible. Nature, we recall, is the womb of history. History arose as men learned to explore and to exploit nature. When within the processes of nature the product of humanity appeared, the processes of nature still persisted, as necessary to history as man's body is to his life. The development of history in nature was preceded by the development of history from nature. Even as we are to close with the discussion of death, we began with the discussion of the birth of history in nature. Nature has provided the condition for the coming to be of selves and communities. It has been the necessary condition for freedom through its offering of responsible choice. Man's choice has been real and risky because his vision has been limited both by his finitude in nature and by his sinful response to his dependence on it.

But God has not only made nature the condition for freedom; he has also made it the means of controlling freedom. Let us emphasize this point by expatiating. Man can be responsibly free because he is God's creature with a nature fixed in its need for fulfilment within a community of creative concern. By means of man's original endowment and by means of the kinds of experience that follow as consequences of his choices, God made it possible for man both to choose genuinely in nature, and yet to be within God's ultimate control. When man comes to himself, he comes to God's purpose for his life. When man finds full freedom, he finds it in the fulfilment that is the right relation to God and man, and the proper use of nature. Thus God created man both authentically free, according to man's measure of need, and yet also responsibly directed toward man's own eventual fulfilment through freedom.

Since God is sovereign love who bestowed freedom responsibly on his creatures, neither determinism nor unstructured freedom is a true option in the understanding of man's relation to God. God made nature in such a fashion that dependence upon its resources would bring out in man creative initiative and responsible concern. The more man develops nature, the more he seems to be independent of it, but the more as a total human community he is actually dependent upon it. Not only is there an irreplaceable division of labour that becomes a necessity for the increasing population in man's new dimensions of using nature, but man can now also be threatened over ever vaster areas because of his technological mastery of nature. Man is a bundle of need in nature under God. To forget this fact is dangerous. Man's dependence on nature has made him a worldwide community of need, met only by the complexity of the human community of interdependence.

We have now considered nature in relation to man with reference to development and dependence. We are not concerned with producing any full account of nature as such. Our task, rather, is to try to see whether the creative reason can find meaning in man's relation to nature. Such meaning can have both objective and subjective aspects. Such is the case with respect to the third term under which we now consider nature: destruction.

'The destruction that wasteth at noonday' needs no documentation. It is an overwhelming fact. Can this fact of destruction in any way be integrated with meaning in the total interpretation of experience? For one thing, destruction gives room for new growth or new work. The plants that die in autumn make room for the flowers that bud in the spring. The fire that sweeps the forest lets the saplings grow. Some animals, as life ebbs, are moved from within themselves to go off to die.

The improving of medical services in India has worsened the problem of over-population. What chance would future generations have if the old did not have to make room for the new?

Then, again, if manufactured goods did not wear out there would be little for man to do. Man needs useful work to give meaning to life, particularly as he grows into maturity. Few in this life reach the stage where friendship and purely creative activity can satisfy their need to know themselves as persons. Their meaning in life centres in being needed. Therefore constructive work is necessary to their well-being as persons. One side to destruction is the fact that things that are made have to be replaced as well as plants and persons. As a matter of fact, we are now facing the need for 'inbuilt obsolescence', not only to maintain markets but to maintain human dignity. We have 'benevolent conspiracies' to slow down work in order to provide wider employment. Automation threatens man's meaning in life unless man can answer the push of process in terms of a creative and mature pull of purpose. Thus destruction has meaning in terms of replacement.

Destruction in nature also has meaning in terms of the consequences that follow the sinful or irresponsible use of freedom. If a man hates and murders his fellowman, creation precludes his escaping the consequences of his hate. On the objective side, at least, the murderer has to face the natural consequences of his deed. In a fit of anger an author may put to the fire the only copy of a manuscript on which he has worked long and well. No tears will bring it back. Or a careless driver may wreck a new car. Such consequences of sin and irresponsibility represent the continuous destruction in nature which man must face. Collectively man faces the wasting of his natural resources or the incalculable destruction through war. Such destruction, however, need not be entirely evil. When sections around Saint Paul's Cathedral in London were blitzed, much of historic value and of aesthetic enjoyment were lost. But a new section can be raised, far better to live and work in than the one that was there before.

This context is not the proper one for the discussion of the problem of natural evil, but only for the consideration of meaning in nature. We do need to see, however, how deeply intermeshed are the consequences of man's evil in nature. In the above illustration, destructive and constructive results intermingle. Meaning is seldom one-dimensional. Nature abused makes possible nature restored or nature improved. The seriousness of life, both destructively and constructively, is contained within man's relation to nature. If painful consequences did not follow the abuse of the body, freedom would not be responsibly structured in such a way that we might learn from it. If sin did not objectify destruction, man could sin without coming face to face with its nature, especially in that indirect way in which God lets us have freedom in nature that we may learn for ourselves by means of the consequences of our actions. If careless choices were not followed in some way by hurtful results, freedom itself would be irresponsible in nature. Thus besides the meaning of replacement, destruction in nature also finds meaning in terms of the consequences which follow the misuse of freedom.

In addition to these two kinds of objective meanings of destruction in nature, there are at least two kinds of subjective meanings. The first is the eliciting of sympathy. If God means to develop community in history, objective togetherness is only the condition for it. Propinquity is invitation to community. Common dependence calls for mutual aid. Community itself, however, is born only through a human fellow feeling. Community requires more than helpfulness. Community demands the opening of persons to each other on the level of entering into each others' lives. Community requires sharing of selves, of spiritual participation. The peculiar thing about life is that nothing draws people closer together than suffering, at least until they are ripe for mature love. Not even nature can be understood in its relation to man except through human nature. Being sinful, we are naturally envious. Therefore, except as we are within the reality of God's common love for all by the power of the Spirit, our natural response to the success or joy of others is invidiousness. The success of others calls out in natural man self-reference and doleful comparison. Co-operation brings out strength of individuality and satis-

R

faction in collaboration. It achieves a certain experience of belonging together, of needing one another, and of common achievement.

But real congruence of spirit needs the deeper call of suffering and sorrow to strip us of the need and desire to puff ourselves up. In suffering we can share the other person's plight. In sorrow we can become one with the other on a level below the striving for self-sufficiency, let alone superiority. Destruction in nature brings suffering and sorrow. These, in turn, call for sympathy. Wherever human beings win the victory within themselves and become capable of experiencing sympathy, there community is being made. But community is the central meaning of history. The eliciting of community is history's central purpose. For this growing of community, we believe God created the world. Therefore destruction in nature should never be used to deny meaning in history. Such destruction illustrates profoundly the indirect way in which God works. Whether such suffering is necessary to sovereign love and whether nature illustrates an excess of suffering incompatible with such love are questions concerning evil that we shall have to face in terms of the critical reason before we leave this section. The one thing we must not do is to claim that destruction in nature is only negative evidence.

For the faith that makes love central to life, and that sees love exemplified at its highest in the kind of love that identifies itself with the people God has made, all the way to a suffering death in nature, it is altogether improper to use nature's destruction as an argument to show that there is no God. On the very contrary, creative reason centres its understanding of meaning in history and nature particularly in the way in which God has bestowed freedom on his creatures, in such a real manner that he does not force or coerce man's freedom, even for man's sake, but, rather, works indirectly in nature to evoke in man the love which can make mature response to God and relate itself maturely within persons in all their problems and sufferings, as well as in the creative and co-operative aspects of human community.

The fourth aspect under which we discuss the meaning of

nature in relation to man is insecurity. In previous writing I have called this aspect 'precariousness', saying that nature exhibits a balance of predictability and precariousness that seems to be the very condition for growing responsibility without self-seriousness, or dependability without self-sufficiency. In different terms we now affirm the same basic truth that insecurity in nature is the prerequisite for the development of community. If men could plan responsibly with no problem of nature within themselves in terms of health, and no problem of nature outside themselves in terms of unexpected destruction, they would need neither each other nor God. Then independence would be the greatest virtue. Responsible selfhood would be man's central need. Then, indeed, self-centricity could rest satisfied with self-protection and self-promotion. If there had been implanted in man an incurable desire for community, man could not, to be sure, then rest content in such self-attainment, however satisfying such achievement would be to his physical self. But he would be in a dilemma between external satisfaction and internal unrest, with no objective way leading from one to the other.

As it is, man has within him this incurable drive to community. Man is not man except as a social being. Life cannot satisfy except on social terms. As it is, the natural order serves the social. Man cannot remain secure in nature. He cannot predict with certainty that when he sows he will reap. He cannot plan and know that his plans will succeed no matter how much care he himself may take. The most careful driver on the road is at the mercy of his fellowman. The most self-protective person can be wiped out by an 'act of God'. The social importance of destruction in nature can be symbolized by the mammoth work of insurance or assurance companies. The fellow plight of human beings within an insecure nature drives them together in terms of need to meet nature's threat. It also draws them together in terms of a community of insecurity engendered by nature's precariousness.

The religious importance of nature's insecurity is, therefore, basic to its meaning. Nature threatens man with destruction. He needs realities and powers beyond ordinary experience to help him. The dentist can help nature's threat to our teeth, but finally nature will destroy the dentist's most skilful struggle against its decaying powers. For the insecurity in nature is consummated in death. Death is the final symbol of insecurity in nature. Unless we can see meaning in death, nature will eventually bury all meanings. It will bury forever not only all means for community and meaning in community; it will bury community itself. Therefore we come face to face with the fourth of the terms under which we are discussing meaning in nature in relation to religion.

Death is the destroyer. Destruction is partial death. If all and everything ultimate die, religion, as we have defined it, is wrong at its centre. We have to make up our mind about ultimates. Either we define death in terms of life, or we define life in terms of death. If life characterizes reality at its inmost self-being, death must have meaning in its terms. If death describes what is most real, life cannot have ultimate meaning. We have no right, to be sure, to make human death the final criterion of the ultimate nature of reality unless we are also willing to make humanity the final index of what is most real. If God is ultimate, God's living or dying is the final question of the nature of self-being. But the nature of God has definite implications for the destiny of creation. If God is the dramatist enjoying the play of human history, death might be of convenience to him. Beyond good and evil, he cares not for what the players feel or how they fare. In eternity God amuses himself with watching ever new players try an infinite number of combinations in carrying out their respective roles, to the constant relieving of his monotony.

In this view, there is no reason why man should be spared suffering, why justice should reign, or why anyone should succeed in life. Death is God's means of getting rid of players and of affecting other players. Man's role is to play the part assigned him for the time being. Or God can be concerned with his own glory and power. Nothing can then prove his power more than the might to condemn to eternal suffering those who have disobeyed him. His glory, in such a position, is represented by his rule over all, and by every kind of condition from

250

fullness of finite bliss to replete final agony. Under such conditions, to die from earthly life and to face the results of one's choices of life eternally can be understood as part of the wider pattern of human history within God's eternal plan. But all such theories make mockery of the kind of meaning that we have discussed, legitimately, we believe, in terms of which we have chosen our religious ultimate as the sovereign God of love concerned with effecting the fully open and inclusive community of creative concern and satisfactory life.

Closer to our view of God, and still affording explanatory power to accept human death as final, is the view that the living God is finite in power. He has then sufficient power to create, or at least to work in creation, but not enough finally to control it. God, within this view, meant the best for man when he created him, but he could not foresee man's abuse of freedom. Or God, from this stance, may not even have created man in a direct sense. God is himself part of the creative process of reality, struggling to make the most out of it, but with no ultimate power to control its final outcome. According to such views as these, death could spell the end of man while man's life could still find meaning in pleasing God, in helping him to create the conditions in terms of which he could help others the more, or in helping others by a direct participation in God's struggles on man's behalf. Death, within such views, is the fate of all men as creatures, but life nevertheless has ultimate meaning with relation to the realities and powers beyond ordinary experience which help and harm man.

Or death can be thought of as the means whereby the frustrated life of estrangement from God turns again back to its origin in God to rest in him beyond the pains of alienation in human history. Such a view sounds good and may lull us into a sentimental acceptance of it. Nevertheless death is now not seen in the light of the ultimate perspective. It is viewed only as an emotional response of time-weary man. On such a view nothing has been accomplished in human history or in nature, and therefore neither death nor life has reason for being. To be sure, the nature of ultimate reality may be such that the infinite cannot help creating. The original unity may be only one side of self-being, while the other is the striving for concreteness, which is the ground for tragedy both for God and man. Creation into nature and the construction of history are then the outflow from unity, while religion at its highest is God's striving ever to regain his lost unity and to find for himself the peace of perfect togetherness. Then death, indeed, has meaning to both God and man as the fulfilment of return, which is ever frustrated by the estrangement of the escape of the finite. God is then working through nature and history for his own unity and for the release from suffering of his own creation.

Both self-love and love for the finite can then characterize the experience of the suffering God, who yet knows, not only within history but beyond it, the joy both of original unity beyond the power of its total loss, and of struggling back toward unity and helping others to find release and complete being in him, as the finite creatures also participate in the joy of the struggle of return, in some instances even participating in the ecstasy of the unity that transcends the fragmentation of human experience and the limitations of finitude. Ecstasy in life and death might then have something of release and attainment in common. There is no denying that such an interpretation of experience can give meaning to death within a definitely religious orientation. At its best, indeed, it comes close to the kind of understanding that is in line with our own religious ultimate.

The basic questions as to the meaning of death in our interpretation of nature in relation to man is whether or not man merely participates, partakes and even contributes to God's life, or whether man actually has meaning in terms of a destiny of his own within the life of God. If something man does has meaning in the ultimate perspective, there is, as we saw, at least partial meaning in history. If something man is or does lasts beyond human history, caught up in some manner in eternity, human history, we recall, has more significance still. Particularly is this the case if the order of human history and nature contribute by their workings toward the eternal meaning and contribution of man. If man himself, however, has not only meaning, but being beyond human history, and if human history helps to create that meaning and shape that being, then human history has supreme meaning for man.

If death, in such a case, is not only a door between human history and man's life beyond human history, but also a means for history's transformation, then death in nature takes on a new dimension of meaning. If man is actually made different within the experience of death, so that death is an agent of history, the nature of death takes on critical significance within the ultimate perspective suggested by our analysis. If creative reason can, on solid ground, point to positive meaning in death, which without such positive meaning threatens ultimate meaning, it has, indeed, reached its supreme triumph.

Obviously, any such suggestion has to remain a faith indicated by the totality of what we know. It is beyond our powers to prove or disprove. And yet death is the basic fact that reason must meet or stand frustrated with regard to ultimates. I believe that a steady gaze at the significance of death in the light of man's total experience in history and nature will disclose that it has two meanings: it is a door and a means of transformation. Death is the destroyer. Within the purpose of infinite Love to make finite love perfect, through the experiences in history and nature, death, we shall find, is the kind of destruction that discloses the depth and patience of God's indirect work by means of man's freedom. Apart from the meaning that death holds, in any case, the Christian faith lies discredited and itself dead.

Our full perspective of God as sovereign love cannot countenance final meaninglessness. Death as total meaninglessness means nothing less than that. God is not a computing machine, a vast thinking mechanism co-ordinating the activities of the universe. Nor is God the magnification of man's struggles on some ultimate plane. God, as sovereign love, is neither unfeeling thought nor unresolved struggle. God, as sovereign love, must accomplish in and with creation a result commensurate with his intention. For God to create those with enough understanding to call him children only to let them suffer and die, along with whatever good life has brought, is an inadmissible supposition. If our ultimate is correct, therefore, death must have meaning beyond itself. Death has, in fact, meaning both as transition and as transformation.

Death, we have proposed, is a door. Death leads somewhere. We can call it a door only if there is real continuity between life on this side and on the other. Such continuity must characterize the person who goes from one room to another, and the conditions in both rooms must be of such a nature that the same person is preserved and able to develop there. The meaning of life must go on beyond life, if death is to have meaning in our full sense. Since we know knothing beyond death except by implication from our experience—apart from the resurrection of Jesus and whatever other experiences of similar kind there may be which we have no right to rule out arbitrarily—we must know what is beyond death mostly in terms of what is consistent with our ultimate perspective. Life beyond death is thus basically known through a faith judgment based on the totality of our experiential interpretation. Knowledge of life beyond death is, at its heart, based on our knowledge of this life.

Our best image of God comes from the kind of life we saw in Jesus in this world. Possibly we should put much more emphasis than we do on the rising of Jesus from the dead. The resurrection of Jesus was in line both with his life and with the kind of view of God we get through it. As history, we saw, the resurrection is at best probable. It is more probable still in the light of our understanding of God and the understanding of the integrity of the witnesses through the faith they confessed —a faith for which they were willing to die. In any case, however, it is from knowledge in this life, whether from life generally, or more especially from the life of Jesus, that we come to understand the meaning of death. No mere objective rising from the dead supplies us with the meaning of death. Whether from general implications of the nature of God, then, or from the resurrection of Jesus, we arrive at basic continuity between this life and the next.

Such continuity demands that death does not determine man's fate once for all. Such a teaching is both unjust to people and a denial of the meaning of God as love. People do not have equal chance in this life to prepare for life beyond; therefore any teaching that death settles man's fate once for all is grossly unfair to man and unworthy of God. The least that can be expected is that God will lead every man to the same opportunity to decide for life to come. People would then need the opportunity after death to reach sameness of chance for their eternal decision. But such equality of situation would at best be a matter of justice. It would fall immeasurably short of our ultimate of God as sovereign love. The God of sovereign love is by nature so fully concerned with each life, to perfect it, that the least that can be expected of him is that he keep on helping each life until in freedom it reach its own highest fruition.

If each life is continued beyond death until it becomes capable of being utterly fulfilled, and if each life, once fulfilled, would then be completely satisfied to give up its being into the hands of its creator, there would at least be fully inclusive meaning in eternity, involving maximum realization of meaning for each person as well. Justice would then be filled out by love. In such a case, death would be a transition from one kind of existence to another, with sufficient continuity to involve further growth in man toward God's purpose for him.

The question is then inevitable, however, why, in such a case, should the perfected life be done to death finally? The better the life, the more worthy it is to be preserved. The higher the life, the greater loss death becomes. If God is boundless in possibility, if death is release from the pedagogical needs of nature, why should we die after being perfected? If we are spirits, participating in God's kind of being beyond objectification, there is no problem of time and space. Why should we fall prey at last to the lure of the grave of the undifferentiated, if the least that love can accomplish to be sovereign is the perfect fulfilment of each life? Although on this side of death we cannot know what God has in store for us in eternity, sovereign love can be trusted to provide such fulfilment, as the more it is attained, the more its continuance is desired. Perhaps our fullest surmise may be that God will perfect eventually, within cosmic history, all the lives he has created, in such a way that no life can be fulfilled until all reach their destiny in God. Beyond such cosmic history lies eternity; and what that can mean must surely, for us, remain the mystery of God.

Death, however, is not only a transition but also a transformation. Continuity is necessary for sameness of being. The person is the same person before and after death. But surely the same person will also be radically changed. Basic continuity is subject to discontinuity. Death is not only a door, but a door into a new room with different kinds of conditions. The continuity is enough for sameness to obtain, but basic sameness will know unimaginable transformation. Death is not only the means of obtaining freedom from our kind of nature. It is also the shock of our kind of freedom which helps to set us free from the conditions of our nature. Death is God's shock treatment whereby he delivers us from all our false self-securities. In this life, our freedom is real enough and safe enough to allow us to find freedom, even from God, in terms of the securities we build up for ourselves, either within ourselves or in terms of external protection from the insecurities of life.

We take care of our health by doctors and medicines, we guard ourselves from hunger and want by bank accounts, we protect ourselves from being outside human community by the friendships we make and the positions we hold. We work diligently to make ourselves as secure and as satisfied in this life as we can. We then proceed to forget about God or to interpret him to our liking. Or we struggle to be on good terms with God by what we are, do and give, while still putting first, as practical people, the tangible securities by which we believe we can live. But death levels all such securities. It takes a complete toll of them all. Death cuts us loose from all securities in history and nature, and makes us face life anew before God in the kinds of conditions that he will provide for us.

Death, then, means transformation of life both through the shock of being deprived of our usual securities, and through the facing of new conditions of existence. We cannot know whether we are to be reborn into another kind of space-time existence or into some unimaginably new situation. Spirit is not basically dependent on space-time. Spirit in other lives may be free of our kinds of objectification. We may be born successively onto other planets under conditions entirely hidden from us now, for God can have countless planets and countless kinds of planets for our use, or we may be born into conditions of existence, by whatever name, beyond any imagining that God has in store for our endless future. Even our kind of time may last only through a certain stage of pedagogical purpose. What we are saying is that enough continuity will remain to make further growth meaningful while enough discontinuity will obtain to make death from this life meaningful.

For this reason, we cannot accept reincarnation as an adequate doctrine. In reincarnation not enough of the person remains to make growth a meaningful category. On the personal level, certainly, enough memory must characterise personality to make such personless rebirth into another life in this world, as pictured by the doctrine of reincarnation, waste motion. We cannot rule out such a possibility entirely unless we hold that life must be reborn in the same form as that in which it died. But then we believe that in the teaching of reincarnation there is not sufficient discontinuity either. In reincarnation death is mostly transition and not enough transformation. It seems more adequate to think of life beyond death as beyond our earthly bounds. The magnificence of God as creator invites us to think of more basic fulfilment, or more radical frustration of our failing stubbornness in making this life ultimate in the first place. Faith in reincarnation, especially in its modern Western optimistic form, seems indeed to be still another form of trying to make this kind of life ultimate. It seems a faithless clinging to the securities of our space-time conditions. It is a refusal, perhaps, to face God's larger invitation, even in this life, to become radically transformed beyond the conditions of this life. The Eastern form of reincarnation is mostly accompanied by fear of the weary cycle of life, at least according to interpreters, but certainly even in the Eastern experience there must surely be strong dominance of the present life along with elements of self-justification on the part of the fortunate and hoping for such fortune on the part of the rest.

Probably the most consistent way to approach this problem

of death is to believe that the person as a whole dies, but is reborn by God. Whatever of the person belongs basically to the pedagogical situation of earthly life will be done away. Whatever belongs to God will remain. Each person is spirit. He is related to God as spirit. There is an earthly spirit, and there is an eternal personal spirit. Spirit is man's inmost nature as capacity for God. Whatever of permanent significance man's personal spirit has taken into itself remains after death to be used by God in the life or lives to come. Whatever belongs merely to this life is left behind. It is difficult for us to envisage different kinds of permanence and of perishability from what we now know, but there obviously is truth in Hinduism's understanding that life goes on beyond death in accordance with its deserts here. We are born again into some kind of existence perpetuating this one.

Rather than accept reincarnation, let alone transmigration, however, we take for our model of life after death the biblical picture of the risen Jesus. He was the same person, yet under new conditions, and hardly recognizable except as a spirit even by the disciples who had known him most intimately. At that, he reappeared under the conditions of this earthly life sufficiently to communicate within it. Earthly death should lead to some such perpetuation and transformation. We may, of course, die and be reborn countless times in eternity with innumerable kinds of conditions for further growth and glory. Eternity is the generator of endless time. God need be in no hurry. If God is sovereign love who wants to share his own creative eternity, we cannot know more, in any case, than the most primitive beginnings of eternal life even from our best understanding and most creative imagination beyond that.

What we have been saying is that death is both transition and transformation. Enough sameness persists to make creation accumulative, to make justice real, and to make love triumphant beyond all justice. But also enough newness must surely be part of God's creative purpose to make life an endless appropriation of God's endless resources of creative community. In such a case death is a consummation. It finishes one kind of existence to make ready for the next. However much in part we may see, we see no true part unless we see at the centre the creative reality and richness of God, who has promised eternal life by his own faithfulness in nature, and by his own incoming in human history in a kind of life and a kind of community that are open, inclusive and unconditional in their resources. Such is the vision of creative faith, a vision man cannot sustain except he be inspirited by God.

We have then reached the summit of meaning in the discussion of death. History and nature witness together to a kind of community in the making. Our creative reason has been allowed to soar in its seeing of life in the light of the larger purpose and the longer future. Having established the main lines of our faith, can we, however, give genuine weight to the critical reason within our main perspective? Must the critical reason always write *nihil obstat* once we have allowed the creative reason to organize experience in its light? To answer this question we turn now from our creative construction of history and nature to consider in terms of the critical reason the problems of evil in history and nature, and the weighing of our findings in the light of our total seeing. How far is our interpretation due to faith and how far to fact? How much right do we have to call what we have done in this section 'knowledge'? Only the considered, if not necessarily correct, answer to this question of knowledge will finally count for our investigation of reason in religion.

The critical reason raises three strong objections to the interpretation we have advanced, namely that the totality of human experience is best understood in terms of a sovereign God of love. The first of the three main objections is the fact that God took too long time with creation before he created man, and that he started at too low a beginning. Why should billions of years have elapsed before God got down to creating man? Why should he have begun with the inorganic, then brought life into being at levels practically indistinguishable from non-life, and then waited for the long ages before he even began to create animoid life? Besides, why should a sovereign God have made seeming mistakes in the evolutionary process? Some species have perished, to be no more. Evolution seems to have made false starts. From within our presupposition there seems to be no need for subhuman life at all. It seems hardly consistent with sovereign love to make animals for man to kill and to eat. Hunting may be a joy to man, but hardly to the prey. Should the creature of sovereign love, for that matter, enjoy hunting and killing instead of helping and curing? When critical reason looks at man's actual appearance in the total history of the cosmos, and when it takes a close view of the man whom God has made, it raises serious objections to thinking that creation is the work of the sovereign God of love.

What can the creative reason answer? It had better be both honest and humble. It seems that God could have begun creating on the level of man with a proper environment to perfect community and still have preserved man's full freedom. It will not do to reduce the total cosmic process to an exclusively man-centred pedagogy. This contention even the creative reason should admit. We can, to be sure, accept the fact of the unimaginable ages of preparation, and wonder at the patience and care of God's preparatory work. We can say that God began purposefully at the very opposite of his own burning life and intensive consciousness, with non-life having only a potential 'within' to be developed with all deliberateness on the part of the creator. We can claim that all life is accumulative. None of it, it may be believed, is ever wasted. We can affirm that every life is passed on at death to some other form of life, until life, as a totally steady stream, rises to the point where God can impart to it the individuation of self-consciousness and potentiality therewith for eternal life.

In such a case, even though forms of evolution perish, life itself does not perish and the results of learning do not disappear from the earth. We can then learn from science the long history of God's care, whereby he made the earth itself for life, and then promoted the sensitivizing process of noogenesis until the 'within' of matter could think, plan and become the free participant of the process of mental and spiritual evolution. An expert scientist like Teilhard de Chardin, can, indeed, grow eloquent over the several stages of evolution whereby

God prepared for the final break-through of man into the midst of cosmic history.

Creative reason can thus produce a plausible account of the low and long beginnings in the creation of man, based on the facts of the case and not without serious meaningfulness; but when all is said and done, this is factual thinking making the best of a situation. The critical reason still has the right to maintain that such a start is both wasteful of time and indifferent to pain. Unless animal life has meaning in its own right, for instance, there seems to be no reason to infer its creation from our main presupposition, while there may be good ground for contending that it should not have been created. We might possibly say that animals do not suffer because they have no consciousness of our kind, or that on the whole they experience more pleasure than pain. But we cannot know with certainty that either statement is true. Some believe that neither statement can be affirmed as a positive universal. But beyond all such questions, the fact seems obvious that a sovereign God of love could have created the animal world with no possibility of experiencing pain. In spite of strong advice to the contrary, I believe that animals do in fact suffer, even though perhaps not in our way or kind of suffering.

If it is then said that the experience of pain is protectively necessary, the question remains why the world should be such that the animals should be threatened and need pain to learn how to survive. If the point is further made that each life, although not surviving in its own form, will be fulfilled within the total stream of life in its eventual self-realization, through evolution or through life beyond the evolutionary process, we have to ask ourselves if, in the light of our main presupposition, such a long and painful process seems necessary and justified. And why not maintain, in such a case, that man, too, can be similarly fulfilled within the result of the whole process of life, without the need of any personal participation in the end result?

If we aver that the reason man should be exceptional in surviving is that he differs from the animals, and even more from all non-life, in his self-consciousness and moral and

261

spiritual capacity, may it not be that in the light of coming forms of evolution higher than man, the same argument might be even more convincing as to the present undeveloped nature of man, that can be fulfilled in the totality of the life process? Thus the argument still persists. The critical reason has grounds for objecting that a sovereign God, aiming at a community of concern created in freedom, could and should have begun at a higher level. If then, even man's present life should not be deemed high enough to merit perpetuation, even within its transformation, the argument of the critical reason could be sharpened to pose the problem whether God could not have begun at an even higher level than with man's creation. Could he not have begun at least on the level of Jesus' special background and kind of endowment? The total interpreter, listening to both the creative and the critical reason, can own that both have some soundness in their contention, but that the critical reason at this point has the stronger case. With regard to this problem we shall simply have to admit that the cosmic process, although it can be interpreted in the light of God's purpose in the creation of man, nevertheless, cannot readily be reduced to this purpose. On this point there remain both a partial negation of the interpretation produced by the creative reason and an unsolved mystery.

The critical reason can prefer to think of some primeval force creatively fighting and finding its way, making mistakes in so doing, and trembling even now on the brink of possible failure in its achievement in humanity. The creative reason can reply that such an answer begs the whole question as to where the purpose and the power have come from in the first place, whether the best we know can come arbitrarily from out of the vast womb of nothingness, with respect to every level of development beyond the previous attainment of process, and why there should have been such an incommensurate shifting of creative gears in terms of the production of meaning within the last few cosmic seconds. Thus the negative caution of the critical reason is balanced by its own counter-argument, leaving us both caution and mystery, and yet both within the need for a faith large and genuine enough for interpretation of a process as yet hardly begun, according to its own indications, and for direction of constructive life and civilization. At the end of this section we shall have to weigh the total, and present as true a case as we can in the light of the total evidence as far as we can see on behalf of the dynamic tension within which the creative reason must necessarily work.

The second main objection the critical reason has to offer is that the process exhibits an excess of evil. Nature need not be so destructive as it is, claims the critical reason, and man need not be so brutal as he is in order to learn love in freedom. A sovereign God of love, aiming at the creation of a free and concerned community, zestful with creative adventure, should certainly not have needed to make a world where life devours life, where the cat not only eats the mouse but teases and tortures it first, where human beings not only destroy each other but exhibit undreamed-of depths of sadism century after century. Why, if God be both good and powerful, wise and holy, should human history, let alone nature, be such a record of evil? Why should man incline to self so stubbornly that even after he has learned that satisfaction comes only from living within a community of faith and concern, he nevertheless seems caught and doomed within the prison house of his own drives? Why, at least, when man is finally ready to own God's way, both in heart and in mind, does not God fulfil him as an example of the good life and an inspiration to others? Why should the fulfilled life be almost a mockery to those who seek it with constant dedication and who stand ready, at that, to alternate between trying their hardest or completely letting go of self-will and self-effort?

Again, the critical reason commands respect for its caution to creative faith. We know no full answer to its objection. From our perspective at least, and from within our stage of experience, it does seem reasonable that God could have made nature less destructive and man with a far stronger drive to others, to righteousness and to peace. The creative reason, of course, has already found meaning within such seemingly negative considerations as dependence, destruction and death. We shall not here repeat the arguments, or even review their

s

main line of attacking these problems. We saw that they are indeed the main instruments of God's creating community with freedom.

When we have readily admitted this fact, however, we have to own that we can see no proper proportion between specific learning and specific experience of evil. Some are helped, it seems, by such experience and some are hurt; some learn from it and some become hardened because of it. Nor is there any balancing of the scales before people die. People of seventy and eighty still murder each other. Some of the best-living people, as far as we can tell, die young and suffering. Why some families should have idiots born to them while others who seem less deserving have all the strong, healthy children they want is a mystery. If this life is the end of any human life, there obviously can be no solution of the problem of evil worthy of the name. Thus we are left with the inscrutable problem of excess evil and what seems a faulty distribution of it as well.

The creative reason, of course, has its own reply. If God is truly sovereign and if this process is but the beginning, it is presumptuous for us to prescribe the measure of evil which is most effective. We are not God to see the far future. We cannot even observe the inner result of any experience. And who are we to determine the distribution of trials in the learning process? Can we know the long past of any individual before he becomes the man he is? Can we see the total result of his life on the life of others? Do we dare to assess how he himself is affected in eternity by his earthly experience? If life, furthermore, is social in nature, who can tell how any person fits into the total picture of God's work with man? Do we have a right to isolate any man from God's total purpose before his birth, during his life and after his death?

If the highest understanding of the creative process in its aiming at community, furthermore, focuses in love, is not sacrificial self-giving the key to what seems aimless destruction? May not even life's living on life be a symbol of the fact that no life lives for itself alone? At the very fabric of life is the participation of life in life, even to the point of external physical incorporation of other life by the living on it. May not such taking and giving of life by life point to the ultimate oneness of life, which is the goal of life, whether through conflict or co-operation, whether through destruction or development?

To the critical reason these arguments are not empty. They carry some power of conviction. Nevertheless the critical reason must insist that we have in this case a good deal of argument from ignorance as well as no sufficient meeting of the original charge. To be sure, man cannot know the will of God in its full reaches or in its particular application. Such argument to ignorance contains some truth. But if we are to argue at all we must think as men. Faith may venture to hold a position where none better can be had. Such faith, however, cannot command the critical reason to admit that it has full right to hold it in the light of our best interpretation of experience as a whole. Therefore the critical reason must caution creative faith at this point.

Unless there is a more probable faith, its task stops at this point; but critical reason must perform its task boldly and assiduously up to this point. In so doing, it will point out that much of the argument of the creative reason to the inscrutable nature of God's will is from ignorance rather than from accessible data. As such, the argument is legitimate, granting the presupposition with none better available, but it is also weak. Besides, the creative reason has not answered the basic objection of the critical reason that although such evil as destruction and death have meaning for the creation of community, nevertheless they seem in excess of what such a God and such a community seem to require. Granting the main meanings that the creative reason rightly found in dependence, destruction and death, nevertheless the interpreter torn between the creative and the critical reason, must frankly face the fact that reason has no adequate answer to the charge that evil is excessive and faultily distributed.

At this point, faith has no right to coerce the critical reason for the sake of unity of believing and seeing. The believer must consequently make some choice for knowing and living that of necessity contains within it both light and darkness. In this kind of world we can see no way that faith and knowledge can come together without tension. And yet, we have claimed, we must keep them as far as possible together for the sake of wholeness of life and constructiveness of civilization. We can let go neither honesty nor concern. We must, consequently, leave this objection, as well as the first one, for the final summation of reason in religion in its bearing on history and nature.

Only one main question remains: can reason in its interpretation of religion use legitimately the category of 'the compossible'? The compossible is the category of necessary relationship which the theologians are prone to use in their justification of evil, as for instance, to use a complex and therefore ample illustration: If there is to be love, there have to be genuine personal beings; if personality is to be real it must be free; if there is to be freedom there has to be risk; if risk is to be real there have to be bad choices with hurtful consequences; if man is to understand what freedom means for himself he must make bad choices; in order for man to make bad choices there must be ignorance; but for man to make bad choices only out of ignorance leaves the will still untouched; therefore for man to become willing to live in a community of concern from within his own self, through learning, he must desire to make bad choices as well as to be ignorant of them, and come to desire through his own experience to make good choices instead, and willingly and appreciatively to live the good life.

Or because of the importance of the usage of the compossible by theologians, let us take other examples. If God is love, he will not manufacture children but train them in freedom. In his humility God gave man sufficient freedom to go on revolting against his will, to distort his revelation, and to harm himself. Since freedom cannot be forced to love, but only won to love, God had to identify himself with man in his lostness and sin, and, by sharing man's suffering, win man to himself and lead him to his own true fulfilment. Thus love and suffering are compossibles. Learning freedom and riskful choices are also compossibles. The redemption of faithless freedom and suffering love are compossibles.

One more example. For God to create responsibly is so to weight human nature both toward immediate satisfaction centring in self, and toward eventual good centring in God, that man might first become a genuine self through freedom and then be fulfilled by love. In order to control the process in between, God needed to answer bad choices with evil consequences, especially indirectly through man's life in nature; but in order to keep man a total community and to break up man's natural individualism, God needed an order in which the consequences were distributed generally and where vicarious good and vicarious evil, working together from opposite sides, would help men to find their social natures under God. Therefore a sovereign God of love is a concept consistent with natural evil, such as destruction and precariousness.

We have deliberately lingered on these examples of the compossible, for this reason: unless reason can legitimately use this category, we can see no adequate way in which reason can deal with religion, assuming, of course, that the interpreter is both competent and honest with all the facts. The position has, indeed, been taken that the God who can effect the same result eventually without the need of any painful process is in principle greater than one who has to depend upon such partial and evil means. For a sovereign God of love the means must be as good as the ends, it is held; the ends never justify the means. What can the creative reason say to this charge? If we admit that we cannot begin with a theoretical world speculatively, but within the actual world we know, have we not already made the actual world the basis and even criterion of ultimate knowledge? At least this world, in such a case, lays down the conditions within which the ultimate must work.

Certainly it is true that we have to interpret from within our own knowledge situation. We have to begin with the fact of a created, finite world. To begin with an indiscriminate infinite where 'anything does' is no solution. We have seen that, in one view, the infinite can never become related to the finite without being limited by it, in which case, we found, such an infinite cannot even be, since the infinite having by definition to be everywhere must accordingly be in touch with any and every finite, which is contrary to the original definition of the infinite. We have called such a view of the infinite 'the Illicit Infinite'.

But there are other illicit infinites! To suggest that a sovereign God of love must by presupposition be a hedonist is in effect to exchange the God of love for hedonism as ultimate. 'Good means' is then defined not as appropriate to the end as understood in terms of the ultimate, but, rather, as incapable of suffering and of any kind of deficiency. What really has happened, then, is that we have accepted some such proposition as the following: perfection and pain are completely incompatible. Since God is perfect, therefore, and this world has pain, he cannot have created it—how easy it is to follow such argument! It also appeals to one part of us existentially at a very deep level. To be sure, to wish to avoid pain is natural for man, and therefore to refuse to believe that a perfect God can be responsible for pain is altogether understandable.

But hedonism has now become ultimate, and not the God of love. If love as ultimate chooses to create persons and community in faith and freedom as its prime goals, pain can indeed be a good means. It is the appropriate means, the best means we know, as we have shown, to the end. The further inquiry remains, of course, whether pain can also be part of the perfect world when it is completed. Can there be pain in the perfected community? This poses the problem of the compossible in its two basic parts. To the theoretical affirmation that a sovereign God of love should be able to achieve the result of creation with perfect means in the hedonistic sense, the answer is clear. Such a charge has already accepted as ultimate good the total absence of pain and of all partial and painful means, however good and appropriate they may be to the best ends we can conceive. We grant freely, however, that we are not thinking in a vacuum or in pure speculation. We are interpreting the world we know. If the same result could be obtained without any evil, and if we have to try to explain the nature of our existence, this kind of creation seems either the result of bungling or of sadism.

Perhaps, in such a case, description of experience in its totality is all we can legitimately undertake along with such prescription for life as can come from evaluative interpretation of our ordinary experience. As it is, we start with the actual world of human experience and cosmic process, and interpret its data within a creative faith judgment which takes as its lead line the creation of meaning and goodness, as directive for life from the past toward the future, and as the truest indication of life and process. The best we can do is to present a pattern from within what we know. Within such knowledge, persons cannot multiply by mere fission and God cannot split off children like an amoeba. We feel, too, that this pattern offers the best conceivable kind of human fulfilment, the potential solution to our human problems and to the evils of nature. From within the highest of human experience, love and pain are not contradictories. In the depths of experience they can be seen as supporting factors in process but not in product.

But our solution requires both faith and concern, whereas theoretical hedonism in its ultimate demand for love, does away with all the heights and depths of love. As a matter of fact, it makes love a meaningless term. Such is the choice we are offered: the denial of the compossible as a legitimate category for reason in religion, and the dismissal therewith of whatever central light on experience and process we have seen; or else the acceptance of the fact that once we have identified and chosen our ultimate in the light of our best interpretation of the totality of experience, we have to see all things resolutely in its light. There can be no mixing of ultimates. A finite God, for instance, is such a mixture of ultimates, between goodness and power, and between ultimate reality and temporal fact; it presents no ultimate beyond others that can synthesize them.

The second main problem with regard to the compossible is this: have we actually presented a tenable ultimate in the light of the kind of compossible we have ourselves proposed? If we grant that evil can be means but never end, or that a perfect world cannot in the end, or as a product, contain any evil, have we not with such an admission also marked our own position a failure? We cannot entirely deny this allegation. The problem is simple. If in eternity God created only this world, the arbitrariness of the act is beyond sturdy faith to accept. In such a position, certainly, the creature has created the Creator! In such a view, God is surely a doctrine due to rationalization. But if God creates out of nature, sharing his fullness in all eternity, will there not always be a world in process, at least some new creation in prospect, where love will have to suffer, and where all who love will have to be involved in such suffering? If God is by nature creator because he is love, can there ever be full and final consummation?

There are, of course, partial answers to this contention, which is nearly lethal to our thinking, but they may not suffice as adequate replies. Therefore the critical reason may after all prevail over the creative. One partial answer is that God is not in time, and that, therefore, the problems of time begin and end with time. Creation is simply a free act of love in time which may never be legitimately generalized. Eternity is not intrinsically affected by time. We have dismissed such a view as arbitrary and cannot rest content with it. Why should eternity ever choose to create time just once, and if it did so, is creation more than a bagatelle? In this view, creation is not the serious work of a sovereign God of love.

Another attempt to solve this ultimate mystery is to claim that God's love knows nothing of our kind of hedonism, that indeed perfect love glories in creative and redemptive suffering, and that perfect love when suffering, lacks all the evils and imperfections that we experience. Therefore as we become perfected in love we shall ourselves be able to share God's joy in suffering and become worthy, by his grace, to share in the responsibilities of creation. Thus our ultimate can accept suffering both as love's perfection in self giving and as pedagogically necessary to the learning of love in freedom. All we can say is that our best experiences confirm this contention, and that we can see the truth of it with our minds as well, but even so we must leave this question open.

For us the slowness of natural creation and its low beginnings in comparison with human history, and the final meaning and place of cosmic process in eternity, no matter how much meaning the creative reason may suggest, will stand out as profound mysteries. They are the given data for reason to interpret, but the ultimate 'why' eludes us. The critical reason in the last instance refuses to bow to any creative vision that we have seen yet. The meaning of faith, however suggestive and in many respects convincing, is at last swallowed up in the mystery of faith. Therefore we have to choose beyond any full agreement between the creative and the critical reason as to what we are to believe and do. We must relate ourselves to the world process and to human history. We are forced to be free. Our freedom cannot be forfeited, but only used or abused. Therefore we turn to the final summary of the extent to which we judge that history and nature can give us knowledge of realities and powers beyond our ordinary experience that can help and harm man. Can history and nature in the last analysis give us religious knowledge?

Our considered answer is definite and short: No. From history and nature, rightly interpreted, we can conceive and believe God, but we cannot know him. The reason we cannot know God is simple: the problems of history are never answered in history. Does our negative answer, then, involve the changing of our conclusions for the first two main sections? The reply to this query is equally definite and brief: No. Such seemingly contradictory answers call for a fuller elucidation of our conclusion.

If we look at history and nature alone we see no full answers in terms of human life, and *a fortiori* in terms of God. *Coram hominibus* or *coram deo*, history and nature, in themselves and by themselves, have no answers. But not only that! If history and nature are all, we can see conclusively that there can be no answers commensurate with either the fulfilment of human meaning or the perfect intention of divine purpose. Obviously we are not concerned with the interpretation of history in scientific terms. History by nature is no science and can never be handled adequately as a science. A science can control its data, make rather precise generalizations that can be tested and from which predictions can be made. History can have no such equivalence of events because history cannot be recalled, to be put under controlled conditions and tested. But more than that, it is not a natural subject like geology or astronomy that lends

271

itself in ample measure to scientific pursuits. Without idealizing scientific method and the possibilities for its actual application to date, there is such a realm as the natural which lends itself exceptionally to measurement and to checking on results, within publicly accessible areas of experience. History is no such subject.

History combines within itself the forces that shape it, from nature and its own past, and the freedoms that make it in relation to those forces. History is neither merely the scene of determined data nor the stage of dramatic choices. It is the total continuum of countless choices and counter-choices concerning natural conditions and historic situations. Therefore history can be neither natural science nor biography. It can be neither merely the story of sociological factors nor merely the story of men. Historic method, at the least, must accept such minimum conditions for its proper operation. If, on the level of mere fact, history remains unorganized activity needing at least minimum selection and shaping to become meaningful at all, how much context must be introduced to write any history of meaning within history! A common human nature, a common cosmic process, increasing intercommunication, and intensified interdependence can combine to give us some such meaning as we have traced in terms of extensive and intensive modes of community.

In such analysis we take account of both the shaping factors of nature and the choosing factors of humanity. We have found facts of history interrelated with nature that cannot be denied. Our facts are standard data generally acceptable. Our proposal, however, that open, inclusive and concerned community is the potential answer to fulfilment of meaning in history, naturally contains a value judgment, but one which claims to represent the deepest drive of history itself, and to speak to man at the depths of his life. Such a claim cannot be proved, but it can be put forward as an hypothesis that has been discovered from careful observation of the historic process and of human life.

But even if we grant that such an hypothesis commends itself to both the creative and the critical reason, as a drive and condition of history wherein history itself is made, there can nevertheless be no solution within history precisely in terms of the hypothesis which we have offered. History buries all human community as far as its participants go. Therefore there can be no answer within history. A creator concerned with history as community as such, with no regard for its concrete participants, would be unworthy of and unequal to the best we see in history. Therefore there can be no answer to history outside history, either, in terms of realities and powers beyond ordinary experience apart from the consummation of history itself. But neither history nor nature gives or can give, according to our knowledge of them, any such consummation.

On the contrary, we know that nature and history decidedly deny such consummation within itself. Any final arrival of community at the expense of all who made it possible is a goal in itself as unworthy as that of a God who delights in the consummation at the expense of its concrete participants. Seen alone, history and nature cut off the facts that point beyond history. We can say either that we cannot know the fulfilment beyond history, which is correct evaluative description of process, or that nature and history prove that there is no fulfilment, which is a naturalistic faith judgment. In neither case does history provide knowledge of God based on history.

If, moreover, we take the meaning of history as we have proposed it, and understand God to be the creator of nature and the guide of history, we can conceive and believe him, but we can have no knowledge of him. If history is taken in the aggregate sense, without organization around the focus of its most intensive meaning with the greatest power for universalization, the life of Jesus, then even his death and resurrection become only isolated, unexplained incidents, showing the strange power of nature and history to produce the noble with the cruel, the high and wide view of life along with the sordid and the narrow. From history as a whole taken aggregatively, then, there can be no knowledge of God and no reason for conceiving or believing him. There seems to be no authentic meaning.

But from history organized around the focus of its highest attainment in terms of its deepest drive, the love of Jesus and the drive to community, there emerges meaning universally potential and applicable both to illumine and to explain life, even if this meaning cannot be particularized concretely. But such meaning is not only largely unrealized in history but frustrated by death. Therefore there can be no dependable reasoning from it if reason is limited to the scope of history and nature. Consequently we have given our definite and short answer to the question whether God can be known from history and nature. The answer is No.

We can, accordingly, find no adequate philosophy of history, since history cannot by its own nature answer its own questions. What I have proposed, instead, is that there can be a theology of history. In this case, history is seen resolutely not in its own terms, but within the perspective of its highest attainment or emergence. God is not seen in the light of history, but history is seen in the light of God. The knowledge of God, we have suggested, stems basically from our knowledge of the highest kind of life and community we know, but cannot be tested except as a potential by life and community in general. Such knowledge, rather, is vision receiving context from a concrete instance, and reinforced by such instances as approximate this normative meaning for life and community.

The knowledge we claim is based on the principle of sufficient explanation of the arrival of the whole creative process and the producing of this kind of life. It is also founded on the fact that this kind of love is man's deepest need, and the vision of how creation and history seem to conspire toward the creation of wider community that increasingly needs the open, inclusive and concerned dimensions for its successful attainment. God as the ground and the goal of creation and history are thus suggested by such a vision. In line with and through such interpretation, men testify that they have been grasped and changed by this reality and power beyond ordinary human experience. Faith can accordingly generate creative reason to organize, evaluate and direct experience according to such an ultimate presupposition whom we have called God. The kind of understanding of nature and history which we have assayed has assumed this context and found answering meaning. What is the status of this knowledge of God up to this point of our investigation?

Can anyone claim such loose assertions of general interpretation, of subjective vision, and of partial experience to be knowledge in the strict sense of ordinary empirical or rational knowledge? No matter how fallible and fugitive all other forms of knowledge may also be, particularly when concrete events and life are involved, they are yet more worthy to be called knowledge than any and all claims of religion. We shall not tire of stressing this basic and obvious fact. Nevertheless we maintain that there is religious knowledge.

Religion, we recall, is the interpretation of the ultimate meanings of the cosmic process as a whole, and of nature, history and life within it. Such interpretation is inescapable by the fact that we must organize, evaluate and direct life with reference to the totality of our experience. The choice is, therefore, between the blind acceptance of some traditional faith, the arbitrary following of some untested faith claim, possibly with the honest belief or the escapist relief that no knowledge of ultimates is possible anyway, on the one hand; and, on the other hand, the open, patient, and as far as possible, competent weighing of candidates for our ultimate allegiance in thought and life. Such open and careful use of whatever material can be interpreted we call knowledge.

The second choice may be more difficult and painful than that of unexamined tradition or blind choice, but it is the only one that leads to increasing clarification of what can be known and what cannot. What we are saying is that, although our final stance must be a choice of faith through lack of conclusive evidence, nevertheless it should be the most deliberate as well as committed choice ossible. This is to say that in the use of reason the religious interpreter must necessarily rely mostly on the creative reason, the organ of faith, but he must not, on that account, in any way belittle the critical reason or fail to use it as competently as possible in whatever manner it can be used.

Our finding, so far, is that God as love, the creator and sustainer of nature and history, who purposes fulfilment in community, is a truer lead in the understanding of nature and history than any other that we have found. But even this claim is contingent upon a certain kind of faith judgment. It cannot be true unless God is immeasurably beyond what we now know, and unless eternity overwhelms time. We cannot accept the idea that God is love unless we see nature and history within unimaginable reaches of God's pedagogical process, which in this earthly life has no more than its feeble, first start. If so, all of nature and history are only roughly related to this central fact of God's purpose in the long ages, sidereally immeasurable in our terms. Therefore we see only fragments and fractions, not the whole process in its majestic fullness. In order for reason to find fulfilment of its vision, we must, therefore, go on from all attempts at philosophies of history to theologies of history, based mostly on faith's creative seeing beyond history.

The only other choice that seems open to us is to believe that some mysterious power fumbles for meaning in history, pushing and pulling it to its present attainment. Such a view would account for the failures of nature and history, and be congenial to their possibly imminent destruction at the hands of man; but it would not adequately account for the long growth of creation, and most certainly would not explain the sudden upward surge in the creation of meaning within the last few cosmic seconds. Agnosticism concerning the meaning of history, moreover, may be honest, but never integrates history and nature within any examined ultimate, whereas the ultimate that the agnostic actually lives by in effect determines what view of nature and history he in fact holds. On the whole, therefore, even the critical reason must own that if a choice has to be made, the choice for the most relevant and explanatory theology of history is in significant measure in line with reason as well as with constructive faith.

Pragmatic attestation must be used with great care. Nevertheless, it is of genuine significance that the ultimate that we find in the life of Christ, as well as in his teaching, death and resurrection, is of such a nature that the more it is believed and lived the more man and society are helped. Since man's deepest need and fullest satisfaction come within the creative acceptance of a community of integrity and concern, open and inclusive, and sustained within the meaning and power of faith, the more the nature of the ultimate is accepted and lived, the better life becomes. The more man trusts and accepts the will of God in his concern for all men, the more history is transformed in fulfilling directions, and the better nature becomes used for the common good. Such a God ought to be real even if he were not! Since our most careful findings point along such lines, we cannot but help man in his deepest need for evaluation, interpretation and direction of life when we make a reasoned faith judgment of acceptance of the God of creative concern.

Thus the creative reason has our final word. The critical reason must keep insisting that history and nature cannot give us the knowledge of God. But the critical reason should also own that the meaning we have actually proposed as facts of history and of nature—their making for community based on choice of content but not of circumstance, of extensive situation but not of intensive modes—gives more meaning to total history than any other we know. Both history and nature are therefore best seen, as they are in themselves, when their deepest drive and highest meaning are seen from beyond themselves.

I, therefore, stand by both our answers: history and nature by themselves cannot give us knowledge of God; we can conceive of and believe God, but not know him from within the processes of history, for knowledge of his nature and ways depends upon our seeing the meaning of history completed beyond history. On the other hand, such a denial of knowledge of God in history and nature does not deny that, in the dimension of the ultimate, we can have the best knowledge available to interpret and guide life in terms of the kind of life Jesus lived and recommended. We do not claim that such knowledge is identifiable with ordinary kinds of knowledge, but only that it is far preferable to accept it within the limits of its possibilities than to rely on mere authoritarian tradition or on arbitrary choice. If in this sense of knowledge, the light of open, inclusive and concerned love is our best candidate for ultimate allegiance, reason should also admit that although

277

nature and history do not give us knowledge of God, the push of process and the pull of purpose, in their interrelations with nature, are in line with the nature and purpose of God. Therefore even though reason in religion cannot claim the knowledge of God through its examination of history and nature in themselves, nevertheless it is persuaded that the more knowledge is lifted into the dimension of the realities and powers beyond ordinary experience, the more history and nature are seen, as well, within their own fullest meaning and destiny.

Thus we are left with the ambiguity of history and nature, as such, not giving us knowledge of God, while, nevertheless, history and nature, seen in the light of our fullest presupposition beyond themselves, help to attest the legitimacy of that presupposition. This is all the more true since the whole purpose of God, as we see it, is to perfect a community of love through history by means of his indirect work in nature. But the earthly scene is not long-lasting enough, even though serious enough, to do more than begin man's transformation in history. Human history only begins on earth.

With respect to our not having and yet gaining knowledge of God through history and nature, there is yet one final consideration to recall. Knowledge of ultimates, we remember, is from within the whole self with respect to concrete choices in life, history and nature. Therefore it can never be the kind of knowledge that either science or philosophy handles. Religious knowledge is always within man's full involvement; it is never either merely thing-knowledge or merely thought-knowledge. Therefore even conceiving of God is different within the dimension of decision and of concrete living. Religious knowledge, in its inmost sense, is thus different from theological knowledge, which comes closer to philosophy in that it is, after all, objectification. Unless such objective knowledge is possible in science, in philosophy and in theology, communicable interpretation both for the sake of knowing in itself and for the direction of life and history is impossible.

We decided in our first main section that such knowledge is possible. But we must never forget that it is the cold, *post-factum* attempt to recapture the full dynamic situation, especially

278

in theology, which deals basically not with thing-knowledge nor with thought-knowledge, but with the knowledge of spirit, with 'the within' of reality, with living meaningfulness at the centre of history and in our relating ourselves to nature.

Thus in affirming that we can conceive and believe God from within history, but not know him, we may even have used far too many non-religious models and standards for knowing. Within history, we obviously cannot know God in his full nature and purpose, as indicated by the highest self-revelation and made knowable only by the completion of the purpose of history and nature in eternity. We can come to know God, in this sense, only as we ourselves find fulfilment through transformation. Faith, seeing in the light of the life of Christ, can project its meaning on the screen of eternity and glimpse something of what the fuller vision may be. Yet such faith is still secondary, 'speculative' seeing in the light of the creative reason, and not the existential knowledge of God's presence and will, which come only within life and history. Thus, in one sense, no knowledge of God is as real as the existential, while, in another, the existential is too far compromised by being in the midst of the struggle to give us the vision of God beyond history and at the completion of the transformation of history.

The God of theology, on the one hand, can easily become, and already all too much is, the encrustation of dogma based on fear and on the dead past. The God of religion, on the other hand, can easily become limited, in our existential understanding, to the scope of our struggle, and be framed within its dimensions. God is God both of eternity and of history. This fact constitutes a major problem for religious knowledge. Knowledge of God needs both creative thought, consistent ever with the fullest vision of him in accordance to the truest revelation in history, and also the creative reason which struggles within the frustrations of actual history. Only when the two are dynamically combined within the total self and within the living community can we speak of effective knowledge of God.

Freely we acknowledge that in the usual sense of knowledge, religious knowledge, particularly in history and nature, is weak and weary while, on the other hand, it is particularly

T   279

within such weakness and despair of full seeing that faith grows strong in its resolute identification with the will of God in life and history. Such identification of spirit with Spirit alone can provide the first-hand vision and experience, engendering creative faith that can convince the critical reason not to shirk its proper task of checking and challenging, but to co-operate in concerned conflict. Religious knowledge in history and nature is borrowed knowledge. History and nature cannot provide it primarily, but they can find it when they are put in living contact with the Christ as the fully inclusive and concerned life of God in human history.

PART IV

Reason and World Religions

Chapter XV

Can we Establish rational Relations among Religions?

One of the main objections to ascribing objective, universal nature to religious knowledge is the fact of many basically differing world religions. What can the creative reason do with this stubborn fact? Can it evaluate and organize it in such a way that the critical reason can judge its solution of the problem both honest and competent?

Our plan of attack is first to analyse the main possible relationship among the religions. At these we must look both straight and steadily. To be sure, we must not disregard our previous findings. We work within a given perspective. Seen in its light, do the differing religions offer resistance or support to our main thesis, namely that the nature of religion consists in powers and realities beyond ordinary experience that can help and harm man, and that these powers and realities at heart are constituted by Universal Concern creative of an open, inclusive and co-operative community? Our inquiry into the relation between history and nature in the light of the ultimate perspective has already resulted in our seeing the development of such a universal community of creative concern as the key to the workings of both history and nature. Does our thesis also draw into a unifying pattern the developments and inter-relations of the religions of the world?

Theoretically it is possible to suggest that one religion alone is true. All others are then false. But such a claim disregards the actual problem itself. The problem is how there can be objective, universal religious knowledge in view of the fact of the many basically differing religions. If one religion alone is true, there is no such category as religion in general. In such a case, there can be no appeal to general experience.

283

Every claim to uniqueness on the part of a religion is necessarily esoteric. Such a claim debars the possibility of reason's finding universal, objective religious knowledge.

But cannot one religion first discover and release the universal objective nature of religion? If this nature has been discovered by man, or revealed to man, must it not have entered history at a particular time in a particular form? Why, then, call the claim to uniqueness on the part of a particular religion esoteric? Could not the acceptance of such a discovery or revelation by man in general, moreover, take a long time? Both these affirmations are true as far as they go, but they do not go far enough. Any special break-through of such understanding of the objective, universal nature of religion involves in its general relevance as the potential, or deepest truth, of all the other religions. Therefore, although the special truth, to be sure, needs general acceptance, it exists already for such general acceptance by all the other religions, which themselves exist at their deepest drive only because of their participation in this universal, objective nature of religious reality. They may, in fact, be false religions. They may result from misdirected religious desire rather than from basic religious need. They may have so sprung from fear and fleeing of God that they, in fact, misrepresent true religion. Therefore they may not point toward the true nature of religion, but on the contrary give misleading evidence as to the nature of religion. Thus one religion could alone be true, even though all other religions, at their original drives, would nevertheless be related to it.

All such considerations, however, are of no real importance. A deep enough, thorough enough, and comprehensive enough investigation of the facts will then reveal what is genuinely religious and what is the ignorant use or wilful abuse of the religious drive. If any religion is true in the sense of universal, objective nature, it must necessarily be true for all men. My own interpretation comes out of history, but must submit to the test of universal relevance for humanity as a whole and for man as man. Therefore it must face up to the facts of other widely differing world religions.

For three reasons, my own perspective as well as all candidates for the universal, objective interpretation of religion, cannot evade such a test: (1) the ultimate must be related to all proximates; (2) religion is based on basic human need common to all human beings; (3) the deepest meanings of history and of nature have to do with a common human experience. The stages of development or of acceptance may vary considerably, but the fundamental reality of religion must be at least potentially related to all religions. Such a relation may then be either correcting or fulfilling, or most likely a matter of both. We shall, therefore, devote no more space to a position that by its own claim forfeits universal, objective knowledge and consequently evades our fundamental problem: in view of the many basically differing religions, how can there be unity of religious truth?

A second position holds that there is a rationally ascertainable nature of religion that becomes expressed in all religions, and yet is never fully attained by any of them. This view is the 'liberal' or essentialist position. This stance uses the ultimate nature of truth and the highest use of reason together as insurance that a true and normative religion can indeed be found. The ultimate unity of truth and reason's natural allegiance to it makes it possible to hold that there is one God and one right religion, although we may fail fully to find it, to agree concerning it, and to practise it. There may be many answers to its nature, but a frequent approach to 'the essence' of all religions is in terms of love, reason and experience.

Within this viewpoint it may, furthermore, never be necessary to have one actual universal religion, and thus do away with the concrete and creative differentiations of history; but all religious people should learn empathy and co-operation. They should fight irrationality and unworthy doctrines and practices by means of science and education, philosophy and high religion. The best way to grow in any religion, therefore, is to study the other religions, to be eager to learn from them, to rethink one's own faith continually, and to be ever ready for new creative experiences and understandings, as these may result both from creative contacts with other religions and from a fresh and fearless re-evaluation of one's own. No religion is then alone true, for truth alone gives religious meaning and power constructively to any religion. But neither are all religions equally true, and beyond rational and moral comparison. Religions do differ within themselves and among themselves, but they all have to give allegiance to truth and right in such a way that some may have to be radically repudiated or transformed. In fact, as man in history matures, and education becomes general not only in knowledge but in attitude, there may spring forth some religion-for-one-world that releases both what is commonly true in religion and what is historically different and enriching.

Is not such a liberal position so thoroughly in line with both the spirit and the findings of our search up to now that we ought simply to adopt it as our own? The position is, of course, conglomerate to begin with, since it is composed of the attitudes and views of a number of liberal and concerned thinkers. Obviously it contains much truth from many angles. The problems connected with it, nevertheless, are many. The definition of religion is far too intellectualistic. It is not sufficiently historical. Reason is assumed to be the handmaid of a good heart. The depth of sin never oppresses this kind of interpretation. Reason in religion is treated apart from rationalization in religion. Men are assumed to seek God and to want to find common reality in religion. The good-hearted interpreters in their good intentions seldom see fear's compulsive fleeing from the Creator or hate's depth-repudiation of the Saviour God. Instead, immaturity and ignorance are considered the strongest opponents of rational and effective religion. Science and education are accepted without depth scrutiny as friends of rational religion. Nor are the stubbornness of historic overagainstness and the at-homeness in a group through ingroup animosity treated as weighty problems. Therefore there is not enough relation between such high-minded interpretation and the ugly images of historic religions.

We have, therefore, to repudiate a highly attractive interpretation of the relation of the world religions. Would we could hold it! Religions, however, have always been mostly man's interpretation of the ultimate and man's living of this relation to the ultimate. Most of religious interpretation has, therefore, reflected man's actual nature as sinner, both seeking and fleeing God, both trying to love him even while far more fearing and hating him. Man has sought adjustment to the terror of the unknown, safety from evil forces threatening him, ways of finding satisfaction in life without incurring guilt, even when such satisfactions have been basically self-centred or collectively group-centred, and ways of being forgiven and right with the world in its deepest dimensions without having to repent too radically and to reform too drastically. With such main drives at the centre of the concrete religions, on the part of most worshippers and functionaries, no amount of comparing or co-working can arrive at true religion as man's right relation to God. Man's deepest relation and longing is for God; but the depth dimension in man is usually so undeveloped, so obscured, and so lengthily buried under guilt repression that, all in all, what really drives the great masses of religious men is the urge for self-protection and self-promotion. Accordingly, love, reason and experience consequent to such motivations are not the dominant realities in concrete religions in terms of which they can be interpreted and steered toward effective, if not unity, at least constructive co-operation.

Another main contention as to the relation of religion and the religions is that since religions differ basically among themselves they can provide no consensus as to universal, objective religious knowledge. Perhaps all are equally true since all are relative. Religious pluralism may preclude establishable religious knowledge of a common nature and inclusive importance. Such a charge aims straight at the heart of our conclusions up to this point. If it is true, whether we are deceived or deceiving, we are left with generalized, limited data. If such be the case, there is no universal, objective religious knowledge, even in our existential approach to it as the choice of faith for whatever content of experience can best organize, evaluate and direct the totality of experience.

The supporters of this position offer three main reasons:

(1) Eternity itself involves religious relativity. Since there is no way in which any finite can ever reach the infinite, or

no way in which time-conditioned existence can ever attain unconditioned eternity, and since the realities and powers of religion are on the side of eternity, not human history, no relative degree of nearness or distance has determinate meaning for the nature of religion. No relative content of religious confession or practice can ever constitute the ground for universal, objective knowledge of the nature and truth of religion itself.

(2) All religions involve specific historic conditions that make them integral wholes beyond rational comparison. Religions are not theoretical truths that can be intellectually examined in rational categories, but the concrete products of man's particular response within specific historic contexts. Because of such historic specificity as well as because of their relation to eternity, religions are at their inmost reality incommensurate.

(3) No common core of religion, as such, has been isolated that can adequately serve as the reliable basis of comparison. Religions are so diverse in development and expression that there is no congruent area of nature or truth, within them or outside them, that can be used in the rational discussion of their interrelation. If such a basis for comparison were there, it certainly would have been found by now. All attempts up to the present have either presupposed the truth of one of the religions, or else have been guilty of some *tour de force* interpretation that has resulted in no more than some unrealistic syncretism. Religions are not made; they grow. All attempts at rational reconstruction become no more than clumsy constructions, dead corpses of religion, anatomically possible, but lacking all possibility for living faith.

Before answering these three claims for religious pluralism, we shall have to consider another position that claims to belong to our first main division of one unique religion, but which analytically belongs in this our third category. This position claims that whatever religion understands itself and all other religions to be relative, by such understanding becomes, in fact, universal. The universal nature of religions, in this view, and the universal nature of religious knowledge consist both in their universal partaking of relativity and also in their realizing and accepting this fact. Much of Hinduism's contention is of such a nature. Accordingly, it claims no universal nature or truth for its own religion. The absolute admits within itself no such historic plurality of religions. Religions are human and historical and therefore relative. Paul Tillich holds a similar view. He claims that the Christian faith is ultimate because it refuses to make itself ultimate. Its central symbol is the Cross, the dying to self. Accordingly it refuses to make itself superior or most important. By accepting instead its own finitude, it announces its universality and ultimacy.

All such claims to ultimacy, however, have to do with a universalistic attitude, and not with concrete universal content of religion. What is truly espoused is religious pluralism. No religion, the claim goes, is ultimate because all religions are relative. However, the fact that interpreters of one religion see and accept the fact of universal relativity does not mean that they genuinely claim their religion to be ultimate, except as an ultimate attitude toward religions. Their *religion* is relative and *all* religions, in their view, are in fact relative. Both an empty ultimate, a universal negation of concrete religious content as ultimate, and an undifferentiated ultimate, which amounts to the same thing, afford no final or universal reality to historic religions, let alone organic relations with them; and therefore the advocates of positions which use such ultimates do, in fact, contend for religious pluralism as the classification in which they should be put. For this reason we have not discussed them under our first division, that of one only true religion, but under our third, that of religious pluralism. The whole discussion up to now gives reason for our refusal further to discuss the Great Negation in this context, while the ensuing discussion will deal with the claims of religious pluralism, or that all religions in the light of eternity, history and knowledge are equally true and best for their own people.

My own answer to the three grounds for religious pluralism can be concise. The first charge is that eternity itself involves religious relativity. Infinity, according to this charge, admits no degrees of significant differentiation among religions. Eternity, the contention insists, is sovereignly distinct from time and obliterates all approximations. But such a view operates with what we have called the Illicit Infinite. Such an infinite, given any finite, cannot be known; it cannot have any being. Its meaning is purely theoretical. It cannot be held by any being, except as a *tour de force* paradox, which is, in fact, nothing but an illicit contradiction. Therefore such claims must abandon all knowledge of the infinite. As an escape from religious or rational responsibility, or both, such a position is understandable. It can also be had as a reminder of the difference, beyond imagination, between God's vision and man's. As a whole, however, it mostly bedevils man's thinking about religion, and ought to be declared once for all as out of bounds.

According to our view of God, time is real and serious. Religious differences matter, and choice is important. Human relativity is real, but it does not preclude reliable religious knowledge. We need not, however, repeat here a discussion to which we have devoted major attention already.

My answer to the second reason advanced in behalf of religious pluralism can be equally direct. The second reason, we recall, was to the effect that the historic conditionedness of the differing religions involves an incommensurate relativity. Such relativity I grant freely. I also agree that religions are not rational constructs but religious developments. Religions are not planned but grow. Fortunately this volume has already answered at some length the charge of religious relativity, and weighed carefully the kind of reliability that can be had with regard to religious knowledge. Therefore my answer can be brief. Historic development is only one form of relativity. It precludes in no new way whatever our attaining religious reliability. We still have one common human nature at the base of human understanding, and one common world in which we live. What is common to human nature all over the world is more important to the understanding of religious reality than the relative concomitants of historic development.

Every person is unique, and yet we dismiss neither medicine

nor psychology. Every people and culture have their own differentiating characteristics, and yet we assay both anthropology and sociology. Every fingerprint is different, and yet we study criminology, just as we keep on studying botany in spite of every leaf's being different. The more complex the subject, the more difficult the interpretation; but there is no reason that we should be reduced to mathematics and inventory just because of the ubiquity of disconcerting difference. Extreme nominalism appeals to an uncritical matter-of-factness. Critical thought knows that it is logically impossible either to describe or discuss apart from universals. The obvious fact of religious relativity and of actual pluralism, due to the concrete development of religions in history, in no way, therefore, abolishes or basically undermines the fact of one humanity in one world reaching for religious reality in different settings and within diverse religious backgrounds.

Our problem of interpretation is exactly how to acknowledge to the full those differences and yet to find what is common in the search and the finding. If the differing religions come to basically irreconcilable conclusions, the reason is very likely not that there is no common human nature or common world to which this nature basically responds, even within the varieties of historic conditions, but rather that there is no such objective realm as religious reality beyond man's ordinary experience. Or, perhaps more deeply, the ground for differentiation may not be merely historic differences, but a common phenomenon among religions according to which they are more the product of man's fear than the result of trust, or more rationalizations than open-ended interpretations. The decisive issue as to whether there can be objective, universal religious knowledge is, therefore, neither the denial on the ground of the nature of eternity nor the denial on the ground of historic conditionedness, but rather the claim that no common basis for interpreting the widely differing religions has in fact passed intellectual muster.

The fourth and last position, my own, contends with the main charge of religious pluralism. I hold that there is no rationally and morally normative religion. Nor is there a rationally constructive religion. But there is a religiously normative event in human history which is both the judge and the fulfiller of all religions. The more it is accepted in life and truth, the more religion is a help to man. The more it is lacking through ignorance or rejection, the more religion harms man. The only relation between this event and historic religions, apart from historic accessibility and continuity, is the creative rule: by their fruits ye shall know them. The fruit witnesses both to its own reality and to the tree of truth that bore it. That normative religious event is the life of Jesus, as power for history and perspective on eternity. With whatever elements of historical ambiguity, that life illustrated and taught God as universal love, a Father to be trusted, and an open, inclusive society, engendered by faith and generating creative satisfaction.

We have already discussed in Part One our understanding of the life of Jesus. We do not know and cannot claim that he lived dominantly throughout his life the full measure of the universal love of God. The unconditional nature of God pervasively present would shatter human finitude, transforming it into some eternal fulfilment of spiritual participation in the life of God, surely reserved for some eventual, far-off, post-mortem existence. All such claims for the life of Jesus are the creation of uncritical devotion, whatever the motivation. They are ecclesiastical pretensions limited to no denomination. They have basis neither in history nor in sound interpretation of God's relation to man. But we do know and we do claim that he lived and taught that God is love, to the point where God's presence in his life and teachings has become the revelation of God for countless believers over the centuries, a revelation that is still spreading to the ends of the earth. Our analysis has shown that such love, fulfilling life and creating community, is what man most deeply needs. In Part One we analysed the implication of this love for our understanding the cosmic scale of religion. In Part Two we related this love more fully to man, as such, and to his knowledge of God. In Part Three we treated this love in its relation to history and nature. We are now ready to suggest that this love is also the best key to the study of reason in its bearing on the religions of the world.

The strongest objection to such a standard is, of course, that it seems too high. To be sure, it will be said, if all lived such love realistically, creative and co-operative life would flourish, within which our feelings would be so drastically changed that we cannot now even imagine what we would feel. There is now no climate of opinion for accepting such universal religion. To us now it seems basically irrelevant. It seems to be so far removed from our feelings of anxiety and constant conflict that, in fact, it appears to be no religion. At least it seems to be the faith for only saints and sages, who least need it. Such love means fullness of life, the objection runs, without the depth of anxiety which is at present our common lot and which even makes life interesting for us. We are human beings full of fears and hostility, who read most avidly the bad news in the morning paper and who respond more strongly to conflict and defeat than to reports of fulfilled satisfaction and hospitable runways of final arrivals.

Wanting the answers, we even more dread finding them. For us a world of fulfilment is the world of no problems to solve, no battles to win, no threatening evils to engage. The fact is that more than rejecting such a tame world of constant, for us routine, attainment, we deem it irrelevant and even unreal. God and the Gospel have living meaning within the needs of constant conflict, the actual world we can understand, while they become largely emotional abstractions if they are proposed as real in themselves and attainable realities for us. Because we have not faced up to this primary fact of how far removed confession is from life, we have pushed from us our highest confessions as actual options in life and history. If we have not called them mythical in so many words, we have behaved toward them as at best aspects of life rather than the final declarations of the nature of reality.

The natural response to our proposing God as universal love, sufficiently seen in Jesus Christ to give us objective reference for our faith is, consequently, that such religion is idealistically irrelevant. It cannot become universal as confessionally and motivationally effective. The fact is, however, that it was at least once lived with power enough to have proved itself

293

already historically relevant. Without being fully understood, this life created a following of disciples who understood it sufficiently to produce exasperatingly and movingly an account of it in the New Testament. Even the distorted message in the New Testament contained enough authenticity to occasion a community that with all its frustrations and failures confessed the love of God that dies and lives for man's salvation. The Spirit who moved the Master to compassion for man, within his trust in God, kept breathing on the world, seeking the continuation and expansion of that love in the life and teachings of Jesus, and finding some success in lives that preferred death for him to life without him. To be sure, the deeper anxieties of the heart, in order to relieve the tension of the relevance of this life of God's love on earth, deified him out of his effective relevant humanity; but in spite of his rejection by both the world that repudiated him and the church that confessed him, in ways and measures beyond our tracing, that actual life of the man from Nazareth still haunts the world and keeps calling men within the church to ever-new dedication to the God who lived at the centre of his own trust and commitment.

If Christ is made either irrelevant, or inaccessible, it is not on account of historic fact, but on account of false religion and misleading theology. The Christ of historic Christian theology offers no general relevance for life, for he is unreal. Christianity is schizophrenic between its high confession of Christ and its low power over life and society. It is largely bankrupt and repudiated by modern man. But 'classical Christianity' has always been ineffective in actual practice. It has been powerful and weak at the same time because it has failed to understand and to accept its own foundation. It has feared God and barred itself behind theology against the genuine Gospel of the relevant love of God for all men, that was made accessible in history through a life which humanity tried to get rid of, by physical killing, by outward persecution of his followers and by inward distortion of the meaning of this life. The answer to the charge that Jesus Christ is irrelevant as the standard for all religions of the world, including Christianity, both to break and to remake, both to kill and to bring new life again, is that

294

this life is, to begin with, historic and fully human. Therefore it cannot be irrelevant for genuine faith and following. It can be idealistic and inaccessible only to fear and evasion, or to lack of understanding and following. Starting in, and with, actual history, therefore, we start with a standard fully relevant to all.

The reason that this standard does not seem or feel relevant is that it has been falsely presented and falsely experienced. Jesus loved strugglingly as well as serenely. He was full of tensions as well as full of peace. His was no humanity beyond problems. His was no power beyond human defeat. On the way to death he struggled over death, and in dying he agonized over being deserted by God. Even so, he saw the devil falling like lightning and offered a peace to his followers beyond circumstance to touch. His love was so real and so satisfying that it spoke to the disciples' deepest relation to God, and, through them, to all kinds and conditions of human experience and to all times and parts of the world. If this life and this teaching are presented as 'idealistic' and removed from the world, it is not their fault, but the fault of those who interpret the life and teachings of Christ. His was a real human life in the actual world of men, open to the reality of God in trust, and opened to the needs of men in concern. Such trust and such concern are open to all men. The life and teachings of Jesus, expressing the universal love of God, are for all men. They have universal relevance as the open, creative, yet constructively shaping pattern for fulfilling life and community.

But even when this life and this love are rightly present, they fail to be relevant to man's fear-filled feelings and sin-blinded eyes. They must not only be presented, but experienced aright. Sinful man cares not and dares not receive the message made living in the messenger. Such a message calls for radical decision. It demands a fundamental reorientation of life. This living, personal message of God's love actually encountering man in life frightens the sinner. He recoils from it, weighing flight or fight. The message calls for faith. But faith has no background of experience in terms of satisfying associations of feeling. It knows the encounter mostly as a void and an enemy.

Man's general experience of love, at best, is a mixed association of reactions. The message calls for a radically changed basis for experiencing it, which cannot be obtained prior to the experience itself. Therefore, it will seem either irrelevant or threatening, and much of both mixed together within an unanalysable amalgam of response.

The universal love of God calls for reception in trust and creative life. God comes fulfillingly only to positive experience. He comes from the call of the negative to change absence or dread into presence and fulfilment. Therefore the message of God's universal love, meeting us in a concrete life through a pattern and power for our own newness, involves a basic change of human nature. Such change is the deepest meaning of man's life and history, and, therefore, is also the most demanding. For it man must sell all else. When what is best for us comes back to us as we divest ourselves of what previously seemed best to us; it is never the same as before. We see it not only with new eyes, but within a new complex of feelings, where the very self has become basically reconstituted. Such change centres in man's true life and requires right relation to God. Man's intention must be changed, both in direction and in motivation. Because the normative standard for religion is so thorough and so central to life, it is demanding beyond understanding except through the lifelong appropriation of the new life. It can come only through self-offering and self-opening at the centre of life, in full trust in God and within full readiness for inclusive human community.

Such a demand is staggering beyond our imagination, and keeps stunning us as we try to practise it. It becomes sheer sham and unreality apart from God's grace and in humble faith. It has no place for self-attainment and self-righteousness. Such love leads to struggle and to suffering. It seems both foolish and offensive, and often utterly ineffective. Humanly, it seems all too often dismal failure. The problem lies in our own nature and in the accumulated patterns and practices of human emotions, as they become entrenched around historic sets of behaviour. There is, then, no easy or sure way to the transforming acceptance of the kind of standard that both destroys and rebuilds all religions. Faith, worship, and action must reorient life in God, both personally and in community.

But God calls now, it seems clear, for a new level of life for both man and history. When we find that the way we are going is a one-way street to destruction, and when we see that there is another way open to us, although facing about may prove to be history's hardest turn, we believe it can be done in God's power and within the fulfilment that such turning will make. We need have no worry about lack of challenge and failure to find creative adventure if we turn in the direction of true fulfilment. Within the new experience of God's love, fulfilling life and community, the old way of basic self-assertion and competitive conflict will seem, by comparison, not only sin and insanity but empty meaninglessness. There can be no levelling commonness and no boring monotony within the creative newness and rich diversity of God's love for all, and man's open, inclusive society.

Whatever basic about-face will take place, too, there will be no sudden leaving behind the finitude and sin which beset human nature. Enough that within a co-operative religion for one world, rooted in trust and compassion, there will burgeon forth meaningfulness of life and a surmounting of man's enemies beyond mere survival. Such realistic understanding of religion within the world religions will provide the creative reason with its highest challenge in the interest of both truth and life, and will accept the companionship of the critical reason in man's most difficult task of expressing his relation to the ultimate, both in terms of the universally central and unifying, and also of the completely concrete and creatively different.

The best we can do from now on is to let the creative reason approach this problem of togetherness within the creatively different in terms of the actual main religions there are. If our analysis is correct, no religion can be built rationally nor changed rationally. Religions grow from within man's confession and commitment, but such growth becomes real and fruitful only when it results from faith's seeing rather than from mere groping. Reason has its proper place within religion and within the religions. Even as a standard informed by a

297

normative life, reason is a servant in the world of faith, correcting and redirecting it mostly by its offer of truth for life.

How, precisely, however, are we relating this discussion of
the world religions to the function of reason in religion? We
have already suggested certain relationships among the religions which we cannot accept, and have given our reasons for
not accepting them. Then we have proposed that there is a
normative event in history in terms of which we can organize,
evaluate and direct all religious experience. This event, we
found, is more than suggested and less than assured by history.
Therefore it is concretely relevant to history and yet requires
faith, a faith in ultimates from within history for the world.
Relevant to all religions by its universal nature, this event is
yet revolutionary by its depth of reach. Therefore, because of
its very fullness of humanity and genuineness of experience,
this universal love of God seems so far beyond ordinary experience as to be irrelevant. Yet mankind now faces this choice
in actual history: to perish for lack of being its true self sufficiently to meet radical new demands of a new era in history; or
to find the resources for the fulfilment of its needs for this new
day. Resources for the need can be found only in the reality that
underlies man's own true potential: the open and inclusive
community within the faithfulness of God.

Having proposed this thesis with regard to reason and the
religions of the world, how can we now develop and test it
concretely with respect to the historic religions? Obviously,
we cannot entertain an exhaustive or even lengthy treatment
of any religion. What we propose to do is to let the creative
reason find the basic relation of a few major religions to our
normative event, establishing fundamental relevance of nature
and suggesting main lines of creative community. Then the
critical reason can take over to ask whether the analysis is in
fact true, and whether the proposals are both realistic and
effective. And finally, creative faith can have its say at suggesting creative correction and transformation of each religion.

What have we said, then, in this chapter? We have affirmed
that to deem one religion alone true is in effect to doom it, as
an esoteric affair. If no other religion contains worthy truth,

religion is not essential to man; it is not then the universal response of God's call on man. God's revelation in the light of such an esoteric view must be considered to be external and unrelated to human nature in its growing depths. Certainly such a position is also unbiblical, since God has not 'left himself without a witness' outside the biblical revelation; and God is the God of the Gentiles as well as of the Jews 'if it be true that God is one'!

We have also stated that we cannot hold to the proposition that there is basic truth at the centre of each religion, in such a manner and of such a nature that all centres coincide to witness to the one God. The centres of all religions are constituted by the aggregative average, not selectively highest witness of man's response to God within the respective religions. Such response is neither basically rational and isolable from its concrete centre, nor is it the highest response within each religion. Rather, religions reflect man's fear and the fleeing from God, his fighting God, perhaps even more than his full acceptance or understanding of the revelation of God's nature and will. Therefore concrete religions, both in theory and in practice, fall far short of the fullest discoverable religious truth. What is highest in each religion, in other words, does not constitute its pointing centre.

Then again, relativism, open or disguised in terms of a negative universalism, denies that religion is central to human nature, actually or in terms of a discoverable potential. Our whole analysis, however, has found religion to be organically related to God in terms of man's deepest need. Therefore there must be some objective answer to the problem of religion and the religions.

What I am proposing, instead, is that there is a centre in the life and teachings of Jesus, God's universal love for man, which is *for* but not *in* any religion. The contention we are to consider specifically is that this centre does not so much clarify the actual religions as bring to birth their deepest potential. In the light of such reappraisal, even the meaning of the actual religions, in all their partiality and distortion, can begin to be understood. The religions can grow together only as they all

299

find this centre beyond themselves, and in the light of such transcendence commence on a new level to worship and work, to pursue co-operative community and creative reformulation of the faith itself.

Chapter XVI

The normative Event and concrete Religions

Concrete religions are communities of faith. All religions are the expressions of worshipping communities. The communities vary widely, of course, in solidarity and sharpness of focus. To whatever extent we can speak of a religion at all, however, it is a community of confession. In so far as religions definitely differ, they are distinguishable by their adherents' acceptance of differing kinds of faith, that is, distinguishable interpretations of the realities and power beyond ordinary experience that help and harm man. Our problem will be how to isolate and identify the basic determinative faith in terms of which each religion is genuinely distinctive. If our thesis is right, the creative reason must find a universal commonness of faith at the centre of all religions, as at least their depth-potential, and along with this a secondary but important difference characterizing each concrete religion.

If we can find such community of nature below diverging difference of rational interpretation, at the centre of all religions, at least as a depth-potential, and such secondary diversity on the part of each religion, there will be no power in the charge that the variety of the world's religions precludes there being anything objectively essential at the heart of religion as such. As a matter of fact, on the contrary, if the result of our examination is positive, reason will by means of it bear witness to the fact that God as creative love, cherishing man's real freedom, is actually at work within the different religions, synthesizing, at the centre, the unity of truth and the pluralism of creative freedom.

Concretely, from within our thesis, the creative reason proposes that all religions, at their deepest, not only need to become communities living by faith in God's universal love,

301

but also at their depth already potentially express this need at the centre of their confessions, however partially or distortedly. Recalling how prone man is to rationalize his religious interpretation in order to flee from God or to make him seem more congenial to man, we find that even the rationalizations, at their base, bear witness to the truth of man's deepest needs, in terms of the filling of which alone those who worship within these religions can find the overcoming of their frustrations and the attainment of their fulfilment.

Our assignment will be to seek to uncover the deepest drives of Judaism, Christianity, Islam, Hinduism, Buddhism, the Chinese religions and Shinto. In the case of the last two items the discussion will have to be mostly a matter of postscript. I make no claim to know any of these religions as an expert, and most of them I know mostly from reading. Any discussion of great religions within a few paragraphs is necessarily demanding to a maximum degree. Those who know the religions best must answer whether the discussion has penetrated to the heart of the matter. Our only choice is whether to undertake seriously, within a severely limited scope, a major problem for reason in religion, or whether to avoid the question altogether. I choose at least to suggest an answer as central as I can make it.

We start with Judaism because it is at least the precursor, and I believe the mother, of both Christianity and Islam. However unpalatable such a start may be to the Arabic world, primary creativity with respect to the three great Western religions belongs to Judaism. The formula for our discussion of Judaism and all consequent discussions will be as follows: the creative reason affirms; the critical reason replies; and finally, creative faith suggests. In this way of approaching our problems we can bring out the positive aspects of reason in the religions of the world, then notice carefully the negative considerations, and finally summarize our findings within whatever whole seeing is genuinely available from the facts of the case.

With respect to the thesis of our work, namely that religion is man's evaluative response to the realities and powers that go beyond ordinary experience whether for help or harm, and that those realities and powers are most truly found to be universal love, majestically beyond present grasp, while yet also mysteriously near and effective in human life and history in accordance with our response, the creative reason affirms as fact the following observations concerning Judaism:

(a) Judaism is a community of memory formed by recalling God's mighty deeds in its behalf. Actually, this memory seeks absolute origins in God's creation of Adam and in God's second start within the Noachic covenant of his faithfulness with mankind, symbolized by the rainbow. Added to such mythological gropings for primitive beginnings, mostly general in nature, were the more Jewish-centred legends of Abraham, Isaac and Jacob. Whatever may be the historic ground for these legends, depth-memory reached back to Father Abraham and to Isaac and Jacob. But the community of memory, beyond these founding memories, focused in God's deliverance of his people from Egypt.

Moses shapes most sharply the Jewish community of memory. Real as a historic figure, not entirely as fact, no doubt, but also as a figure created by faith's memory, Moses is nearly a normative figure for Judaism. To this memory of deliverance from Egypt through the wanderings in the wilderness forty years, and by the power of the God who gave the people his law on Sinai, was added principally the strength and glory of David's reign, the heroism and sacrifice of the Maccabees and the intolerable burden of Jesus' rejection and death. 'For David's sake' became present appropriation of memory; Hanukkah lights and music repeat God's majestic 'nevertheless' expressed in the mighty Maccabees to the oppressors of God's people, and even the savage story of Esther and the celebration of freedom from oppression fit better into the Maccabean story of national liberation than into the earlier exile; depth-consciously, furthermore, the Jewish people keep being terrorized by the memory of having incited and assented to the killing of him whose life is the paradigm of right religious response, a son of their own people, released for the light of the whole world. All these events must be lifted to the level of God's mighty deed, whatever be the response on the part of the people in acceptance and obedience, or in rejection and faithlessness.

(*b*) The creative reason also finds that Judaism is a community of hope, based not only on memory but on the faithfulness of God. Israel faced not only the past, but also the future. Abraham went out seeking an unknown land, Moses and his people set out for the promised land. The nation looked in hope for the kingdom that God promised to David and his seed forever; the exiles longed in hope for the rebuilding of Jerusalem; God's people, through long frustration, looked in hope for the coming of the Messiah; the modern Jew has hoped for the restoration of Palestine, and now he hopes for such fulfilment as can come in connection with its development.

(*c*) Similarly, Judaism is a community of faith. Possibly we should put first its grim determination to maintain monotheism. The great prophets saw the very nature of righteousness as grounded in the God of all the earth, who cannot but do right, and whose will is the plumbline of righteousness for men and nations. Over and over again, the people were called upon to choose between the one God and the many gods of the neighbouring nations. The first commandment of law was the worship of the one God, and the first commandment of love was the total love of the one God. The first historians in the world, the authors of the Book of Kings, derived their meaning of history from the way in which the rulers responded to the will of God. Memory and hope were both grounded in faith in the God of history, the God of election, who had chosen his people in faithfulness and who promised to honour his covenant with Israel.

The reason that we have, in fact, suggested Judaism as a community of faith only in the third place is that we want to stress how concrete and historical was the faith of Israel. It always went beyond man's ordinary experience, centring in the God high and lifted up, but the faith was no speculative abstraction, created through the analysis of experience in the scholar's study, nor was it basically the faith of the priest in the temple, performing ritual, but the lively faith of God's whole people before him in the concrete choices of national decisions, and only secondarily in personal life. Persons were part of the people of God. The people themselves were the community of faith.

(*d*) The creative reason continues to point out that Judaism is also a community of law. Judaism is the people who have received and are grateful for God's law. The law for the Jews, at least of biblical times, was not any legalism to be endured nor any oppressive moralism to be suffered. The world 'law' lacks the connotation of torah. Neither is nomos an equivalent concept. The Jews felt privileged to be picked by God to be his people and to know his law, which was the way of salvation. The Jews delighted in the law of the Lord and had it for their song in the night. To be sure, the disobedient and the unjust had the law to fear. The law judged the unrighteous guilty, without equivocation and sentimentalism. The prophets thundered the majesty of the law of God and the heinousness of its breaking. But the law in itself was good, God's gracious gift to his own people, whereby he led them in his own way for his name's sake.

Nor was the receiving of the law merely God's favouritism to Israel. To the best among its interpreters—the only concern of the creative reason—the law was given by God as a special privilege involving a special responsibility. It was a way of walking in obedience to demonstrate the righteousness of God. Its precepts reached out beyond the Jews to love of neighbour even in the case of the stranger in the gates. In Leviticus 19 the Jew is admonished to love his non-Jewish neighbour as himself, remembering that the Jews themselves were once slaves in the land of Egypt. In Second Isaiah, Israel can understand the problem of its catastrophe in exile only on the ground that it is the suffering servant bearing the guilt of the world. Such explanation is not mere rationalization, but the viewing of election in the full panorama of monotheism newly born. The highest peak of the law became its consummation in the love of God and neighbour, admonitions which became central to Jewish worship in their intimate and continual repetition. Surely the creative reason can come close in such instances to finding in Judaism the full stress on universal

305

acceptance and concern, expressed graphically in such books as Ruth and Jonah, with regard to foreigners; and in Hosea, with regard to God's unwavering concern for Israel in all its waywardness.

These four positive affirmations concerning Judaism as a religious community before the living God—of memory, hope, faith and law—have to be balanced by the response of the critical reason. In fairness to fact, what reservations or negative considerations does the critical reason have to offer?

Regardful of our suggested normative definition of religion as an unconditional life of inclusive and creative concern within an open community of faith, the critical reason makes its considered reply:

(a) The Jewish community, based on the memory of God's mighty deeds, failed to retain or to make sufficiently emphatic the universal phases of that memory. Adam and Noah became mostly mythical characters at the beginning of Jewish genealogy. Abraham, instead of being first of all the father of faith, in whose seed all the nations were to be blessed, became mostly the founder of an in-group who prided themselves on their special privilege in having him as their father. The Book of Esther, the account of nationalistic triumph and revenge, became the occasion for celebration, rather than of repentance and shame; while the Book of Ruth, with its message of David's non-Jewish ancestor, has never occasioned similar general appeal. The Books of the Maccabees give occasion for holidays, but not the Book of Jonah with its protest against nationalism.

As a consummation, the Christ who called anyone and all who did the will of God his kind and kin, however near by birth or far by race, was crucified at the hand of Jewish as well as Roman nationalism. Nor is that crucifixion officially repudiated by Judaism as a religion even yet, or Christ accepted for the prophet he was. All this nationalism, in religion, it may be objected, is all too natural; and this is precisely the objection by the critical reason to Judaism as a community of memory. The memory contains universal humanity under a universal God, but this part of the Jewish memory never became dominant in its religion as a whole. Normative religion, however, grounded in what is more than man always makes man more human, inclusively as well as intensively.

(b) As a community of hope, the critical reason continues, Judaism has been similarly centred in the Jewish community. It has been more of a political, cultural, religious hope than a liberating hope within religious universalism. The Messiah became a hope of national deliverance and triumph rather than a deliverance from the feverish drive of nationalism. Without forgetting the many factors which enter into the conflict between modern Zionism and the American Council of Judaism, the leading difference is surely their respective attitudes toward the national and the universal nature of the Jewish faith. For us to make nationalism all important to Judaism, or to produce a Jewish God of wrath, wreaking vengeance on the enemies of Israel, is to misrepresent the situation and to bear false testimony against a neighbour. Not to notice and to report the fierce nationalism which has motivated Jewish faith, however, is equally to distort evidence. The critical reason must also report that the Jewish community of hope, as a whole, failed to extend its most inclusive expectations into worlds beyond this life, because its main drive was not universalistically religious but particularistically and politically religious. Judaism never developed at its centre of hope the expectations of universal consummation within eternity. Naturally, therefore, Christ, who stood for the transcendence of both human and earthly barriers, never found ready acceptance within Judaism as such.

(c) The critical reason also reports that the Jewish community of law was never graduated into the community of love. The law as a way of life under God has never basically been broken and fulfilled by love as the fulfilment of both law and life. The way of the law, however wide and good, has to make room for love as the leaven of an accepting and concerned community. The reality of love leaves the law, as law, a dead skeleton, but includes it within the strong and flexible life which needs the skeleton for its support. Both before and after Christian times, the relation between law and love in Judaism as bases of community has been indistinct; indeed law and love have overlapped.

The critical reason has to admit that in modern, and particularly in liberal Judaism, there is often ardent confession of the God of universal love; but reason, in its truly critical role, knows also that such profession is generally some faith in a religious pluralism of the kind we dismissed as not truly universal. Full religious universalism maintains that religious maturity is not only a matter of live-and-let-live or even of live-and-help-live, but of a common life with diversity in response to a common God within common basic need, generating a religious community at its common base, which is itself more foundational than are the consequent concrete religions. This base is the universal love of God suggested by our normative religious event, which breaks every concrete religion continually in order to reconstruct it for fuller attainment of universal community.

In the case of Judaism, creative faith, moreover, can suggest that to witness positively and powerfully to the thesis of our investigation, it need only become its true self by proceeding in its own development to accept and to pursue creatively its own universal elements. At its highest, Judaism is the kind of universalistic monotheism which we have found to be basic religion. Love to God and to man can find consummation in him who, while accepting such faith as basic in law, yet turned the equation into a more fulfilling community grounded in love from God for man and through God for man. Judaism also needs to cleanse its memory of the crucifixion of Christ and to lift its hope to the consummation of the kind of community for which he lived and died. Then its community of faith and of law will reach out, without limit in God and man, to shake itself free from its in-group nationalism and invidious culture loyalty, even while maintaining and glorying in its culturally creative distinctiveness. Judaism can come to terms with Christ and universal love by an honest treatment of history and a creative pointing to its own fulfilment, for Judaism itself, at its highest, points unmistakably to the reality and regulative adequacy of its own normative event, while its falling short exhibits its failure to accept the meaning and motivation of this event at the centre of its faith as a community.

In a way, we have been discussing the Christian faith throughout the book, but in accordance with our assertion in this section, namely, that no religion can meet the standard of our normative event, we are obliged at least to suggest in what way Christianity stands under the same judgment as all other religions. But first we should at least list the main points wherein the Christian faith accords with our normative definition of religion.

(*a*) Christianity is founded on the normative event, the life and teachings of Jesus as the central way to know God. In him reason in religion finds its central focus.

(*b*) The Christian Scriptures stress that apart from love, no faith and work are of any worth. Man's love is possible only because of God's love.

(*c*) Christian history has kept the Cross as its mainline for worship, life and thought; and the Cross stands for God's self-giving love for the world.

(*d*) Christianity, by the power inherent in its motivation and message, has spread to the ends of the world, and has penetrated and coloured every aspect of man's life. Human worth and work were increased in value immeasurably by being grounded in the love of God. Concern for human welfare has consequently become intensified and spread throughout the world, most clearly visible in the indirect products, such as science, democracy and medicine, of such faith in the God who cares.

Our task, however, in this section, is not primarily to speak for the creative reason, but to listen to the critical. How does Christ repudiate Christianity as an actual religion?

(*a*) The critical reason judges that it is more difficult for Christianity than any other religion to make Christ central to its faith. The reason for this astonishing fact is that the Christ of Christianity is the creation of false faith. For this reason we shall later consider the use of the word 'Christ'. Possibly creative faith can salvage it. Jesus seemingly was never understood by his own disciples, and those who founded the religion in his name continued to misconstrue his mission and message. How so? The critical reason cannot know that Jesus fully lived or taught the universal love of God. We do know that his life and teachings suggested it, and that this theme has been the highest in the history of the Christian faith. But pious devotion and uncritical imagination made the life and teaching of Jesus into a mystery religion. Increasingly they saw Jesus as God himself walking on earth in one of his aspects, or even personalities, in such a way that Jesus was no longer considered to be an ordinary human being subject to human sin and weakness.

Thus Christianity became guilty, without deliberate plan or conscious guilt, of developing a blasphemous idolatry, against the growth of which the critical reason was powerless. The critical event, which is normative for faith and normative for human psychology and sociology, therefore, never came to full historic expression. The New Testament writings are themselves such a mixture of high and holy faith and truth, on the one hand, and uncritical mythology, on the other, that the normative event became basically obscured and distorted. Judaism, Islam and all high-grade religions must forever reject the uncritical primitivism and paganism of much biblical faith. Such especially is the case since Christianity incorporated into its doctrine the Old Testament as well, as replete with factually reliable information and an adequate standard for guidance. No matter what protestations were made as to the full humanity of Christ and the fulfilling reality of the New Covenant, the actual main drive of the Christian faith was to make Jesus God, and to dilute the New Covenant of the universal love of God by accepting on equal footing the rest of the Bible. In this way, Christianity at its very beginning failed to accept and practically repudiated the normative nature of its own distinctive event.

(b) The formulation of the faith, the critical reason finds, increasingly separated Christian confession from the Christian foundation. The creeds kept correct formulae of relationship only to omit completely the normative Gospel of God's universal love. They also made polite bows at Jesus' humanity, while more and more failing to stop his being worshipped as a god. Such progression can be understood as the creation of myth by the worshipping community. It is still going on, as in the preposterous claims that even the mother of Jesus was born without sin and was taken directly into heaven. Religion seems to thrive on myth matched with uncritical faith. The powerlessness and poverty of the critical reason in religion can perhaps best be illustrated by the way in which God's revelation of man's saving truth for himself, and for all human needs to be and to know, became waylaid, robbed and nearly destroyed by fear's highwaymen of uncritical piety and creative myth. It is not for the critical reason to judge whether religion can live and have power apart from such piety and myth. Creative faith, listening with integrity and competence to the critical reason, must struggle with this basic question as to the nature of religion and the religions. The critical reason can report unhesitatingly, however, that the Christian faith has never developed the full meaning and reality of the normative event as central both to its life and thought.

(c) The critical reason reports, furthermore, that in spite of critical scholarship and a generation that has produced foremost theologians, who stress the centrality of the love of God for the Christian faith, the World Council of Churches has perpetuated and indeed intensified the stress of Jesus as God, now even without explicit acknowledgment of his full humanity, while ignoring, in its central formula of confession, contemporary recognition of the universal love of God as alone central to the Christian faith. Therefore the World Council has more than driven deeper the wedge between the normative event of revelation and the historic defection on the part of the Christian religion; it has nearly severed the Christian faith from its founder and substituted for him a pious myth.

Nor has official leadership repudiated the doctrine of eternal hell as the destiny of most men, a doctrine which nullifies at the centre of faith any confession in the sovereign God of love. More and more, the leading Protestant theologians have been sensitive to this basic contradiction within the biblical and the historic formulation and the undeniable implications of the Christian faith as to God's ultimate faithfulness with his own creation and his own children; but the critical reason must report that the institutional machinery is still basically arraigned confessionally against, and not for, its own normative event.

x   311

Recently the World Council of Churches has further complicated the problem by adding 'according to the Scriptures' to
its Christological idolatry, thus plainly refusing to make the
event normative to the Scriptures. There can be some hope in
this proceeding since the Scriptures also teach other traditions
than Jesus as God and eternal hell, but the critical reason, in
the light of our analysis, can settle for nothing less than the full
truth of the inclusive community of concern, open to all truth
and to all men, within faith in the God of universal love. Therefore Christianity as an historic religion is judged severely by its
own normative event.

(d) The normative standard for faith and conduct, the
critical reason continues to drive home, has also become effectively thwarted and in effect denied by the practices of both
personal and collective life. Instead of upholding the indivisible humanity in Christ, as did the original church at least,
Christianity has succumbed to nationalism and even supported
war in its official main line of pronouncements. Similarly, it has
generally accepted segregation of races wherever this practice
has been culturally dominant, and all too often Christianity has
sponsored class churches similar to social clubs. It has even
sanctioned capitalism as consistent with Christian motivation
and distribution. In short, the Christian faith, instead of espous-
ing the indivisible humanity in Christ and complete concern for
all men in the open community of faith in the God of universal
love, has in the overwhelming number of Christian practitioners
collapsed into the *status quo* of political, cultural, social and
economic behaviour.

There can be no question, therefore, that if Christ belongs
to *status quo* Christianity, the honest and informed worshipper
must renounce the name and the religion. Creative faith confronts no smaller problem. Fortunately there has always been
a remnant who have striven to understand and to accept the
Christian faith at its centre. Perhaps the remnant has a right
to the name.

The main question is whether the normative event is irre-
levantly too high for humanity to accept for life and thought.
We have already discussed this problem and suggested how

312

both Scriptures and institutions are accommodations to actual human nature at its present level of attainment. We have also suggested that we stand at a corner in human history where we need either a new religion and a new level of religious reality and power, or a recovery of the highest in the old, along with a new level of understanding and living of it. The problem, however, is not so much analytical as decisional. Whether we can change effectively remains for faith to determine. Our analysis at least shows that the resources for such an effective change are available. For such a change creative faith can suggest three basic recommendations:

(a) We must acknowledge how complicated the historic evidence is as to the historic Jesus and refuse to be arbitrary at this point, whether defensively or aggressively. Genuine love also refuses to be anxious about an institution. The love that gives its own life for others does not withhold the surrender of its own name. Certainly we should send to the slaughterhouse mythological Christianity, and dare to put the knife unshrinkingly even to our own ideological son of traditional Christianity. We must heed the Jewish and Muslim protest in the name of genuine monotheism and declare once for all that we do not worship Jesus of Nazareth. We worship only the God whom we see in his life of love. Reverence and honesty must both lead us to humble repentance at this central point of our faith.

(b) Creative faith can then accept the normative event as the chief focus on God for life and thought. It seems that life must now preclude explicit formulation of doctrine. Once again we must let Christianity, by whatever name, be the way of universal love, repudiating war, segregation, class structures, exploitive economics, and whatever practices tear men apart. Creative diversity is possible within a universal community of co-operation and concern. We may have to pay the price of commitment, perhaps the price of the constant cross, for our human self-seeking and group invidiousness, walking long and painfully in the way; but nevertheless keep walking with a spirit that finds real and ready spiritual meaning and historic victories. We cannot tell how long and arduous may be the way to a basic new mode of living this constructive civilization, until feeling and seeing become habituated to a new climate of evaluation and direction of life. We have no illusion within our creative faith as to how near failure can be at any point. But creative faith knows that in this direction lies the way of health for persons and civilization. A new reality of worship and spiritual experience has to come, before we can find the motivation for such open and inclusive community as is now demanded of us.

(c) Along with such commitment to the kind of faith that is needed, we can begin increasingly to formulate the universal faith. If names block universal acceptance, we must find creative language for human fulfilment within the universal faith of one world. Great modern theologians are already tearing down the outworn ideological structure. The traditional institutional arrangement may also have to undergo basic transformation at the hand of creative faith.

I believe that in the life and teachings of Jesus we have the normative event that has never been accepted, even for the formulation of its meaning. The Spirit pants to write better scriptures for a new age. For the old we must be thankful, and let them become fulfilled in God's new directives for a new age of human history. One aspect of such formulation, I believe, will be to take the normative event of universal love and create a world of thought productively consistent with the event. Traditional Christianity has employed alien philosophies and fought sham intellectual battles as a consequence. The Christian faith has always been weakened by being forced into foreign thought forms. Within them we cannot worship the Lord our God with all our minds and therefore we cannot worship him either honestly or competently. I should like personally to retain the word 'Christ' and give it its due. All religions, including the Christian, should then wrestle honestly with the historic facts, and find ways to formulate the heart of the universal faith, relative to their own needs. Human history and cultural continuity should have their own proper relevance. Such heritages as Hebrew transcendence and Greek immanence, or Jewish particularity and Stoic universalism, which were drawn into the original formulation of the Christian faith, for instance, still speak with quiet insistence as we come to face other religions like Islam and Hinduism. In the light of such heritages, the main motif for formulating God's highest relation to man, I believe, is Incarnation; but the Christian faith has never dared to take its focus in Christ and then to release for general use God's most important relation to humanity.

If creative faith can count on openness to historic data and flexibility as to name, a deep and general commitment to the way of open community in inclusive concern, and full freedom in its creative wrestling for a faith adequate for one world under one God, we shall find, I believe, that reason constructively witnesses to the basic place religion has in man's experience and history. Certainly the Christian faith, as traditional dogma, presents both strong pros and cons as to the nature and help of religious reality. But creative faith finds that if the creative reason had listened long and well to the critical reason, the Christian faith would present far more conclusively positive evidence for our thesis. The problem seems to be not so much the fact of many religions as the fact of fear and ignorance which beset all religions. Life seems to have been lived on so low a basis that much ignorance, not only on the part of the masses but also among the professional interpreters of religion, is actually due to the fear of the available truth from which man must flee and hide. The content of religions is not unimportant, but increasingly man's fundamental problem as to reason in religion is the power for distortion on the part of both finitude and sin.

When we turn to Islam we find yet another religion that centres in God. The realities and powers beyond man's ordinary experience are sharply focused in monotheism. Once again Judaism's 'thy God is one' rings clear and strong. The creative reason in the light of this basic fact finds the four following positive points that are in line with our main analysis:

(a) Islam is a community of high faith in the one God. It arose in large measure as a revolt against the Christian dilution of monotheism. The humanity of Jesus was affirmed by Islam, not negatively, but in positive acceptance of Jesus as a great prophet. Having made personal will the ultimate category, even

315

metaphysically, Islam resolutely and consistently rejected the category of incarnation. The mysterious majesty of the infinite God could not really be personally present in a human being. Even more offensive was the Christian claim that the Son of God died on the Cross. Certainly God cannot suffer or, *a fortiori*, die. One strong reason for the pulsing power of early Islam was the fact that its dramatic protest gave unhesitant outlet to man's deep longing for ultimate unity.

(*b*) Islam also developed a God-centred faith. In history, Islam became total surrender to the will of God with determinism at the heart of its faith. In nature, Islam espoused occasionalism, or not only the constant control but the continual re-creation of nature by the will of God.

(*c*) In worship, such severe monotheistic faith engendered exceptional emphasis on prayer as the personal and communal acceptance of God's will. No-one can estimate the power for Islam of this stress on prayer. Pilgrimages to the places where the only true prophet gave the authoritative revelation of the one God dramatize importantly the concreteness of the high and holy revelation. Islam lacks no stress on the personal in God or in the communication of God's will. The figure of Mohammed serves this need for concreteness, and he is, as well, the giver of the holy scriptures. Then, too, the community of worship, based on prayer and pilgrimages, using the means of scriptures, tradition, analogy and common consent, evinces its intrinsic universal nature by its motivation of universal zeal to convert all to the true God. The frustration of the successful original method of the sword, although damping to the heart of its faith in will, in the sense of power as ultimate, nevertheless has not doomed the faith to inactivity. The rapid spread of Islam in modern Africa is a sign of its adaptability.

(*d*) The Islamic community also reflects its monolithic monotheism by the way in which it has taken all of life under its auspices. Here again it is akin to orthodox legalistic Judaism. The totality of life must be lived unto God and according to the directions of the revelation or of the religious community. There is no room for personal decisions whether or not to

316

accept the faith. Islam, where it has power, is rigidly exclusive. Or, to put the same fact from within the faith: the people of Islam are totally committed to the final revelation of the one God and the one revelation, and are unreservedly concerned with each and every member of its community. There is no room for personal choice in the matter of God's own revelation; nor is there room for personal mores rebelliously or indifferently independent of the faith. The family and the community cut off the defecting member, and religiously every detail of life matters, even how to eat a watermelon.

The foregoing positive points show that Islam is definitely religious in the sense of our definition. It sees all of life in the light of the realities and powers beyond ordinary experience that help and harm. What, then, of the report of the critical reason? Its findings may be listed under three charges:

(a) Islam, although passionately religious and remarkably monotheistic, is not a community centring in the love of God. Its shaping image is that of a potentate. Its regulative pattern is power. Its sovereignty is of the self-sufficient Will. Therefore, as far as man is concerned, Islam stresses surrender, not fulfilment in freedom. The nature of creation becomes for Islam God's direct activity as well as direct creation; there is, therefore, neither room for an intelligent meaning of nature nor ground for an insightful accounting for evil. The nature of man and history for Islam never become interdependent with the processes of nature in the total indirect work of God in nature-history as a pedagogical process. The failure of Islam is the failure to understand the nature of love. It has shared this failure with all religions, but its own distinctive failure has been an overemphasis on personal will in terms of power. Some branches of the Christian church have indeed been closer in 'feel' at this point to Islam than to distinctive Christianity according to its own normative nature, but Islam in general has suffered from this defect.

(b) The Islamic community, moreover, not only suffers from the failure to make God's love central to his sovereignty but also from its denial of universal community. Its community of faith, not understanding how love includes presently and prospectively all men even in their lovelessness, becomes inflexibly exclusive. God, according to Islam, can shut out on the same level as he can take in; and so can the human community in his name. An Islamic family, not understanding the nature of God as the Father of Love, or ultimate concern, will shut out unreservedly the member that renounces the faith. True religion, we have seen, is inclusive community. We recall that inclusive community does not mean sentimental community without standards of righteousness or power of exclusion; but love's exclusion is only for the rehabilitation of those who shut themselves out from the fellowship by their own refusal to be inclusively accepting. From the point of view of the inclusive community, the lines of communication and concern are never broken. Islam has not as yet accepted such universalism.

(c) The critical reason also discovers that Islam is not an open community. It is mostly a religion of authority without room for creative growth, in its present reliance on the past and on the Koran. It is, as a matter of fact, to a great extent a book religion. Its authority is heteronomous. In the same way it has attempted to be a theocratic faith. It has tried persistently to impose its faith on the total community, using the state to enforce orthodoxy and to protect it from outside religions. A theocratic religion springs from the heresy of not taking history and creation seriously as present works of God on the pedagogical level. The heresy comes from a failure to understand the way sovereign love works. The freedom of history as a place of decision, and the freedom of man as a creature finding out for himself that God's way alone is best, find little place within a theocratic conception of the relation of religion and the state. Islam has had its own cultural flowering within its own kind of cultural conditions, but it has never come to its own highest fruitage because of its basic lack of understanding and faith in the sovereign God of love.

If such are the reports of the creative and the critical reasons, what can creative faith do with them? It can rejoice in Islam's determined monotheism. Christianity needs almost desperately Islam's help at this point. Creative faith can also be glad for the universalism, even though it be one of power, of Islam. In this respect it can help Judaism. The stark and stern universalism of its monotheism is surely a sturdy basis for worldwide religion. Creative faith can also take delight in the personal stress in Islam. Reality at its heart is purposive, and the purpose is all-embracing of nature and history. This aspect of its faith Islam can offer to the Oriental religions, where the stress on the personal has not often been clear and pervasive. Creative faith also can take deep satisfaction in the way Islam is rooted in worship, particularly in prayer, and the way it pervades all of life.

With such strong basis for rejoicing in Islam, creative faith can go on to suggest that Islam relate itself fulfillingly to the normative event of all religions. Without losing its basic continuity, and while developing its own historic past, Islam can recreate its central conception of the sovereign will of God in terms of God's universal love. In so doing it can begin with the first words of the Koran itself. 'In the name of the most merciful God.' Mercy can lead to love. A potentate can be merciful without loving, but love is ever merciful. If God is the most merciful, or all-merciful, such an affirmation should indicate that his nature ought more consistently to be understood in terms of love rather than of power. This theme, literally and in other forms, keeps recurring in the Koran and ought to be made into the central doctrine of Islam. When this is done, in faith and life, Islam can solve potentially all its other main problems. It can then create and develop new and deeper views of nature, history, man and destiny. Worship and practical life also will be transformed and enriched. Then Islam will be headed for the true and full monotheism of the one sovereign God of which it is the central historic exponent. Creative faith, indeed, discovers that the critical reason can help the creative reason within Islam to find its own true intention and to witness, at its heart, to the truth of our basic analysis.

Before such a transformation as we have suggested can take place, however, *status quo* Islam, as well as *status quo* Judaism and *status quo* Christianity, must be discredited and discarded. Science and the historic method can lead to the basic kind of demythologizing that is needed. Restrictive faith in the prophet,

319

in the Koran and in the traditions of the community must be shaken and thoroughly cleansed. Whether or not this can be done, while still keeping the historic faith, is as much of a question as whether or not traditional Christianity can make room for its own universal message, or whether or not its name must be sacrificed to its reality. Possibly in both instances there can be continuity of institution with a radical reformulation of the faith.

Turning from the regulative nature of Islam with its all-pervasive monotheism to the more amorphous and highly diversified phenomenon of Hinduism involves seemingly an abrupt break. Islam is characteristically Western; Hinduism is typically Eastern. The problem of religion and the religions, then, appears to centre in the difference between the religions we have considered up to this point and the religions we are about to discuss. And yet the difference is not so great as at first it appears. Hinduism, in spite of its vastly divergent branches, is a religious community, springing from the womb of Hindu history and culture. Creative reason reports the following considerations that are in line with our normative analysis of religion as a basic response of the human spirit:

(a) Hinduism is a religious community *par excellence* in terms of what lies beyond man's ordinary experience. Hinduism roots passionately, almost fanatically, in the eternal and the universal. Ordinary experience, as a matter of fact, consists of the fugitive unreality that can never satisfy the deepest in man. Religion refuses to rest in the relative. History is transient and fails to satisfy man. The worshipper seeks that which is eternal and real beyond appearance. Hinduism exemplifies centrally our definition of religion as man's response to the realities and powers beyond ordinary experience that can help and harm.

(b) Secondly, Hinduism affirms at its centre that man's deepest reality and his only fulfilment come by identification with the eternal and the universal. 'Thou art that' is no mere sophisticated insight reserved for the esoteric mystic. Popular and crass religious forms of Hindu worship and life obviously fail to make such insights central. The way beyond the illusions and temptations of the ordinary is not easy on any level. But

320

at the heart of Hinduism is a burning rejection of the seeming sources of satisfaction. The admiration of the Hindu community as a whole is kindled most readily and deeply in the presence of those who seek the wells of reality too deep for ordinary drilling.

(c) The creative reason also appreciates the fact that freedom is real and responsible in Hindu thought. Not only is freedom real and responsible in the doctrine of karma, but it also rests in reality far beyond earthly life. Life is responsibility from before earthly life, and the consequences of freedom's choices follow into future life. Out of the continuum of the earned past comes life ever again, to challenge the living present with choices continually significant for the future. The reason freedom is real and responsible is that justice is inherent in the nature of things. Sooner or later, in this life or another, the consequences of choice, for better or for worse, come to all. In this way, life and evil are dealt with in serious dimensions both for life and for thought.

(d) But justice in Hinduism is not the final hope of man. The wheel of deed and consequence can be broken by the enlightened identification with the eternal and the universal. The finally real goes beyond life's burden of choice, and offers the freedom of the fulfilment of the finite within the bosom of the infinite. The nature of the fulfilment cannot be known from this side of its reality. The finite thinkers may call it being plus intelligence, plus bliss. The self becomes fulfilled within this indescribable reality which is beyond anything we can even imagine in terms of relation. Such release from partiality and strife, from what we have called, in our own way, finitude and sin, is no work of man, but something that comes to the self from beyond it. We might call the obtaining of enlightenment in our language 'a gift of grace'. It must be prepared for, but it cannot be seized. At the proper time inmost reality opens itself to receive what is its own in man.

The creative reason has now exhibited a strong show window as to the positive nature of the Hindu religion. What objections can the critical reason muster? The central reports of the critical reason are as follows:

(*a*) Hinduism may seem universal because it accepts good in all religions and understands that no religion is final since all religions are relative. But the ultimate universalism of Hinduism is negative in nature; it is due, in fact, to its employment of the Illicit Infinite. At Hinduism's highest reaches, the road of revelation to reality peters out into the *via negativa*. Hinduism, therefore, has no positive content of religion in terms of which to interpret, evaluate, organize and direct the rest of experience; hence its universalism is really specious. No religion, it holds, is universal, because all are relative; therefore there is no universal religion; and neither is Hinduism itself universal. Such, indeed, is the full logic of Hinduism at its summit.[1] Hinduism even lacks finality of context in terms of which continually to reinterpret and reorganize experience as content.

(*b*) Nor is Hinduism's concept of eternity adequately revelatory to be religiously clear and effective. Because time and history are not real in the first place, Hinduism's grasp of eternity is amorphous and vague. No-one acquainted with Hinduism, with even partial penetration, can claim that there is no reality to time and history in any of its literature; but, as a whole, ordinary experience lacks the sturdy stuff of reality in terms of which to interpret eternity. Love is not sufficiently real as a substrate of eternity in, with, and under, time and history. The personal aspect of reality lacks status as an ultimate category and is generally thought of as narrowly local and limited in nature. Hinduism, in general, has not seen how the personal can be a finite category and yet intrinsically eternal as adjectival to God as love and spirit. The critical reason finds, therefore, that Hinduism lacks an effective category of the eternal as well as of the universal.

(*c*) The critical reason also discovers that with all its stress on the inviolate nature of responsible freedom within its categories of karma and samsara, or deed and consequence seen in the larger perspective before and after earthly life, Hinduism nevertheless lacks full understanding of the nature

---

[1] I am aware, of course, of the diversity of Hinduism and that there are forms of Hindu faith that would definitely repudiate the Illicit Infinite. In such cases the critical reason raises no such objection. The stress on the *ultimacy* of the personal, not only in Ramanuja but also in Śankara, may be stronger than the stress above. Recent readings of them have left this question open as well as the fuller meaning of grace.

of freedom. It never takes freedom with sufficient seriousness. This is true in both the ultimate and the proximate perspective. The ultimate cannot be free if it is burdened with the mass of evil choices in creation. Therefore creation itself is a fall into evil. There is no organic and intrinsic relation between freedom as an ultimate reality in any universal sense, for whatever ultimate freedom can come must be by the release from and oblivion to the world of creation. Ultimately there is no freedom because man is released from choice, not in the sense of the release of fulfilment of the personal, but in the sense of the loss of the personal and all life of freedom. Freedom presupposes choice; choice presupposes the personal; where the personal is not both regulatory and intrinsic to what is ultimate, there is ultimately no freedom.

At the same time, freedom is taken too seriously and normatively on the level of created life. Freedom is not sufficiently rooted in grace as the releasing reality even of created life. There is certainly a doctrine of grace in Hinduism, but there is not enough organic, saving relation between man and the ultimate order to make man's freedom basically a privilege. As a whole, the wheel of life with its necessity of deed and consequence, or birth and rebirth, is a burden to be borne and a fate to be escaped. Freedom in terms of karma is not a matter of delight, as is the Jewish law. It is not fulfilled by love through grace and faith, as in Christianity. Freedom as karma is all too much a description of the inexorable nature of things that explains why things are as they are. The inescapable doctrine of karma is partly also a rationalization of the social order and a tranquillizer against social reform. The nature of things is just, and only harm can come from trying to redo the order externally. Quiet acceptance and the wise working within things as they are, therefore, become the rule of wisdom. Even nature and animal life are governed by this truth, an obstacle to man's destined rule over the animal world and nature, as, for instance, in the Eighth Psalm. Freedom therefore lacks effective relation to the fulfilment of life, either ultimately or proximately. There are genuine elements of pedagogical preparations for final release within Hindu thought, but eternal and inclusive love not being ultimate, the Hindu doctrine of freedom also lacks fruition.

(d) The critical reason further contends that these three basic lacks of Hinduism have resulted in a quiescent culture lacking in positive strength. Hindu culture has been sensitive to life and generally tolerant of the *status quo*. Modern India rises into leadership to a great extent because of the noble and positive protests of men like Gandhi who were steeped in Christian unrest. India now rises as a nation of heroic dimensions, having pioneered in the revolt against colonialism; but the driving incentive to independence came through contact with the drive to progress and change within Western religion at its best, whether in Christian progressism or Marxist messianism. The contagion of universal concern based on God's being universal love never sufficiently touched the Hindu social order until recently. The critical reason finds that the doing away with untouchability, for instance, came basically out of the modern contact of India with Christianity and science.

Creative faith, nevertheless, is not daunted by these serious charges of lacks and faults.

(a) Even though Hinduism's understanding of the universal, as a whole or at its typical manifestation, is finally negative, it has even so a positive fulfilment on this side of the knowable reality. Reality at its highest is not only unknowable by determinate thought, but also graspable in terms of being plus intelligence plus bliss. Man can identify himself with *saccidananda*. *Tat tvam asi*, thou art that, is not merely a going beyond ordinary experience. It is also a fulfilment beyond thought and description of the essential self.

(b) Therefore the final negative in Hinduism is similar in nature to my use of paradox to suggest that not even analogy is enough to indicate the distinction between God and man. Both the negative and the positive are needed. Hinduism needs only to work out this relation of being plus intelligence plus bliss more explicitly in terms of love. Hinduism is at the forefront in its feeling for transcendence. It is amazing in its power to put ordinary experience into its own place of transiency and precariousness.

(c) Its failure comes partly from its not making eternity accessible to thought. There is an anti-rationalism in Hinduism in general that comes, no doubt, from too much thinking about the ultimate nature of things and from a lack of constructive concern for the total life of man on earth. Hinduism needs to take reason with far more seriousness within the balanced disciplines of whole response. Life surpasses reason, and love transcends thought; but only when reason is fully satisfied within the fulfilment of life as a whole. In Hinduism reason has both been overused and underestimated.

(d) Hinduism can also learn to take freedom more seriously, not as forced choice alone, but as the opportunity of learning and living love. When the ultimate finds a face, and that face is life's strongest hope and help, then life on earth takes on unending and inexhaustible meaning. The here and now is then not to be considered as unimportant or impeding, but as the chance for ever-increasing concern for community, where the losing of self in love is the finding of self in life. When Hinduism learns at its depths that God is love, universal and eternal, who offers freedom as a gift, both personal and social life will be stirred with ever growing meaning and vigour. There will be increased traffic in transformation.

Does Hinduism, however, refute our thesis that religion is man's response to realities and powers beyond ordinary life that can help and harm, and that right religion is seen in the kind of life that Jesus lived and taught, engendering the inclusive, open community of creative concern? On the contrary, it seems that our normative definition of religion and our normative religious event-meaning go to show how Hinduism illustrates centrally the reality of religion, and that our normative event-meaning indicates how Hinduism itself can become fulfilled by being corrected and transformed. All religions are under the judgment of God as universal love and of the open, inclusive community of creative concern motivated by faith in him, but all religions, too, can be helped and led toward consummation of their own inner quest by being seen in the light and power of Christ, when Christ ceases to be an in-group symbol of a debased and discredited community, and becomes instead the symbol and true way to full religious reality for all peoples of the world. Hinduism historically contains the personal category in some of its thought as well as the Illicit Infinite, and contemporaneously has giant spirit-thinkers like Radhakrishnan, who find it meaningful, at the centre of things, to develop the fuller meaning of God as love against the Hindu background. Hinduism may, in fact, lead the way to the true religion for one world, where Christ will be freed from idolatry and released for the universal truth and way of love which he centrally was and taught.

Inasmuch as we are not discussing the religions as such, but only illustrating a thesis and suggesting an approach to the problem of reason in religion with respect to the religions of the world, we are free merely to list some positive aspects of Buddhism, then to let the critical reason make its proper objection, and finally to leave the whole matter in the hands of creative faith. Such is the approach of this work throughout.

(a) The creative reason rejoices in the fact that Buddhism refuses ordinary experience as religious criterion. At the centre of its faith lies its affirmation, 'not this, not this', declaring man's ordinary experience as such to be deceiving as to ultimates. It may seem at first that Buddhism's 'not this, not this' is the direct opposite of Hinduism's 'thou art that'. One seems to stress the absence of relations between the finite and the ultimate; the other seems to emphasize essential relations at the heart of things, reaching deep into man's innermost being. But Hinduism, as we have seen, has its own final negative, rejecting the grasp of the ultimate in terms of determinate categories of thought, whereas Buddhism, on its side, is open to dispute among Buddhist scholars and branches of Buddhist thought as to the meaning of nirvana, whether in negative or positive terms. Both religions, however, in general uphold the main stress of our thesis that religion is man's response to realities and powers beyond ordinary experience.[1]

(b) While it is often charged that Buddhism is the one

[1] For our purposes there is no need to discuss, for instance, the nihilistic forms of Buddhism. What we are doing is to consider the main drive or intention of the different religions. For this reason also I have used Theravada Buddhism as the main line. Such procedure would be impossible if the discussion were more than suggestive.

religion that shows how true transcendence outruns the personal category in religion, on the very contrary, the creative reason reports, Buddhism shows how necessary the personal category is by its very use of the Buddha figure. No-one can feel himself into Buddhist art without seeing how Gautama penetrates the religious consciousness of Buddhism as the way to serenity and release. When Buddhism developed critical theology, in truth, it took on idealistic thought forms. Instead of merely using the common term 'idealistic metaphysics', we have purposefully used the word 'theology' for thought concerning ultimates. But this aspect of Buddhism can be seen not only in speculative thought, but also in the personal allegiance of Amida Buddhists to their personal saviour, who saves them by grace when they call believingly upon his name. Buddhism witnesses, in fact, to the truth that when a vital religious category is suppressed in one way, it returns in some other form or stress.

(c) The creative reason presents with proud confidence the fact that Buddhism makes compassion a basic category of religion. The central legend of Buddha's own renunciation of nirvana for the sake of benighted and suffering humanity highlights this truth. Buddhist scripture, recommending the cessation of hatred by love, throws further light on this subject. It simply is not enough to claim that such sayings are entirely a matter of self-concern, where the person who hates is concerned only with his own deliverance from the passion and poison of hate. Such deliverance Buddhism promises, but its concerns include the implications of this truth for man as man, and therefore also for others. A major stress of Mahāyāna Buddhism is also its concentration on compassion and on the Buddha as the compassionate one. Added to these facts is compassion's stress on peace for the world in both historic and contemporary Buddhism.

(d) Buddhism also recognizes the existential nature of religion. We have stressed the existential as a foundational element of primary religion. Socrates and Jesus exemplify the elementary nature of existential response. Creative faith thrives on it. The Buddha, as far as we know, peculiarly both lived and taught the existential approach to religious reality. He considered that pulling an arrow out of a wounded man, instead of discussing the situation, was not only narrowly practical but also essential to religious sanity. The eightfold path to salvation is not only a matter of pragmatic wisdom, but illustrates, in large measure, the existential avenue to religious fulfilment. As in Hinduism, so in Buddhism, redemption, whether it be called moksa or satori, comes as an existential appropriation beyond thought or deed. Few religions show greater variety in the delicate interrelation between thought, habituated practice and the existential than does Buddhism.

To these positive considerations the critical reason retorts:

(a) When all is said and done the *neti, neti* of Buddhism denies both dependable meaning for religion and also final fulfilment. Nirvana offers either escape from life or ultimate agnosticism, but no reliable revelation as to man's consummation within an ultimate purpose. Therefore it is in fact the denial of our thesis as to reason in religion.

(b) The critical reason also contends that the personal in religion is given its historic importance in Buddhism, but never constitutes, except in popular thought, an intrinsic aspect of ultimate reality. The personal is ultimately lost in the negative or the unknown.

(c) Buddhism knows compassion, too, as preliminary, but not as the very nature of ultimate reality. Compassion is not the ground of creation, the conditions of history, the controller of providence and the determiner of destiny. It was precisely compassion that prevented the Buddha from immediately reaching nirvana.

(d) With all its stress on the religiously existential, moreover, as well as on the practical ways and thoughts of life, Buddhism has not produced the understanding of the ultimate in terms of universal concern, grounded in ultimate reality, and engendering the open and inclusive community of creative co-operation.

But creative faith answers these charges boldly. The 'not this, not this' can be made to stand for the preliminary denial of the fugitive as fulfilment. Such is the radical requirement of adequate religion. There is, then, beyond such preliminary preparation, room for the development of the positive meaning of nirvana, which some Buddhist scholars believe is genuinely intended by the faith itself. To synthesize Christian resurrection with Buddhist nirvana may involve no syncretism or mixed perspectives, but the fulfilment of both faiths in terms of the universal combination of the positive 'yes' and the negative 'no' which must characterize every assertion by finite man as to what lies beyond ordinary experience in ultimate reality and destiny. Certainly what God has in store for us is not only personal fulfilment in terms of present life, but some discontinuity, as we saw in our discussion when Buddhism was not even in question, which makes denial of basic continuity in some sense necessary. Resurrection suggests such discontinuity more readily than immortality. Nirvana stresses it even more strongly.

All Buddhism has to do is to make its own stress on compassion theologically central. It need not do so abstractly, either, but can do so in terms of its own central legend of the Buddha who renounced his own salvation to save the world. The two major religious figures of the world will then witness together not only as to the nature of religion but also as to the normative nature of love. Actually it is a far shorter journey from nirvana to Christ than from eternal hell to Christ. The struggling Christ on the crucifix shows God's love in history; the serene Buddha barely touching the earth with his finger can become a symbol of the external assurance of love's victory.

Barthianism has fired the religious imagination. Its negative stress on the infinite qualitative distinction between God and man and its positive stress on inscrutable mystery are too near the 'feel' of Buddhism for Christians to wonder at the relevance of Christ for Buddhism. Similarly, there is much common appeal in Amida Buddhism and Lutheran piety, where faith in the saviour and salvation by grace dominate the religious consciousness. In some definite stretches of Lutheran thought, moreover, Christ is limited in his revelation to the forgiveness of sin, in such a way that the use of Christ to interpret the whole of experience or to give a 'world view' is called speculation and philosophy. There is much empathy between Buddhism and Christianity. Buddhism can, in any case, witness to both the general definition we have made of religion and also to the normative nature of Christ as universal love. Its power as a religion would be deepened, as it would fulfil its own depth-drive, by becoming impenetrated by the universal love of God. The key to Buddhism as a branch of the religion for one world is its own creative development of its own concern with compassion, in both ultimate and proximate categories.

Our thesis is not, we recall, that all religions are naturally fulfilled by universal love. Such a claim would involve their being basically the rationalization of man's main attempt to find and to serve God. But the full fact of religion, we recall, is that all religions, being the response to God on the part of both ignorant and fearful men, are at their centre both a search for God and a twisting of this search into some form of accommodation with the actual attainment which men have chosen and reached. Fulfilment, therefore, involves the frustration of the overt faith, at its broadest formulation, the release of the deeper witness of need, and the meeting of such need as is indicated by the religions themselves. Up to this point we think we have seen that there is no religion which does not at its centre suggest that its deepest drive, if redirected and re-motivated, would not be fulfilled by universal love in life, thought and faith. In the case of Chinese and Japanese religions we add only a postscript to the preceding analysis.

Those who know Chinese religions expertly tell us that their strands interweave almost beyond untangling. Chinese culture seems to be broad and hospitable to overlapping religious communities, permeated by a healthy practical this-worldliness. I shall, therefore, not try to illustrate the thesis of this book in terms of the Chinese religions except by a comment that is merely an addendum.

Confucianism, which seems indigenous to the Chinese religious approach, stresses the communal nature of religion with its systems of loyalties, like subject to sovereign, servant to master, and family obligations. Confucianism is almost a community of loyalty in law. This law transcends mere legalism, and fulfils man by both his affections and obligations. At its highest, it can rise to concern; at its lowest, it falls to the level of duty. According to our thesis, Confucianism is too far committed to these practical, personal relations to be centred in the realities and powers beyond this life. But the transcendent element works its way by having the Confucian ethics supplemented by Tao mysticism and 'ancestor worship'. Ancestor worship is not a formal religion, but the feeling for the fuller meaning of life and its fulfilment beyond this life. The chain of being cannot be cut by death. There is more to life than our conceiving, rearing, living and dying.

Confucianism also becomes fulfilled by either Buddhism or Taoism. Buddhism supplies preeminently the more-than-ordinary experience. Taoism is itself a highly variegated religious phenomenon, stretching all the way from a most mystic form of worship to an intellectualistic philosophy. Both heart and mind find their creative expression in this Chinese variety of logos relations. Taoism therefore serves as a peculiarly strong counterpart to Confucian this-worldliness. The sensitive and concerned religious admonitions of some Chinese scriptures like the *Tao Te Ching* are among the highest reaches of religion, according to our thesis, anywhere and any time. It seems that the Chinese religions, as a whole, have stayed closer to the actual world, with its conflict and constant balancing of good and evil, than it has to the eschatological, which has received no more than occasional and precarious emphasis.

Mohism, with its stress on universal love, may come as close as any historic emphasis to both our descriptive and normative definitions.[1] But its stress seems to have been too high and holy, and too inclusive to be accepted by the fear, indifference and hostility of ordinary experience. China can, however, recover its own Chinese 'Christ', at least in much of his central stress. If 'capitalist' motivation can be destroyed in some real measure and the Chinese reoriented and re-motivated politically and economically in terms of their present era of high idealism, alongside of the deliberate material orientation and practices of even this present revolutionary

---

[1] The appearance of Mo Ti in the fourth (or fifth) century B.C. is a great mystery of history.

drive, China can recover the central drive of Mohism, and focusing on the meaning and power of the eternal Christ, who is our final standard, can develop creatively its own branch of the religion for one world, which must be built on faith in the universal God of love, who covets an open and inclusive society of creative concern.

Japan is another country of many religions. For one thing, it has developed many forms of Buddhism that enrich the religious landscape. Its distinctive creation, however, is Shinto. Once again, I am in no position to discuss this wide-ranging faith, with its many reaches into the main areas of life. It is of interest to note, however, that Shinto is also a community without clear borders and barriers. Its devotees can supplement their Shinto practices by means of other religions. Its own three main stresses, however, bear strongly on the thesis of this book. The political and social aspects root historically in the emperor's representing the powers and realities beyond ordinary experience. To think crassly of emperor worship as founded on any literal descent from heaven, or in terms of the 'Son of Heaven', is to miss man's reaching to interpret all life within the religious realities beyond rational comprehension. The rest of Shinto loyalties are derived from this deeper identification of the national and the social order with religious reality. Samurai codes of conduct, accordingly, become sacred.

In the kamiway, moreover, nature is understood as more than material. Sophisticated religious thinkers often scorn the primitivism of this kind of combination of pantheism and animatism. But the deepest drive, here again, is the understanding of nature itself as purposive, as 'intending' toward man. The pathetic fallacy is surely less false than the apathetic. A shallow naturalism, instead of being hard-headed, is far less adequate, and separates man from nature. Thus we see both history and nature, our first two Shinto categories, as related to the fuller religious realities.

The third aspect of Shinto is its intimate dealing with the dead: how concretely they return, even expected at specific times, and how they must be honoured and included in present life. Here we see how the religious drive reaches out for fulfilment beyond this life. All national, shrine or family ceremonials are touched penetratingly by some aspect of these three emphases in Shinto: history, nature and what is more than either history or nature. Shinto, therefore, fits well our descriptive analysis of religion, but it needs at its centre the universalism and intensive inclusiveness of our normative event. Shinto needs the Christ, whom to know is to be both at home and a stranger in every land and every religion.

Some might now expect at the end of this volume concise summaries of reason in religion with respect to God, man, nature and history. To give such summaries in this place, however, would be, in effect, to deny the living nature of religion. We are not dealing primarily with logic or with science. We are not looking for precise rational systems or for prefabricated religious structures. We are dealing with the living reality of religion as man's historic response to the realities and powers beyond ordinary experience that can help and harm him. We seek neither to defend nor to offend any religion, but to treat them with integrity and rigorous concern. Even the historic encrustations of institutional religions can more refute than vindicate our normative definitions of the community of inclusive concern open to Creative Being, illustrated by a life of love; even seemingly secularized revolts against religious thwarting of historic creativity in basic areas of life, like economic communism and anti-colonialism, can be closer to the all-illuminating event than the religions that fight such secularism. Cold winds of secular power, in fact, may have to move on the face of the earth, chasing away the debris of discredited religions, which by their identification with the *status quo* now obstruct creativity, before the warm sun that reaches all men can again come through the clouds which now veil it for both honest and rationalizing men.

No-one can predict the course of the future of religions, for religion lives on a creativity that defies prediction and develops in a climate of faith, engendering its own supporting climate of opinion, which reason can describe only upon its arrival. In any case, we must leave our discussion open, suggestive for its leading, directive for its findings, but never prescriptive for thought and life in such a way that it prejudges and precludes creativity. History points ahead. Religion is part of human history. If our analysis is correct, reason has its place within the religious creativity to evaluate, organize and direct experience.

The future will surely find that faith right which believes that fulfilling destiny, in life and beyond life, personally and communally, lies along the highway of God's creative concern for all people, offering freedom within integrity of thought and life; for freedom and integrity mature and become consummated only within an ever-enriching and expanding community of concern. Reason in religion can be right only within such integrity and such concern, rooted and grounded in finding faith.

Index

Abraham, 303, 304
Adam, 306
Al Ghazzali, 157
American Council of Judaism, 307
American Indians, 19
Amida, 157, 327, 329
Amos, 20
analytical philosophy, 108f.
animal, 140, 261
animatism, 225
animism, 18, 225
Anselm, 131
Aquinas, 131
atchetypes, 142
Augustine, 131
automation, 246

Barthianism 329
Buddha, 158, 327, 328
Buddhism, 157, 302, 326ff.

capitalism, 214
categorical, 129
Chinese religions, 302, 330
Christianity, 309ff.
classless society, 214
commitment, 32
community, 242ff., 247, 268
compossible, 266f.
Confucianism, 330
conscience, 230f.
creation, 76, 81, 93, 116, 189, 195, 260, 323
creative reason, 35, 260ff., 280, 301, 306f.
critical reason, 36, 99, 114, 259ff., 309f.

Darwin, 139
David, 303, 304, 306
death, 250ff.
dependence, 292ff.
Descartes, 131
destruction, 245ff.
development, 238ff.
dimensional thinking, 57, 94
directional thinking, 56, 94
doubt, 123f., 127, 163

Esther, 303, 306
eternal hell, 311, 329

eternity, 24, 80f., 258, 279, 287, 290, 322
evaluation, 6f., 258f.
evil, 21, 86, 201, 206, 236ff., 263f.
existence, 59, 91
existentialism 215
explanation, 8

faith, 28ff., 96f., 110, 113, 123, 137, 147, 150, 185, 188f., 265
falsification, 151
finite, 122ff., 128, 137, 160f., 195
freedom, 215, 217, 226, 237, 244, 268, 323

Gandhi, 157, 187, 324
Gautama, 157, 327
God, 20, 24f., 59, 67f., 74f., 85ff., 116, 130, 138, 150f., 156, 168ff., 184f., 195ff., 231, 264
Great Negation, 195f., 289
Great Refusal, 195f.
guilt, 180

hedonism, 268
Hinduism, 289, 302, 320ff., 328
history, 66f., 75, 83f., 158, 167, 170, 177, 195ff., 218ff., 238ff., 270ff., 334
Hosea, 157, 306
Hume, 131

Illicit Infinite, 197, 268, 322
imagination, 5
Incarnation, 199, 316
infinite, 20, 195ff.
insecurity, 249
Isaac, 303
Islam, 157, 302, 315ff.

Jacob, 303
Japan, 332
Jesus, 20, 67ff., 74, 77, 110, 157, 158, 179, 187, 254, 292f., 313, 327
Jonah, 306
Judaism, 20, 157, 302, 303ff.

kairos, 212
kalpas, 212
Kant, 130, 131

335

karma, 214-15, 321-3
Kierkegaard, 130
knowledge, 49ff., 96ff., 113, 126, 141,
  159, 278
Koran, 318, 319, 320

language, 79ff., 107, 197
Leviticus, 304
logic, 97, 100, 106f., 130
love, 20, 77ff., 91, 116, 138f., 150f.,
  200, 217ff., 296
Lutheranism, 329

Maccabees, 303, 306
Mahāyāna Buddhism, 327
meaning, 202ff.
meditation, 185, 187
metaphysics, 108, 111, 156
method, 109, 112, 156
miracle, 133
Mohammed, 157, 316
Mohism, 331, 332
Mo Ti, 331n.
Moses, 157, 176, 303, 304
mystery, 26, 78

naturalism, 111
nature, 210, 220, 236ff., 270
New Testament, 68, 74, 176, 294
nirvana, 328, 329
Noah, 306

Old Testament, 69, 74
ontological argument, 131f.
ontology, 131
ordering of experience, 9, 128f.

particulars, 4, 144f
Paul, 67
personal God, 20ff., 89, 138, 199
perspective, 41, 99,
philosophy, 12, 101, 106ff., 285
Plato, 20
pluralism, 287f., 291
prayer, 185f.
presupposition, 39ff., 109, 114f., 196
process, 51, 62f., 87, 111, 262, 270f.
proof, 66
property, 234
pull of purpose, 225ff.
purpose, 55, 200
push of process, 219ff.

Radhakrishnan, 326
Ramanuja, 322n.
rationalization, 165, 167, 172, 179, 185
reason, definition of, 1ff., 96ff., 116, 129
reincarnation, 256f.
relativity, 121ff, 130, 148, 287f., 299
religion, definition of, 16ff., 27ff.
religions, 283ff., 299, 301ff.
religious experience, 23f., 47, 123f.
Resurrection, 156, 329
revelation, 122f., 131f., 199
Ruth, 306

saccidananda, 324
Saint Francis, 187
Sankara, 322n.
scepticism, 124, 163
science, 97, 101ff., 113, 285, 319
Second Isaiah, 314
self, 125ff., 149, 161f., 175, 249
Shinto, 302, 332ff.
sin, 121f., 162ff., 186f., 216
social immortality, 216
Socrates, 158, 176, 179, 327
spirit, 19, 83, 89, 92, 138, 178, 198,
  256, 280, 314
Stoicism, 314
subconscious, 142
suffering, 94
symbol, 79, 141, 172
synthetic experience 146

Taoism, 331
Tao Te Ching, 331
tat tvam asi, 324
Teilhard de Chardin, 260
testing, 9ff., 154
Theravada Buddhism, 326n.
Tillich, 289
totenism, 18, 225
trust, 31ff.
truth, 13, 175, 180

unconditional, 22, 92, 197
United Nations, 224
universals, 4, 144f.

via negativa, 196, 322

World Council of Churches, 311, 312

Zionism, 307